METAMODELING

D1613985

MIT Press Series in Computer Systems
Herb Schwetman, editor

Metamodeling: A Study of Approximations in Queueing Models, by Subhash Chandra
Agrawal, 1985

METAMODELING

A Study of Approximations in Queueing Models

Subhash Chandra Agrawal

The MIT Press
Cambridge, Massachusetts
London, England

This book was printed and bound in the United
States of America.

Publisher's Note: This format is intended to reduce the cost of publishing certain works in
book form and to shorten the gap between edi-
torial preparation and final publication. Detailed editing and composition have been
avoided by photographing the text of this book
directly from the author's camera-ready copy.

Library of Congress Cataloging in Publication
Data

Agrawal, Subhash Chandra.
  Metamodeling: a study of approximations in
queueing models.

  (The MIT series in computer systems)
  Bibliography: p.
  Includes index.
  1. Digital computer simulation. 2. Electronic
digital computers—Evaluation. 3. Queueing the-
ory. 4. Approximation theory. I. Title.
II. Series.
QA76.9.C65A38   1985   001.64   84-19456
ISBN 0-262-01080-1

To my parents
and
to the memory of my grandmother

CONTENTS

FIGURES

Appendixes

BOXES

TABLES

SERIES FOREWORD

System performance has become a major issue in the design and implementation of computer systems. The success or failure of a system often is judged on the degree to which performance objectives are met. Thus, tools and techniques for predicting performance are of great interest.

Subhash Agrawal is one of a small group of researchers who are trying to develop performance prediction tools. The methodology used is based on developing a system model that can be "solved" to produce estimates of response time and throughput rates, both key metrics in determining the performance of a system. This approach, based on mathematical models of systems, has been used in many areas of science and engineering to predict the suitability of structures, etc., before they are constructed. The goal of computer system modeling is the same: to predict suitability before implementation.

In *Metamodeling*, Agrawal has pulled together a wide variety of system modeling techniques and organized them in a coherent fashion. In doing so, he has introduced a consistent terminology and notation so that the reader can focus on the techniques rather than on translating to a familiar notation. In addition he has provided new insight into the properties of some of the approximations. He demonstrates convergence (or lack of convergence) for some techniques where this was not known before.

As with most research, this work builds on that of preceding work, in this case, on previous research in the solution and application of queueing network models, especially as applied to computer systems. This book not only provides new material but summarizes existing work. It does assume a level of knowledge beyond that of the novice in the area, but it is self-contained. The author and his research advisers, Peter Denning and Jeffrey Buzen, are to be commended for the scholarly treatment of a subject of increasing interest.

This book will be of interest not only to students and researchers in the area of system models based on queueing networks but also to practitioners who are interested in applying these techniques to their systems. It could be used to accompany a course on system modeling.

It is appropriate that this book be the first in the new MIT Press Series in Computer Systems. The field of computer systems is maturing; a sign of this maturing is the development of models, using mathematics, which yield insight into system behavior. Additional offerings in this series will address other aspects of computer systems. The field is flourishing; we hope that this series will reflect both the dynamic qualities and the maturing qualities of the field as changes occur.

Herb Schwetman

PREFACE

In recent years there has been a significant increase in the number of approximate methods for analyzing non-homogeneous (non-product form) queueing networks. However, there has been no systematic study of the way these approximations are developed. The goal of the research reported in this monograph is to identify the underlying modeling process and to provide tools and techniques for approximate model development.

The research was done when I was a doctoral student in the Department of Computer Sciences at Purdue University. The monograph is essentially my Ph.D. dissertation.

The publication of this monograph would not have been possible without the support of many individuals and institutions. It gives me great pleasure to acknowledge their assistance. Peter Denning and Jeff Buzen were constant sources of encouragement and advice throughout my graduate studies and the preparation of the monograph. My co-authors of the RTP paper, Jeff Buzen and Annie Shum, and the Association for Computing Machinery, Inc., kindly agreed to let me reprint the paper as an appendix.

BGS Systems, Inc., graciously permitted me to devote time to the preparation of the manuscript.

Research leading to my dissertation and this monograph was made possible by support from National Science Foundation grant MCS78-01729 and an IBM Graduate Research Fellowship for 1982–1983.

METAMODELING

CHAPTER 1

INTRODUCTION

Queueing network models are the most widely used analytical method for estimating the standard performance measures of computer systems. With these models, calculations of throughput are typically within 5% of actual values, and mean response times are within 30% [DENN78]. Their success has been enhanced by simple and efficient solution algorithms and good commercial packages such as BEST/1 [BGS80, BUZE78a], CADS [IRA77] and RESQ [SAUE82a, SAUE82b].

The simplicity of analytic queueing network models limits their utility. They cannot directly represent certain behaviors common in computer systems. These behaviors include simultaneous resource possession, queueing for passive resources such as memory and semaphores, preemptive priorities at some servers, and the blocking of one server by the actions of another. Ignoring these behaviors can lead to substantial errors in the estimates of performance measures. Because of the computational efficiency of queueing network models, analysts have sought ways to represent these behaviors by extending queueing network models. A bewildering array of approximate models has been the result.

In reviewing the literature on approximate queueing models, one is led to a long list of questions. For example:

1. When should one replace a subnetwork with a flow equivalent server?

2. When should one add servers to the model to represent queueing delays for nonphysical resources?

3. When should one split a server into two or more separate servers?

4. Why does iteration show up in some approximations but not in others?

5. If iteration is used, does it converge to a unique solution?

6. Is there any systematic way of analyzing the errors in the solutions of models?

7. Is there any common structure in the processes by which each model was constructed?

The goal of the research reported in this monograph has been to critically study some well known approximate methods and find answers to these questions. The result is a *metamodel* of the process of developing system models.

This metamodel is a general model of the modeling process. We will show, by considering a large number of examples, that the structure of the modeling process envisioned in metamodeling is capable of representing a wide variety of approximations. The central principle of this structure is that an approximation involves mapping a "complex" model into one or more "simpler" models, solving these simpler models, and mapping the solution back into an estimate of the solution of the original model. We employ two general techniques, behavior sequence transformations and state space transformations, to develop, describe and analyze model transformations. Results of our study include a catalog of common transformations, several new methods for analyzing preemptive priority scheduling, the method of aggregate servers for analyzing serialization delays, general theorems about convergence of iterative approximations, and the discovery that some queueing systems may have multiple stable solutions for key performance quantities. These convergence theorems enabled us to prove the convergence of

1) The Bard-Schweitzer approximation for large networks [SCHW79],

2) The Jacobson-Lazowska method for simultaneous resource possession [JACO82] in a simpler way, and

3) The shadow CPU approximation for preemptive priority scheduling [SEVC77].

In the remainder of this chapter, we review analytic queueing network models; they are the focus of the most of the discussion in later chapters. We then review the principal approximations reported in the literature. We next set forth the plan of the subsequent chapters, in which the components of modeling process are taken up. We conclude the chapter with a review of related prior work.

1.1 Queueing Network Models

In this section, we provide a brief overview of queueing network models. We begin with single resource models and then discuss queueing networks, multiple workloads, product form solutions, computational algorithms, and robustness of queueing network models. We conclude the section by reviewing the history of the queueing networks.

1.1.1 Single Resource Models

A single resource model is the most elementary form of a queueing model. It is a description of a service system comprising an arrival process, a completion or service process, a queueing mechanism, a set of one or more units of a resource that renders the service, and a buffer space for holding the waiting customers at the resource.[1] An analytical model typically gives an

---

1. Kendall's shorthand notation $A/B/C/D/E$ is widely used to classify single resource queueing models. In this notation, A describes the arrival process, B specifies comple-

algorithm for computing $p(n)$, the proportion of time n customers are in the queue, given the parameters

λ (or $\lambda(n)$) - mean arrival rate (possibly conditioned on n), and

S (or $S(n)$) - mean service time (also possibly conditioned on n).

If N is the maximum number of customers observed at the server, the solution is [BUZE76a]:

$$p(0) = \frac{1}{1 + \sum_{n=1}^{N} \prod_{k=0}^{n-1} \lambda(k) \, S(k+1)}$$

$$p(n) = p(0) \prod_{k=0}^{n-1} \lambda(k) \, S(k+1), \quad \text{for } n = 1, \dots, N. \tag{1.1}$$

Under the assumptions of Homogeneous Arrivals (HA: $\lambda(n) = \lambda$) and Homogeneous Service (HS: $S(n) = S$) [BUZE76a, DENN78, BRUM82], the solution reduces to

$$p(n) = (1 - \lambda S)(\lambda S)^n. \tag{1.2}$$

1.1.2 Queueing Network Models

A queueing network models is a collection of single resource models arranged in the same configuration as a real system. The parameters of this model are:

V_i - Number of times each customer visits (or requests service at) device i.

---

tion or service process, C denotes the number of units of resources that render the service, D specifies the maximum number of customers that can be queued at the server, and E is the size of the population. Some examples of this notation are

$M/M/1$ - Poisson (Markov) input, exponential (Markov) service times, 1 server;

$M/G/1$ - Poisson (Markov) input, General (arbitrary) service time distribution function, 1 server;

$GI/M/1$ - General, Independently distributed interarrival times, exponential (Markov) service times, 1 server.

S_i (or $S_i(n)$) - mean service time per visit to device i.

An analytical model typically gives an algorithm for computing the solution $p(\underline{n}) = p(n_1, \ldots, n_K)$, the proportion of time n_1 customers are present at device $1, \ldots,$ and n_K customers are at device K. If the arrival rate is specified, the model is *open*. If the total number of customers $N = n_1 + \cdots + n_K$ is fixed, the model is *closed*.

1.1.3 Multiple Workloads

Customers in the network can be differentiated by tagging them with their type or *class* r; a network with multiple classes of customers is called a *multiclass network*. Separate parameters V_{ir} and S_{ir} are specified for each class; separate performance measures are computed for each class. Some classes may be open (i.e., their λ_r's are given and the number of customers of these classes in the system is not fixed), and others may be closed (i.e., their N_r are specified). A network with both open and closed classes is called a *mixed* network. The state of the system is typically defined to be

$$\underline{n} = ((n_{11}, \ldots, n_{1R}), \ldots, (n_{K1}, \ldots, n_{KR})),$$

where n_{ir} is the number of class r customers present at device i.

1.1.4 Product Form Solution

The direct solution $p(\underline{n})$ of a general queueing network would involve a very expensive solution of the global balance equations [HERZ75, STEW78]. Under the following assumptions, however, $p(\underline{n})$ has the "product form" and is efficiently computable:

a. *One Step Behavior*: A state transition can occur only due to a departure of a single customer from one resource to another or outside the system, or due to arrival of a customer from the outside,

b. *Flow Balance*: The number of arrivals (in each class) at a device must equal the number of departures (in each class) from the device,

c. *Device Homogeneity*: A device's service rate for a particular class does not depend on the state of the system in any way except for the total device queue length and the designated class's queue length. This assumption essentially implies that:

- *Single Resource Possession*: A customer may not be present (waiting for service or receiving service) at two or more devices at the same time,

- *No Blocking*: A device renders service whenever customers are present; its ability to render service is not controlled by any other device.

- *Independent Customer Behavior*: Interaction among customers is limited to queueing for physical devices, e.g., there should not be any synchronization requirements.

- *Local Information*: A device's service rate depends only on local queue length and not on the state of the rest of the system.

- *Fair Service*: If service rates differ by class, the service rate for a class depends only on the queue length of that class at the device and not on the queue lengths of other classes. This means that the server does not discriminate against customers in a class depending on the queue lengths in other classes.

d. *Routing Homogeneity*: The customer routing should be state independent.

Because of their intuitive meaning, we will call the assumptions (c) and (d) the *autonomous behavior* assumptions. With the assumptions (a)-(d), the solution has following product form:

$$p(\underline{n}) = \frac{F_1(\underline{n}_1) \cdots F_K(\underline{n}_K)}{G}. \tag{1.3}$$

In this expression G is a normalization constant such that all probabilities sum to 1, $\underline{n}_i = (n_{i1}, \ldots, n_{iR})$, where n_{ir} is the number of class r customers at device i, and F_i is the device factor for device i:

$$F_i(\underline{n}_i) = f_i(n_{i1} + \cdots + n_{iR}) \left(\prod_{r=1}^{R} \prod_{j=1}^{n_{ir}} V_{ir} S_{ir}(j) \right), \tag{1.4}$$

where f_i is a factor affecting the overall device service rate depending on the total queue length.

Another set of assumptions for "product form" solution is provided by Baskett, Chandy, Muntz and Palacios [BASK75]; these assumptions are:

a. *Allowable Scheduling Disciplines*: The following disciplines are allowed: First-Come-First-Served (FCFS), Processor Sharing (PS), Last-Come-First-Served-Preemptive-Resume (LCFS-PR), and Infinite Server (IS) or delay service.

b. *Service Time Distribution*: The service times at a FCFS server should be exponentially distributed; moreover, the S_{ir} should be same for all classes. The service times at PS, LCFS-PR, and IS can have any distribution that has a rational Laplace transform. The mean service times for different classes may also be different.

c. *State Dependent Service Rates*: The service rate (time) at a FCFS server can depend only on the total queue length of the server. The service rate for a class at PS, LCFS-PR and IS servers can also depend on the queue length for that class, but not on the queue length of other classes. Moreover, the overall service rate of a subnetwork can depend on the total number of customers in the subnetwork.

d. *Interarrival Time Distribution*: In open networks, the time between successive customer arrivals for a class should be exponentially distributed. No bulk arrivals are permitted.

Note that the fair service and autonomous operation assumptions are central to this set of assumptions too. These assumptions lead to the condition of "local balance" [CHAN77], i.e., the flow rate into a state due to arrival of a class r job equals the flow rate out of that state due to departure of a class r job. When local balance conditions are met, the system has a product form solution.

1.1.5 Fast Computational Algorithms

The existence of fast computational algorithms is the strong point of product form solution. Two major algorithms are the Convolution algorithm [BRUE80, BUZE71, BUZE73] and the Mean-Value-Analysis algorithm [REIS80, SCHW80, ZAHO81]. These algorithms are alternative ways to exploit the recursive structure of the product form solution and are specified in Box 1.1. Variations of these two basic algorithms are presented in [CHAN80, HOYM82, LAM83].

1.1.6 Robustness and Accuracy

Performance measures predicted by queueing networks are usually sufficiently accurate: utilization estimates are typically within 5% of observed values and response time and queue length estimates are generally within 30% [DENN78].

Closed queueing networks are robust. The errors in the parameter estimates and homogeneity assumptions are usually not magnified in performance measures [GORD80, SURI83b, WILL76]. Open network

Product Form Algorithms for Load Independent Single Class Networks

Notation:

$X(n)$ - network throughput with n customers

$\bar{n}_k(n)$ - mean queue length for server k

$R_k(n)$ - mean response time at server k

The Convolution Algorithm [BRUE80, BUZE71, BUZE73]:

$G_1(0) := 1$
for $n = 1, \ldots, N$ **loop**
$G_1(n) := V_1 S_1 G_1(n-1)$
end loop

for $k = 2, \ldots, K$ **loop**
$G_k(0) := 1$
for $n = 1, \ldots, N$
$\quad G_k(n) := G_{k-1}(n) + V_k S_k G_k(n-1)$ **end loop**
end loop

$$X(N) := \frac{G_K(N-1)}{G_K(N)}$$

The Mean-Value-Analysis (MVA) Algorithm [REIS80, SCHW80, ZAHO81]:

for $k = 1, \ldots, K$
$\bar{n}_k(0) := 0$
end loop

for $n = 1, \ldots, N$
for $k = 1, \ldots, K$
$\quad R_k(n) := S_k(1 + \bar{n}_k(n-1))$ **end loop**
$$X(n) := \frac{n}{\sum\limits_{k=1}^{K} V_k R_k(n)}$$
for $k = 1, \ldots, K$
$\quad \bar{n}_k(n) := V_k R_k(n) X(n)$ **end loop**
end loop

Box 1.1: The Convolution and the MVA algorithms.

performance measures are, however, more sensitive to the errors. Both the parameter estimation errors and the homogeneity assumption errors may be magnified by a factor of the order of $1/(1-U)$, where U is the server utilization [BRUM82].

1.1.7   History

Theory

Open models, usually single server models, have been studied for long time. Kleinrock [KLEI75] provides an extensive treatment. Jackson [JACK57, JACK63], and Gordon and Newell [GORD67] showed that the solution of a closed network of exponential servers has the product form. Baskett, Chandy, Muntz, and Palacios extended the range of the product form networks to include multiclass, mixed networks with a variety of state dependent behavior [BASK75]. Limited forms of state dependent routing are allowed [TOWS80]. The set of product form scheduling disciplines has been extended to include Random Selection [SPIR79], and Load Balancing [AFSH82].

After noticing that many statements about performance are valid without requiring any distributional assumptions, Buzen and Denning developed an *operational approach* to queueing network modeling [BUZE76a, BUZE76b, DENN78, BUZE80a, BUZE80b]. This approach does not require any distributional assumptions; it relies only on the measurable quantities of the system; its homogeneity assumptions are testable. Within this approach, analysis of errors is possible [BRUM82, DENN82, KOWA81, SURI83b].

Practice

Single resource models have long been used to analyze specific aspects of system behavior, e.g., scheduling disciplines, and buffer allocation [COFF73, KLEI75, KLEI76].

The first successful application of queueing network models to computer systems was Scherr's machine repairman model of the Compatible-Time-Sharing-System [SCHE67]. Other applications rapidly followed [BUZE71, KELL76, MOOR71, SAUE75a]. The growth of the applications has been aided by commercially available packages such as BEST/1 [BGS80, BUZE78a], CADS [IRA77] and RESQ [SAUE82a, SAUE82b].

Algorithms

Though the concept of product form solution was known since 1957 [JACK57], queueing network model applications did not really take off before 1971, when Buzen reported an algorithm for computing the normalization constant G for exponential networks and computing performance measures in terms of G [BUZE71]. The algorithm has now been extended to compute performance measures for all product form networks [BRUE80, SAUE83]. The other major algorithm, Mean Value Analysis, computes the performance measures directly [REIS80, SAUE83, SCHW80, ZAHO81]. Some variations of these algorithms are also available. CCNC (Coalesce Computation of Normalizing Constants) is useful when storage is at a premium, and LBANC (Local balance Algorithm for Normalizing Constants) is useful when the number of queues is small but the number of customers is very large [CHAN80]. Tree-Convolution [LAM83] and Tree-MVA [HOYM82] algorithms are useful for analyzing large, but sparse networks. Distributed systems are examples of such sparse networks.

In addition to the exact solution algorithms discussed above, some algorithms have been developed to solve large networks approximately. They will be discussed in Section 1.2.8.

1.2 Approximate Models of Complex Computer Systems

Many practical computer systems violate the homogeneity assumptions required for product form solution. Approximate methods for such cases modify the network model of the system, by adding servers or changing parameters, until a product form model is found that represents the actual behaviors accurately [CHAN78].

In this section we briefly review some of the principal approximate methods. We first present some methods that overcome following non-homogeneous behaviors:

General service time distribution at FCFS servers,

Memory queueing,

Simultaneous resource possession in I/O subsystems,

Preemptive priority scheduling,

Serialization (critical sections),

Internal program concurrency (FORK/JOIN), and

Blocking.

We conclude the section by considering approximate methods for solving large product form networks. Throughout, unless otherwise stated, we assume a closed network with population N, servers $1, \ldots, K$, visit ratios $\{V_k\}$, service functions $\{S_k(n)\}$, and system throughput X_0.

1.2.1 General Service Time Distribution at an FCFS Server

Occasionally, the service time of a customer at a FCFS server has a high coefficient of variation (CV >> 1). Networks that include such servers in general do not have a product form solution because the exponential service time assumption is violated. (The CV of an exponentially distributed random variable is 1.) Consequently, ignoring high CV can lead to significant errors. We now discuss some methods for modeling systems containing FCFS servers with non-exponential (CV ≠ 1) service times.

Shum and Buzen [SHUM76, SHUM77] observed that within a multiplicative factor $F_i(n)$ (Eqns. (1.1) and (1.2)) in the product form solution is, in fact, the queue length distribution for an $M/M/1/N$ queue. They proposed that $F_i(n)$ for a general service time server can be taken as the queue length distribution of an $M/G/1/N$ queue. Assuming a value for network throughput, X_0, they compute arrival rates to each queue and use the $M/G/1/N$ queueing function to compute the device factors. The device factors are then used to evaluate device utilizations from the product form solution algorithms. From the device utilizations, they evaluate the output rate of each queue. If the output rates do not match the arrival rates, the procedure is repeated with another guess for network throughput X_0. The algorithm normally provides fairly accurate solutions but occasionally fails to find a flow-balanced solution.

Chandy, Herzog and Woo (CHW) [CHAN75a] construct K submodels, $M_1, \ldots, M_K$, one for each queue. The submodel M_k consists of the general server k and a flow-equivalent server that represents its complement in the network. The complementary network consists of exponential servers whose initial service function, $S_k^*(n)$, is computed from input parameters by ignoring

Table 1.1: Service function correction in the CHW method [CHAN75a].

Throughput	Queue Length	Service Function
$X_k/V_k < X_0(1 - \epsilon)$	$\sum_l \bar{n}_l > N(1 + \epsilon)$	$\hat{S}_k^*(n) = S_k^*(n)X_0/X_k$
$X_k/V_k > X_0(1 + \epsilon)$	$\sum_l \bar{n}_l < N(1 - \epsilon)$	$\hat{S}_k^*(n) = S_k^*(n)X_0/X_k$
$\|(X_k/V_k - X_0)/X_0\| < \epsilon$	$\|(\sum_l \bar{n}_l - N)/N\| \geq \epsilon$	$\hat{S}_k^*(n) = S_k^*(n)\sum_j \bar{n}_j/N$
$\|(X_k/V_k - X_0)/X_0\| \geq \epsilon$	$\|(\sum_l \bar{n}_l - N)/N\| < \epsilon$	$\hat{S}_k^*(n) = S_k^*(n)X_0/X_k$

> Note: These service functions are used only in characteriz-
> ing the complementary network in M_i, $i \neq k$. The
> two queue model M_k represents the queue k as gen-
> eral server. A rationale for these corrections is pro-
> vided in [TOLO79].

the CV. M_k is solved to obtain the mean queue length $\bar{n}_k$ and the throughput X_k for server k. Because the M_k's are solved independently, the sum of the queue lengths ($\sum_k \bar{n}_k$) may not equal N, the network population; moreover, the local throughputs (X_k's) may not satisfy the forced-flow law ($X_k = V_k X_0$, where $X_0 = (\sum_k X_k/V_k)/K$). When this happens, the $S_k^*(n)$'s are corrected as shown in Table 1.1, and the M_k's are solved with the new estimates of the service functions.

Marie's method [MARI78] is similar to the CHW method. Marie treats each submodel M_k as an $M(\lambda(n))/G/1$ queue, where $\lambda(n)$ is the arrival rate to the queue and equals the throughput of the complementary network with $N - n$ customers. Assuming that queue k's service time has a rational Laplace transform, he computes $S_k^*(n)$ directly rather than by solving for $\bar{n}_k$ and X_k and using Table 1.1. (Marie's method always has $\sum_k \bar{n}_k = N$ and $X_0 = V_k X_k$.) The initial value of $S_k^*(n)$ is obtained by ignoring the CV of queue k, and then, is iteratively corrected.

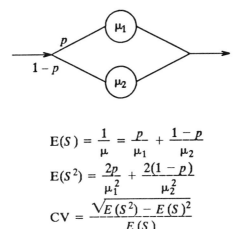

$$E(S) = \frac{1}{\mu} = \frac{p}{\mu_1} + \frac{1-p}{\mu_2}$$

$$E(S^2) = \frac{2p}{\mu_1^2} + \frac{2(1-p)}{\mu_2^2}$$

$$CV = \frac{\sqrt{E(S^2) - E(S)^2}}{E(S)}$$

Figure 1.1: A hyperexponential server.

Balbo has extensively studied and compared these three methods [BALB79]. His recommendation is to ignore the problem if the CV is small (0.5 < CV < 2). Otherwise, Shum and Buzen's method should be used if the network contains only one FCFS server with general service times. If there are two or more non-exponential servers in the network, Marie's method is preferable. The CHW method is not robust and is not as good as other two methods. It is also much more cumbersome to implement.

Zahorjan, Lazowska and Garner's method is based on the theory of near-decomposability [ZAHO83]. We illustrate their method with an example. Assume that the service time at the CPU can be represented as a two stage hyperexponential server as shown in Figure 1.1. With the assumption that $\mu_1 \gg \mu_2$ and $p \gg (1-p)$, the states of the network can be decomposed into two nearly-decomposable sets. The first set represents the states in which stage 2 (rate μ_2) of the hyperexponential is not in service; these states are the states of the network M_1 in which the CPU is replaced by stage 1 (rate μ_1) of the hyperexponential. The second aggregate represents the states in which the stage 2 of the hyperexponential server is always busy; these states are isomorphic with the states of the network M_2 which has $N-1$ customers and in which the CPU is replaced by the stage 2 of the hyperexponential. The conditional probability distribution $p(s \mid i)$, the probability that the system is in state s given that the system is in the aggregate i, can be obtained by solving product form model M_i. The unconditional steady state probability is

$$p(s) = p(s \mid i) \, w_i,$$

where w_i is the probability that the system is in aggregate i; the w_i are given by:

$$w_1 = \frac{\mu_2 p}{\mu_2 + U_1 \mu_1 (1-p)},$$
$$w_2 = 1 - w_1,$$

where U_1 is the utilization of stage 1 in M_1. Other performance measures are the weighted averages of the measures of M_1 and M_2.

1.2.2 Memory Queueing

Memory queueing occurs in two stages. First a job has to wait for memory partition or a scheduling token to become available before it can compete for CPU and I/O devices. Then, once scheduled, it experiences paging delays that depend on the current level of multiprogramming. Because a job holds two limited resources at the same time (memory and CPU or an I/O device), the autonomous behavior assumption is violated and the system does not have a product form solution.

Most approximations for this problem are applications of the decomposition principle [CHAN75b, DENN78]. Consider a network with a subsystem containing non-homogeneous behavior. Construct a flow-equivalent server for the subsystem by analyzing the subsystem in isolation under fixed load. Replace the subsystem by its flow-equivalent server in the original network. If the state transitions within the subsystem occur at a much greater rate than interactions between the subsystem and the rest of the system, not much error is introduced by this replacement [COUR75, COUR77].

In the memory queueing problem, we replace the central subsystem by a flow-equivalent server and equat the memory queue with the queue at the flow-equivalent server. This method is directly applicable to single class networks [BRAN74, CHAN75b, COUR75, COUR77] and is examined in detail in Section 2.5.

A direct application of the decomposition technique to multiclass networks produces a flow-equivalent server with service function $S_{Er}(n_1, \ldots, n_R)$. A network containing servers with such service functions does not have a product form solution. Sauer [SAUE81a] used global balance analysis to solve it. Brandwajn [BRAN82], and Lazowska and Zahorjan [LAZO82] used the following approximation:

$$S_{Er}(n) \approx S_{Er}(\bar{n}_1, \ldots, \bar{n}_{r-1}, n, \bar{n}_{r+1}, \ldots, \bar{n}_R),$$

where $S_{Er}(\bar{n}_1, \ldots, \bar{n}_{r-1}, n, \bar{n}_{r+1}, \ldots, \bar{n}_R)$ is the service time for class r when there are n class r and $\bar{n}_j$ class j customers $(j \neq r)$ in the subsystem, and $\bar{n}_j$ is the average number of class j customers in the subsystem. With this approximation, the network is effectively decomposed into R single class product form networks. These networks are iteratively solved to determine $\bar{n}_1, \ldots, \bar{n}_R$. This approximation is examined further in Chapter 4.

1.2.3   Simultaneous Resource Possession in I/O Subsystems

Memory queueing was an instance of simultaneous resource possession. Another instance of simultaneous resource possession occurs when a disk is blocked and cannot transfer data because another disk is using the channel. If this blocking is neglected, the resulting model usually underestimates the response time. Several researchers have developed approximate solutions for this problem. We discuss some of them below.

Wilhelm [WILH77] models each disk as an (open) $M/G/1$ queue. The basic service time of disk includes the time for seek, preparation (or search), and data transfer phases. It is elongated to include the effect of channel contention. A model for the probability that the channel (the path to the CPU) is free when requested is used to compute elongation of the service time. His model assumes that only a single path exists for each disk and disks are not shared between different CPUs. This assumption simplifies the calculation of the free path probability. Bard removes this assumption and computes the free path probability by using the maximum entropy principle [BARD80].

Jacobson and Lazowska [JACO82] analyze a closed system containing simultaneous resource possession. Their method generates two models that provide parameters for each other. The first model represents the channel queueing as a pure delay whose value comes from the other model; it computes the delay caused by seek, search and data transfer operations. The second model represents the seek-search-transfer queueing as pure delay whose value comes from the first model; it computes the channel queueing. This technique is applicable to a variety of simultaneous resource possession problems and is discussed in detail in Chapter 3.

1.2.4 Priority Scheduling

Computer systems containing devices at which some job classes have priority over others violate the fair service assumption necessary for product form solution.

Sevcik [SEVC77] analyzed such systems by replacing preemptive priority server with a shadow server for each priority class. The service rate of a shadow server is degraded to reflect the contention from higher-priority customers. This method is discussed in detail in Chapter 2. Improvements on this method are presented in Chapters 3 and 4.

Bryant and Krzesinski [BRYA83], and Chandy and Laksmi [CHAN83] have proposed extensions to Mean Value Analysis (MVA) for analyzing priority systems. They introduce no new servers; instead, they modify the formula for response times at priority servers (see Box 1.2). These two methods are further discussed in Chapter 4.

Agrawal, Buzen and Shum [AGRA84] analyze systems with preemptive priority scheduling at CPU by replacing the CPU by a set of equivalent servers, one server for each priority level. The service times at the equivalent servers are such that the response times at the priority CPU assuming Poisson arrivals are equal to that at the equivalent servers. This method is discussed in Appendix C.

1.2.5 Serialization

Critical sections and database record access are two examples of serialized or single-threaded processing. An exact queueing network model of systems with serialization does not have a product form solution because jobs simultaneously hold a "serialization token" and physical devices.

Response time in MVA at a FCFS, PS, LCFS-PR server

$$R_{ir}(\underline{N}) = S_{ir}\left(1 + \sum_{j=1}^{R} \bar{n}_{ij}(\underline{N}-\underline{1}_r)\right)$$

$(\underline{1}_r = (n_1, \ldots, n_R)$ with $n_r = 1$ and $n_j = 0, j \neq r$.)

Bryant-Krzesinski's response time formula
for a preemptive priority server

$$R_{ir}(\underline{N}) = \frac{S_{ir} + \sum_{j=1}^{r} \bar{n}_{ij}(\underline{N}-\underline{1}_r)S_{ij}}{1 - \sum_{j=1}^{r-1} S_{ij}V_{ij}X_j(\underline{N})}$$

Chandy-Laksmi's response time formula
for a preemptive priority server

$$R_{ir}(\underline{N}) = \frac{S_{ir} + \sum_{j=1}^{r} \bar{n}_{ij}(\underline{N}-\underline{1}_r)S_{ij}}{1 - \sum_{j=1}^{r-1} S_{ij}V_{ij}X_j(\underline{N}-\bar{n}_{ij}(\underline{N})\underline{1}_j)}$$

(Class j has priority over class r if $j < r$.)

Box 1.2: Response time expressions for MVA-like priority algorithms.

Agrawal and Buzen [AGRA83] use a shadow server for each critical section in a given computer system. The shadow server's service time is the mean time for that phase of serialized processing. Service times of other devices is degraded to represent concealment of the load imposed by jobs in serialized phases. The details of this method are presented in Chapter 3.

Agre and Tripathi [AGRE82] model reentrant software by representing each software module as a separate server. They allow a module to receive processing only from one device. The service rate of each module server is a function of the number of customers at other modules that execute on the same device. This model is solved using global balance analysis.

Smith and Browne [SMIT80b] divide a job's execution into three phases. Phase 1 is the time from job initiation until the critical section request. Phase 2 is the critical section processing phase. Phase 3 is the processing after the critical section execution. They include a FCFS server WQ (for Wait Queue) to simulate the delay for critical section entry. The service time of WQ, S_{WQ}, equals R_2, the residency time of Phase 2. On switching form Phase 1 to Phase 2, the customer is routed to WQ with the probability

$$ P_{WQ} = 1 - \left[\frac{R_1 + R_3}{R_1 + R_2 + R_3} \right]^{N-1}, $$

where R_i is the residency time of Phase i. This routing is independent of the number of customers presently in the critical section; hence it does not represent the concurrency constraint satisfactorily.

Jacobson and Lazowska [JACO83] use a two level model for the system. The low level model computes critical section residency times given a fixed load equal to the average number of active non-serialized customers and the average number of customers in each critical section. The high level model uses these residency times to determine the average number of customers inside each critical section and the average number of customers outside all critical sections. The two models are iteratively solved.

Thomasian [THOM83] has developed two different techniques for modeling serialization delays. First is an iterative technique that is similar to Smith and Browne's technique [SMIT80b] considered earlier; it uses an improved estimate for P_{WQ}. The second is based on state aggregation: the states are aggregated such that the number of customers in each processing phase is the same for all states in an aggregate state. The aggregate state model is solved using global balance solution techniques. This technique is further discussed in Chapter 4.

1.2.6 Internal Program Concurrency

Internal program concurrency results from FORK-JOIN operations and overlapped CPU-I/O processing within a job. FORK and JOIN operations imply nonautonomous behavior of jobs; the child processes are created together and the parent process cannot continue until all child processes have finished. Similar remarks hold for overlapped CPU-I/O processing. (Compare with nonautonomous behavior of disks and channels). No product form solution exists for such systems.

Towsley, Chandy and Browne [TOWS78] model CPU-I/O overlap by replacing the I/O subsystem by its composite flow-equivalent server. The state equations of the resulting network are solved numerically.

For processes containing FORK and JOIN operations, Smith and Browne [SMIT80a] divide jobs into primary and secondary chains. A primary chain job is the one with the largest expected concurrent execution time (i.e., the one which is expected to perform JOIN last); other jobs form a secondary chain. The time from the process (primary job) initiation until the FORK plus the time from the secondary job JOIN until the primary job completion is represented as pure delay for secondary jobs.

Heidelberger and Trivedi [HEID82, HEID83] have developed approximate models for analyzing asynchronous concurrency (i.e., FORK but no JOIN) and synchronous concurrency (i.e., both FORK and JOIN). In their asynchronous concurrency model [HEID82], forked jobs are represented as open classes. The throughput of the forked jobs should equal the throughput of the parent jobs because a parent process forks one child process of each kind. The model is iteratively solved until balanced throughputs are obtained. They present two techniques for modeling FORK and JOIN operations [HEID83]. The first one involves state aggregation: all states in which the number of active jobs of each type (parent or child process r) is the same are aggregated and the resulting model is solved using global balance solution methods. The second method employs a multiclass model in which each parent and child job is in a separate class. This model also employs additional delay servers to represent the mean synchronization delays between the processes; these delays are iteratively computed. (The second method is similar to that used by Smith and Browne [SMIT80a].) All three techniques are discussed further in Chapter 4.

1.2.7 Blocking

Blocking is a general phenomenon that occurs when the operation of a server is suspended because of the unavailability of resources elsewhere in the network. Examples include:

- finite buffers -- in store and forward communication networks a node cannot transmit a message until the destination node has a buffer available,

- Ethernet -- a node cannot transmit because another node is transmitting on the bus,

- token rings -- a node is blocked until it gets the token, and

- I/O subsystems -- a disk is blocked because the channel is busy transferring data for another disk.

Because of the nonautonomous behavior of these resources, a queueing network with blocking does not have a product form solution. A variety of techniques have been developed to deal with this problem. A brief discussion of some of these techniques follows.

Labetoulle and Pujolle [LABE80] study packet switched networks with finite buffer size at each node by analyzing each queue separately. They model each queue as a $GI/G/1/M_i$ queue with loss (M_i is the number of buffers at node i.). The arrival process (GI) at a queue i is the conjunction of the completion processes (G) of the queues whose output comes to i. If an arrival from queue j to queue i is rejected, it returns to j and a new service of the returned job immediately begins at j. Each queue is solved using diffusion approximation [GELE75, BADE76], and these solutions are reconciled iteratively.

Almes and Lazowska propose a simple markov model for the symmetrical Ethernet control policies [ALME79]. In this model, the message arrival rate is independent of the number of messages already queued, and the message delivery rate of the network when n nodes desire to transmit equals the network capacity times the instantaneous throughput efficiency of the network, E ;

$$E = \frac{1}{1 + \frac{1-A}{A}},$$

where A is the message transmission (the Ether acquisition) probability;

$$A = (1 - 1/n)^{n-1}.$$

Gelenbe and Mitrani [GELE82] model the Ethernet control policies by using a two step iterative procedure. In the first step, they analyze each station in isolation assuming that global parameters, e.g., probability of blocking and probability of determining that a transfer is in progress, are known. In the second step, the results of these single station analyses are used to obtain characteristics of global load and to compute the unknown parameters for station analyses.

Kuehn [KUEH79] analyzes token rings and cyclic service by treating each node i as an $M/G/1$ server. The service time parameters of server i are determined by analyzing token scans in two parts: scans in which no message is transmitted at node i ($c\cdot$), and the scans in which a message is transmitted from node i ($c\cdot$). The means and variance of $c\cdot$ and $c\cdot$ are used to compute the waiting time of the customer.

1.2.8 Approximate Analysis of Large Product Form Networks

Although product form solution algorithms are efficient, their cost rises exponentially with the number of classes in the network. The cost can become prohibitive for sufficiently large networks. As an illustration, consider the MVA equations for a load independent network:

$$R_{ir}(\underline{n}) = S_{ir}(1 + \sum_{j=1}^{R} \bar{n}_{ij}(\underline{n} - \underline{1}_r)), \quad i = 1, \dots, K,$$

$$X_r(\underline{n}) = \frac{n_r}{\sum_{i=1}^{K} V_{ir} R_{ir}},$$

$$\bar{n}_{ir}(\underline{n}) = V_{ir} R_{ir}(\underline{n}) X_r(\underline{n}), \quad i = 1, \dots, K.$$

These equations are solved for $\underline{n} = (\underline{0})$ to $\underline{n} = \underline{N} = (N_1, \dots, N_R)$. The cost of solving this network is $RK \prod_{r=1}^{R}(N_r + 1)$ multiplications and and equal number of additions [ZAHO80]. (The same amount of computation is required for the Convolution algorithm.) This number grows rapidly with number of classes R, number of customers in each class, $N_1, \ldots, N_R$; it can become very large. For example a network with 15 servers, 5 classes, and 10 customers in each class requires about 48 million operations. The storage requirement for this network is 322,102 words for the Convolution algorithm and 1,390,895 words for the MVA algorithm. The computational costs for networks with load-dependent servers are much higher; if all the 15 servers in the above example are load-dependent, the number of required operations is about 1500 times as great, and the storage requirement for MVA is about 9 times (2 times for Convolution) as great.

There are two main approaches to reducing this cost. The first approach is to avoid recursion in the computation by solving for the mean values at a single, given load $\underline{N}$. The second approach is to reduce the complexity by reducing the number of classes (R), number of customers in each class (N_r), or the number of servers (K) in the network. The second approach is discussed and analyzed in detail by Zahorjan [ZAHO80]; an overview of the the techniques appears later in Chapter 4. Following examples illustrate the first approach.

Bard-Schweitzer Approximation [SCHW79]:

The principle is to estimate the queue length $\bar{n}_{ir}(\underline{N} - \underline{1}_r)$ from $\bar{n}_{ir}(\underline{N})$ in the response time equations of MVA, thereby obviating the recursion to obtain $\bar{n}_{ir}(\underline{N} - \underline{1}_r)$. The resulting iterative algorithm is:

Initially assume $\hat{\bar{n}}_{ir}(\underline{N}) = \dfrac{N_r}{K}$, $i = 1, \ldots, K$, $r = 1, \ldots, R$.

Repeat

$$\bar{n}_{ir}(\underline{N}) = \hat{\bar{n}}_{ir}(\underline{N})$$

$$\bar{n}_{ir}(\underline{N} - \underline{1}_j) = \begin{cases} \bar{n}_{ir}(\underline{N}) & j \neq r \\ \dfrac{N_r - 1}{N_r} \bar{n}_{ir}(\underline{N}) & j = r \end{cases}$$

$$R_{ir}(\underline{N}) = S_{ir}(1 + \sum_{j=1}^{R} \bar{n}_{ij}(\underline{N} - \underline{1}_r))$$

$$X_r(\underline{N}) = \dfrac{N_r}{\sum\limits_{i=1}^{K} V_{ir} R_{ir}(\underline{N})}$$

$$\hat{\bar{n}}_{ir}(\underline{N}) = X_r V_{ir} R_{ir}(\underline{N})$$

until $|\hat{\bar{n}}_{ir}(\underline{N}) - \bar{n}_{ir}(\underline{N})| < \epsilon$.

Linearizer Approximation [CHAN82]:

Chandy and Neuse's Linearizer algorithm is a generalization of the Bard-Schweitzer approximation [CHAN82]. It iteratively estimates queue lengths at loads $\underline{N}$, $\underline{N} - \underline{1}_j$ and $\underline{N} - \underline{1}_j - \underline{1}_l$ to eliminate the need for recursion. The estimator is

$$\bar{n}_{ir}(\underline{N} - \underline{1}_j) = \begin{cases} \bar{n}_{ir}(\underline{N}) + N_r D_{irj}(\underline{N}) & j \neq r \\ \dfrac{N_r - 1}{N_r} \bar{n}_{ir}(\underline{N}) + (N_r - 1)D_{irr}(\underline{N}) & j = r, \end{cases}$$

where $D_{irj}(\underline{N})$ is the change in the fraction of class r jobs at queue i resulting from removal of one class j job, i.e.,

$$D_{irj}(\underline{N}) = \begin{cases} \dfrac{\bar{n}_{ir}(\underline{N}-\underline{1}_j)}{N_r} - \dfrac{\bar{n}_{ir}(\underline{N})}{N_r} & j \neq r \\[3ex] \dfrac{\bar{n}_{ir}(\underline{N}-\underline{1}_r)}{N_r-\underline{1}_r} - \dfrac{\bar{n}_{ir}(\underline{N})}{N_r} & j = r. \end{cases}$$

The Linearizer algorithm assumes that D_{irj} is a constant. Note that assuming $D_{irj}(\underline{N}) = 0$ gives the same expressions as the Bard-Schweitzer algorithm.

Bound Analysis [DENN78, ZAHO82, EAGE83a]:

A third class of approximations for the solutions of large networks is based on bounds on performance measures. Bounds are, however, available only for single class networks. Bottleneck analysis [DENN78] gives asymptotic upper bounds on network throughput

$$X_0(N) \leq \min\left(\frac{N}{\sum V_i S_i}, \frac{1}{V_b S_b}\right),$$

where subscript b indicates the bottleneck device, i.e., the device with largest $V_i S_i$.

Balanced Job Bound analysis [ZAHO82] provides tighter bounds by comparing the given system with two balanced systems: a faster one in which all devices have the demand equal to the average ($\sum V_i S_i / K$), and a slower one in which all devices have demand equal to the bottleneck ($V_b S_b$). The bounds are:

$$\frac{N}{\left(\dfrac{\sum V_i S_i}{V_b S_b} + N - 1\right)V_b S_b} \leq X(N) \leq \frac{N}{(K + N - 1)\dfrac{\sum V_i S_i}{K}}.$$

Note that $\sum V_i S_i / V_b S_b$ is the number of devices in a network in which the demand at each server is $V_b S_b$, and $\sum V_i S_i / K$ is the average demand per device in a balanced K server network.

A hierarchy of upper and lower bounds on throughput can be obtained by analyzing system with initial queue length bounds for $\bar{n}_i(n_0)$, and then using MVA equations to compute bounds for $n_0, \ldots, N$ customers [EAGE83a]. A tradeoff exists between the cost and the tightness of bounds: smaller n_0 means higher cost and potentially tighter bounds.

1.3   Plan of the Monograph

Most presentations of the approximations reviewed above begin with the specific nonhomogeneous behavior to be modeled, propose a solution, and illustrate its validity with a few examples. Few try to fit their models into any larger scheme of modeling. Fewer still include systematic studies of errors or validations of their proposals. Consequently, it is difficult for the observer to appreciate the generality of the result or safely apply the method in new contexts.

These difficulties hamper communication among researchers, practitioners, and students. They limit the complexity of the problems that can be solved. With increasing complexity of models, the situation only worsens.

The goal of this work is to set forth a single description of the modeling process underlying all the approximations reviewed above. This description is based upon a general queueing network model of the system. This model directly corresponds to a set of states and state transitions; the transitions are represented as a transition rate matrix. There are three approaches to obtaining a solution of a model:

1. *Direct:* Solve the global balance equations implied by the transition rate matrix on the state space.

2. *Sampling:* Observe a sample path (behavior sequence) of the system, or of a faithful simulation, and estimate the desired performance metrics.

3. *Approximation*: Transform the model to a simpler one, solve it, and use the results as an estimate of the original solution.

This monograph focuses on approximation.

Chapter 2 shows that the modeling process can be viewed as a series of simple steps, each of which is is the construction of a transformation from a given model (M_0) to a simpler but less accurate model (M). The modeler must specify a forward map that gives the parameters of M in terms of the parameters and the performance measures of M_0; and a reverse map that gives the performance metrics of M_0 in terms of those of M. The exact solution of M_0 consists of solving the state space equations for M_0. The approximate solution consists of three steps:

1. Map forward to M.

2. Solve M.

3. Map reverse to M_0.

The goal is that these three steps be much faster than a direct solution of M_0 without significant loss of accuracy.

In Chapter 2 we show that the above basic pattern can be used hierarchically -- i.e., the model M can be further transformed and simplified. We also show that iteration arises naturally in the solution of models -- i.e., the three basic steps may need repetition to solve for unknown metrics in M_0. We illustrate the generality of this description by applying it to some of the principal approximations reviewed earlier.

Chapter 3 studies the class of approximations based on adding extra servers, called shadow servers, to represent the additional queueing delay caused by nonhomogeneous behavior in the original system. An important aid in model development is the behavior sequence transformation, a picture of the way a typical job uses resources as it moves through the system. The method is used to show how the Sevcik shadow CPU approximation and the Jacobson-Lazowska surrogate server approximation can be derived. It is then used to derive a new approximation, the aggregate servers method for modeling serialization.

Chapter 4 generalizes further by characterizing the state spaces underlying models and the ways in which the modeling process manipulates these spaces. The resulting description of model transformations is compact. We use state space transformations to develop a better model, based on a load dependent shadow CPU, for the preemptive priority systems. We also catalog a set of common transformations and illustrate them; they are load concealment, state aggregation, server aggregation, load separation, class aggregation, load scaling, response time modeling, and delay server introduction.

Chapter 5 takes up consistency requirements and convergence proofs for iterative algorithms. We explain why convergence proofs are difficult to obtain in performance modeling. Then, based on the monotonicity properties of queueing networks, we propose two practical techniques for proving convergence. We use these techniques for proving convergence of Bard-Schweitzer algorithm, the Jacobson-Lazowska method for simultaneous resource possession, and the shadow CPU algorithm for preemptive priority at CPU. The basic theorem about convergence predicts the possibility of two or more stable solutions for some networks. This prediction is corroborated with the shadow CPU algorithm, which correctly predicts two possible values for high-priority CPU utilization of a simulated system.

Chapter 6 concludes the monograph by outlining the metamodeling methodology and providing a perspective.

Appendix A presents numerical studies comparing Sevcik's original shadow CPU algorithm, our modifications of the algorithm, the Bryant-Krzesinski priority algorithm, and the Chandy-Laksmi priority algorithm.

Appendix B extends the aggregate server method for open and multi-class mixed networks.

Appendix C presents a general technique for developing approximate analysis methods for a large class of problems. This technique involves replacing a non-product form subsystem by a set of equivalent servers such that the response time at the equivalent servers under an assumed arrival process is same as that at the subsystem. The technique was developed after the metamodeling framework had been formulated. Therefore, it illustrates the usefulness of the research reported in the main body of this monograph.

Appendix D presents some considerations for design and simulation of preemptive priority systems.

As a running example throughout this work, we use a system with preemptive priority scheduling at CPU. In Chapter 2, Sevcik's algorithm applied to this problem illustrates how iteration arises in the basic modeling pattern. In Chapter 3, behavior sequence transformations applied to this problem lead to a better approximation extending Sevcik's. In Chapter 4, state space transformations applied to this problem lead to an even better approximation with a load-dependent server. In Chapter 5, it illustrates the role of consistency requirements, exemplifies one of the techniques for proving convergence and exhibits multiple solutions in some cases. In Appendix C, response time preservation (RTP) transformation applied to this problem yield another efficient solution technique. Each time, we learn something new about the preemptive priority systems and their modeling through the medium of this example.

1.4 Related Work

Our review of approximate solution techniques in Section 1.2 showed a variety of studies employing heuristics that seem to work but which have not been studied systematically for their general properties. Relatively little effort has been made to understand the process of approximate model development. This section reviews the few works that have.

An early approach to solving complex models of computer systems is based on the concept of near-decomposability; it was proposed by Simon and Ando [SIMO61] and applied to queueing systems by Courtois [COUR77]. The basic idea is simple. Start with a state space that accurately describes the system. Aggregate subsets of states such that (1) the transitions within a subset can be analyzed by assuming that the transitions between subsets do not exist, and (2) the transitions between subsets can be studied without regard to the transitions within subsets.[2] Each aggregate can be solved for its state occupancies internally as if it were a closed system. A macro model is solved for the probability of being in each aggregate. The probability of being in a state is estimated as the product of the two foregoing probabilities.

The process of aggregating the states can be recursively applied to obtain a hierarchy of state-models. Courtois has studied the requirements for near-decomposability and the errors introduced by hierarchical aggregation [COUR77]. In many computer system applications, the errors are small. He

---

2. If such an aggregation is possible, then system is *nearly-decomposable*. An intuitive condition for near-decomposability is that the transitions within a subset of states be much more frequent than the transitions from the subset to other subsets (i.e., the rest of the states).

also showed that if the service rate of resource R_{k-1} is an order of magnitude higher than the service rate of resource R_k, resources $R_0, \ldots, R_L$ can be aggregated one by one to obtain a linear hierarchy of aggregate resources $A_0, \ldots, A_L$, where A_k is an aggregate of R_k and A_{k-1}.

Chandy, Herzog and Woo's "Norton's Theorem", discussed in Section 1.2.2 on memory queueing, is another method to aggregate resources [CHAN75b].[3] In contrast to Courtois's method, the Norton's theorem has its roots in complete decomposability of product form networks: any set of resources in a product form network is exactly replaceable by its composite flow-equivalent server. Vantilborgh *et al.* have shown that this approach does not introduce significant errors in non-product form networks if the routing matrix is nearly-decomposable [VANT80].

Another general approach to model development was used by Browne *et al.* [BROW75]. They used a *macro* model of the system in which major subsystems are represented as single servers. They obtained the parameters of these servers by analyzing *micro* models for corresponding subsystems. This approach is hierarchical and permits successive refinements of the model.

Similar to Browne *et al.*'s hierarchical approach is the *isolation method* proposed by Labetoulle and Pujolle [LABE80]. They first partition the system into N solvable subsystems and define the input and output interfaces

---

3. Recall, the service function $S(n)$ of the equivalent server is determined by computing the throughput $X(n)$ of the subsystem in isolation under fixed load n and setting $S(n) = 1/X(n)$. This process is the equivalent of setting the service time of other resources to zero, or "short-circuiting" them. In an analogy with electrical circuits, Chandy, Herzog and Woo call this technique as an application of Norton's Theorem. Denning and Buzen call it "On-line behavior = Off-line behavior" because we have equated its on-line (in-system behavior) with its off-line (in isolation) behavior [DENN78].

(processes) for each subsystem. They then iteratively solve the subnetworks to obtain a consistent solution for the original network.

These approaches are similar in spirit but different in details. The major similarity is their use of the principle of hierarchically reducing a complex model to simpler models. The differences arise from their historical roots, their domains of apparent applicability, and their solution algorithms. The differences can easily mask the strong underlying similarities. One of the purposes of this work is to identify the general modeling process being used and show how existing approximate models illustrate this process.

CHAPTER 2

THE STRUCTURE OF THE MODELING PROCESS

The purpose of this chapter is to set forth a structure underlying all approximations. This structure is based on the concept of model transformation. We first illustrate the basic idea of transformation, then provide formal syntax, and extend the basic process by including iteration, multiple refinement and recursion (successive transformation). These basic structural concepts lead to an iterative hierarchy of models. We conclude the chapter by exhibiting the generality of this structure. The structure will aid the analyst in the formulation of complete (fully specified) models and in the analysis of error introduced by assumptions made during the modeling process.

2.1 Basic Modeling Process

The modeling process has three main components: model construction, solution, and validation. The analyst starts with an initial accurate model that accounts for all relevant aspects of system operation. If, as often happens, no solution of this model can be obtained cheaply, the analyst must transform it into an easily-solved approximate model. The approximate solution must then be validated against measured performance quantities.

There are two potential sources of validation error. One is that the initial model itself is inaccurate; we will ignore this problem by assuming that the analyst chooses a sufficiently accurate starting model. The other possibility is that the model transformation procedure is not exact because the required assumptions are not likely to be satisfied. Thus the critical component in the study of the modeling process is the model transformation procedure.

The initial model will be denoted by M_0. M_0 is typically the system or its associated general queueing network. Corresponding to this model is its state space and state transitions. A direct solution of M_0 involves solving the state equations or sampling (by observation or simulation). In each case M_0 gives accurate values of standard performance measures. In each case, however, constructing and solving M_0 is typically expensive because of its internal complexity and many parameters. Moreover, M_0 is typically unreliable to use for predictions because of the difficulty of accurately estimating its many parameters.

Let P_0 denote the set of parameters of M_0. Let Q_0 denote the set of performance quantities of interest in M_0. The solution procedure is denoted SOLVE, where

$$Q_0 = \text{SOLVE}(M_0, P_0).$$

The foregoing discussion says that, typically, P_0 is large and SOLVE is computationally expensive.

To overcome the complexity of $\text{SOLVE}(M_0, P_0)$ and the size of P_0, the analyst seeks an *approximate model* M with these properties: 1) the parameters P of M are easy to derive from M_0 (i.e., by measurement or calculation from P_0 and Q_0); 2) the solution procedure $\text{SOLVE}(M, P)$ is fast; 3) the

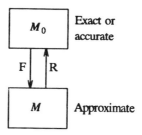

Figure 2.1: The basic pattern in the modeling process.

performance metrics Q_0 are easily obtainable from those of M; and 4) the approximations in transformations between M_0 and M do not introduce too much error. This concept of transforming model M_0 into M is illustrated graphically in Figure 2.1. The *modeling process* constructs the forward mapping F for specifying M and its parameters P, constructs the reverse mapping R, and evaluates error. The objectives are that (1) the cost of constructing M, solving it, and applying the reverse mapping (reverse mapping the solution) is lower than the cost of solving M_0 directly, and (2) the indirect solution does not introduce intolerable error.

The basic pattern of Figure 2.1 can be extended in two ways. First, the model M_0 can be transformed into a set of models $M_1, \ldots, M_n$ whose solutions are combined to form Q_0. Second, the basic pattern can be applied to any of these submodels, yielding still further refinements. The result is a hierarchy (tree) of models, with M_0 as the root, easily solvable models at the leaves, and functional compositions of the forward and reverse mappings to define how Q_0 is formed from the solutions at the leaf models.

2.2   Syntax of Basic Components of a Transformation

There are six components to a specification of the basic transformation illustrated in Figure 2.1:

1. Initial model M_0,
2. Transformed model M,
3. Forward mapping F,
4. Reverse mapping R,
5. Solution algorithm SOLVE for M, and
6. Solution algorithm for Q_0.

A formal description of these components is presented below. Specific examples are provided in subsequent sections.

The **initial model** M_0 is an accurate specification of a system. To fix ideas, we will regard M_0 as the set of global balance equations relating the state occupancy probabilities of the system. The parameters P_0 are then the coefficients of the equations and the solutions Q_0 are the state occupancy probabilities (or linear combinations thereof). The state occupancy probabilities are the most detailed performance measure from which other measures can be derived.

The **transformed model** M is an approximate representation of the system. Its parameters are P and solutions are Q.

The **forward mapping F** defines M and P in terms of M_0, P_0 and Q_0. For simplicity, however, we will assume that M_0 and M are implicit in the mapping and write it as:

$$P = \mathrm{F}(P_0, Q_0).$$

Typically parameters P of M are averages of functions over state subsets of M_0. These parameters may depend on those of M_0 and on the proportions of the time states are occupied; hence, P is, in general, a function of P_0 and Q_0.

The assumptions embodied in forward mappings, which define parameters of M in terms of averages over state subsets of M_0, are often called *homogeneity assumptions* [DENN78], or *aggregation assumptions* [COUR77].

SOLVE denotes any algorithm for computing the metrics Q given model M and its parameters P, i.e.,

$$Q = \text{SOLVE}(M, P).$$

For example, SOLVE is an equation solver when M is directly solved (analytically).

The **reverse mapping R** maps Q back into Q_0:

$$Q_0 = \text{R}(Q).$$

Note R depends implicitly on M_0 and M. It is often an identity mapping for some or all performance metrics. It is sometimes referred to as a *disaggregation function* [COUR77].

Now the solution procedure for M_0 can be defined as a solver for the set of these equations given above:

$$
\boxed{
\begin{aligned}
&\text{SOLVE}(M_0, P_0): \\
&\quad P = \text{F}(P_0, Q_0) \\
&\quad Q = \text{SOLVE}(M, P) \\
&\quad Q_0 = \text{R}(Q)
\end{aligned}
}
$$

When the solution Q_0 involved in the forward transformation is unknown, some numerical techniques must be used to obtain the values of Q_0 from these equations (given F, R, SOLVE and P_0). Henceforth we will generally refer to such techniques as *iteration*. The general schema for an iterative algorithm is:

SOLVE(M_0, P_0):

Choose initial guess $\hat{Q}_0$
repeat
$\quad Q_0 := \hat{Q}_0$
$\quad P := F(P_0, Q_0)$
$\quad Q := \text{SOLVE}(M, P)$
$\quad \hat{Q}_0 := R(Q)$
until Error(Q_0, $\hat{Q}_0$) < ϵ

An iteration starts with an initial guess, $Q_0^{(0)}$, of the solution and produces a series of refinements $Q_0^{(1)}$, $Q_0^{(2)}$, $\cdots$ to this guess. The iteration stops when successive solutions are close enough according to the error function. One of the tasks faced by the analyst is showing that this sequence converges to a unique and correct answer.

It is not unusual for P to be a direct transformation of P_0 that does not require Q_0, e.g., when no additional explicit averaging is performed over states of M_0. In this special case, the set of equations becomes

SOLVE(M_0, P_0):

$\quad P = F(P_0)$
$\quad Q = \text{SOLVE}(M, P)$
$\quad Q_0 = R(Q)$

which can be solved without iteration.

The following sections illustrate these concepts for a variety of common modeling processes:

1) Application of homogeneity assumptions to single and multiple queues, leading to product form solutions without iteration;

2) Sevcik's shadow CPU algorithm, which illustrates iteration;

3) Decomposition using a flow-equivalent server without iteration;

4) Decomposition using a flow-equivalent server with iteration;

5) Representation of Convolution, Mean Value Analysis, and Performance Bound Hierarchy algorithms by recursive application of the basic modeling structure;

6) A full-tree hierarchy of models; and

7) Other examples: state aggregation and diffusion approximation.

We also compare the concept of hierarchy of models as defined here with the one used by other researchers in the past.

2.3   Example 1: Single Server Queue

Let M_0 be a generalized birth-death model of a single server, flow balanced queue whose length is the random variable n. The parameters P_0 of this model, the arrival rate function $\lambda(n)$ and the service time function $S(n)$, can be obtained from measurements of the queue. The solutions Q_0 are the exact state occupancy probabilities $\{p(n)\}$; they satisfy [BUZE76b, BUZE78b]:

$$p(n) = p(n-1)\,\lambda(n-1)\,S(n).$$

M_0 can be transformed into a model M that has Homogeneous Arrivals (HA) and Homogeneous Service (HS) [BRUM82, BUZE80a, BUZE80b]. The parameters P of this model are homogeneous arrival rate λ and service time S. The solutions Q are the state probability estimates $\{\hat{p}(n)\}$; they satisfy

$$\hat{p}(n) = \hat{p}(n-1)\lambda S.$$

The forward mapping F for obtaining parameters, solution procedure SOLVE(M, P), and the reverse mapping R are given in Box 2.1.

Example 1: Single Server Queue

M_0: Generalized birth-death model of a single server queue
P_0: $\{\lambda(n), S(n)\}$
Q_0: $\{p(n)\}$

M: Homogeneous service time and arrival rate model
P: $\{\lambda, S\}$
Q: $\{\hat{p}(n)\}$

F: Homogenizes arrival rate and service time
      (i.e., assume homogeneity):

$$\lambda = \sum_{n \geq 0} \lambda(n)\, p(n)$$

$$S = \frac{\sum_{n > 0} p(n)}{\sum_{n > 0} p(n)/S(n)}$$

R: Identity: $p(n) = \hat{p}(n)$.

SOLVE(M, P): $\hat{p}(n) = (1 - \lambda S)(\lambda S)^n$.

Iteration: Not Required.

Box 2.1: Homogenization of a single server queue:
A basic model transformation without iteration.

Model M is more useful for predictions than M_0. This is so because a change in the speed of the server affects both $\lambda(n)$ and $S(n)$ nonlinearly in a complex way, whereas such a change affects only S in M.

2.4 Example 2: Queueing Network Model

For another simple example, let M_0 be a single-class closed queueing network model of a computer system with K servers whose global balance equations are

$$\sum_{i,j} p(\underline{n}_{ij}) \, r(\underline{n}_{ij}, \underline{n}) \ = \ p(\underline{n}) \sum_{i,j} r(\underline{n}, \underline{n}_{ji}) \, ,$$

where i and j are server indices in the range $1, \ldots, K$; $\underline{n} = (n_1, \ldots, n_K)$ denotes the state of the network with n_i customers at server i; state $\underline{n}_{ij} = (n_1, \ldots, n_i + 1, \ldots, n_j - 1, \cdots, n_K)$ is a neighbor of $\underline{n}$ that enters $\underline{n}$ when a customer moves from server i to server j; $p(\underline{n})$ is the state occupancy probability; and $r(\underline{n}_{ij}, \underline{n})$ is the flow-rate from $\underline{n}_{ij}$ to $\underline{n}$ given that system is in state $\underline{n}_{ij}$.

In general, these equations do not have an efficiently computable solution. But when $r(\underline{n}_{ij}, \underline{n})$ is replaced by $q_{ij}/S_i(n_i + 1)$, the resulting equations satisfy local balance conditions [CHAN77, SAUE81] and the solution has product form. The product form solution can be evaluated rapidly by the Convolution [BRUE80, BUZE73] or Mean Value Analysis (MVA) [REIS80] algorithms. Expressions for the routing probability q_{ij} and service time functions S_i are given by the forward mapping in Box 2.2.

Example 2: Single-Class Closed Queueing Network

M_0: Global balance equations of a closed queueing network.
P_0: $\{ r(\underline{n}_{ij}, \underline{n}), N \}$
Q_0: $\{ p(\underline{n}) \}$

M : Product form queueing network model (Local balance equations).
P : $\{ q_{ij}, S_i(n), N \}$
Q : $\{ \hat{p}(\underline{n}) \}$

F: Homogenize service rates and routing probabilities
(i.e., assume homogeneity):

$$S_i(n) = \frac{\sum_{n_i = n} p(\underline{n})}{\sum_{j \neq i} \sum_{n_i = n} p(\underline{n}) \, r(\underline{n}, \underline{n}_{ji})}$$

$$q_{ij} = \frac{\sum_{n > 0} \frac{\sum_{n_i = n} p(\underline{n}) \, r(\underline{n}, \underline{n}_{ji})}{\sum_{k \neq i} \sum_{n_i = n} p(\underline{n}) \, r(\underline{n}, \underline{n}_{ki})} \sum_{n_i = n} p(\underline{n})}{\sum_{n_i > 0} p(\underline{n})}$$

Sums mentioning n_i are over all $\underline{n}$;
Sums mentioning j (or k) are over all j (or k).

R: Identity: $p(\underline{n}) = \hat{p}(\underline{n})$

SOLVE(M, P):   Product form algorithms: Convolution, MVA, etc.

Iteration: Not Required.

Box 2.2: Homogenization of a queueing network model:
A basic model transformation - without iteration.

2.5   Example 3: Sevcik's Shadow CPU Model

Networks containing priority service cannot be modeled accurately by the product form solution obtained by ignoring the priority scheduling. Sevcik proposed an alternative that produces a more accurate product form solution [SEVC77].

The model M_0 is a two class queueing network model of a computer system. Class H customers have preemptive priority over class L customers at the CPU. For each class $r \in \{H, L\}$, the service time per visit to device i, S_{ir}, visit ratios V_{ir}, and the number of customers N_r are specified. The metric of interest is the system throughput X_{0r} for each class. This model does not satisfy the product form homogeneity requirement because the CPU service rate in class L depends on the class H queue length.

Sevcik proposes to split the CPU into two CPUs -- CPU-H and CPU-L -- each of which is visited by customers of only one class. Because class H customers are not affected by class L customers at the CPU, the processing rate of CPU-H is same as the processing rate of the original CPU. Because class L customers are delayed at the CPU by class H customers, CPU-L's processing rate should be degraded to reflect this contention. The CPU utilization due to class H customers, $U_{CPU,H}$, is the proportion of the CPU capacity used by class H customers; this portion is not available to class L customers. Sevcik argues that the processing rate of CPU-L should be $(1-U_{CPU,H})$ times the processing rate of the original CPU, or, $S_{CPU-L,L} = S_{CPU,L}/(1-U_{CPU,H})$. The service times in the resulting model are assumed to be homogeneous leading to an easily computable product form solution. The reverse mapping is an identity.

However, since we do not know $U_{CPU,H}$ in the beginning, an iterative procedure is required for computing $U_{CPU,H}$. The transformations are summarized in Box 2.3.

Example 3: Sevcik's Shadow CPU Model for Preemptive Priority at CPU

M_0: Two-class queueing network model of system; two queues at the CPU with class H having preemptive priority over class L.

P_0: $\{S_{ir}, V_{ir}, N_r\}$

Q_0: $\{X_{0r}, U_{CPU,H}\}$

M : Same queueing network as in M_0 except that the CPU is split into CPU-H and CPU-L, visited by classes H and L respectively.

P : $\{S_{CPU-H,H}, S_{CPU-L,L}, S_{ir}, V_{ir}, N_r\}$

Q : $\{X_r, U_{CPU-H,H}\}$

F:

$$S_{CPU-L,L} = \frac{S_{CPU,L}}{(1-U_{CPU,H})} \, ,$$

$S_{CPU-H,H} = S_{CPU,H}$, all other parameters same

Since the service discipline at other servers is not priority based, S_{ri} is a parameter of a product-form 2-class network.

R: Identity:
$X_{0r} = X_r$, $U_{CPU,H} = U_{CPU-H,H}$

SOLVE(M, P): Product form algorithms: Convolution, MVA, etc.

Iteration: Required.

Box 2.3: Sevcik's shadow CPU model: An example of simple transformation with iteration.

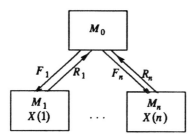

Figure 2.2: Multiple model schema used to construct
an equivalent server for the system modelled by M_0.

2.6 Example 4: Decomposition without Iteration

An important approximation, *decomposition*, is used to replace a
subsystem with a variable rate flow-equivalent server. If the subsystem
interacts weakly with the rest of the system, this replacement will not
significantly affect the queue length distributions outside the subsystem
[COUR77].

The usual approach to constructing the flow-equivalent server is to
consider the subsystem in isolation under a constant load of n customers and
find the job-flow $X(n)$ through it [CHAN75b, DENN78]. This is repeated for
all values of n of interest ($n = 1, \ldots, N$). The flow-equivalent server has a
service function $S(n) = 1/X(n)$.

The modeling process here actually employs a series of models for the
subsystem, $M_1, \ldots, M_N$, one for each value of n. The solutions of these
models are combined to form the flow-equivalent model for the subsystem.
The pattern, illustrated in Figure 2.2, is a generalization of Figure 2.1.

To illustrate, we consider an interactive system with maximum
multiprogramming level N. Let M_{TC} denote its accurate model; "TC" refers
to "Terminal and Central subsystem". M_{TC} contains terminals, CPU, disks,

and a memory queue. When the number of jobs in the central subsystem reaches N, an arriving job must wait in the memory queue. When a job leaves the central subsystem, a job in the memory queue is admitted in the system. Other parameters of M_{TC} are: the number of terminals T, think time Z, and total demand at each device D_i. The desired performance quantity is the throughput X_0 of the system.

Let M_{TE} denote a model consisting of the terminals (T) and a variable rate flow-equivalent server (E) replacing the subsystem. The construction of M_{TE} employs the solution of a number of submodels for the central subsystem. Submodel $M_C(n)$, $n = 1, \ldots, N$, represents the central subsystem with fixed number of customers $J = n$; its solution yields its throughput X_n. This solution is mapped back to one point on the flow through the central subsystem: $X_C(n) = X_n$, $n = 1, \ldots, N$. Model M_{TE} is the model of the system with the central system replaced by a load dependent flow-equivalent server whose service function is

$$S(n) = \begin{cases} 1/X_C(n), & n \leq N \\ 1/X_C(N), & n > N \end{cases}$$

The throughput, X, of this product form model is taken to be the throughput X_0 of M_0 (see Figure 2.3 and Box 2.4).

2.7 Example 5: Decomposition with Iteration

A queueing network with a load dependent server, such as M_{TE} in the preceding example, is more difficult to solve than a model M_{TF} in which load dependent flow-equivalent server (in M_{TE}) is replaced by a fixed rate flow-equivalent server. As shown in Box 2.5, the service time of this fixed rate server, S_F, can be obtained by averaging the load dependent flow rates of the central subsystem obtained from solving $M_C(1), \ldots, M_C(N)$. This averaging

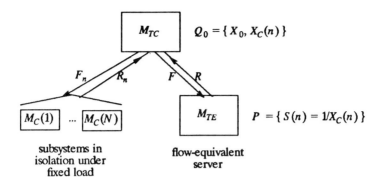

Figure 2.3: A schema for the limited degree of multiprogramming example.

requires that $p(n)$ -- the probability that n jobs are present in the subsystem -- be known. Since these probabilities are initially unknown, an iterative procedure is required. Thus we are trading off the complexity of load dependent server in M_{TE} with the complexity of the iteration between M_{TC} and M_{TF}. Below we examine this trade-off.

For Convolution algorithm implementation, the cost of solving M_{TF} (including the computation of S_F) per iteration is $O(T + 2N)$ additions and $O(T + 2N)$ multiplications/divisions. As compared to this, the cost of solving the load dependent model M_{TE} is $O(T^2/2)$ additions and an equal number of multiplications. Since maximum degree of multiprogramming N is expected to be much smaller than the number of terminals T, the cost of solving the fixed rate model may be relatively small. A simple example illustrating the trade-off is shown in Table 2.1. In this case, the iteration converged rather rapidly (three iterations) and the accuracy is acceptable. The trade-off may be worthwhile.

Example 4: Computer System with Limited Degree of Multiprogramming
(employs a load dependent flow equivalent server).

M_{TC}: Single class queueing network model of an interactive system
with terminals, CPU, disks and memory queue.
P_{TC}: $\{D_i, N, T, Z\}$
Q_{TC}: $\{X_0, X_C(1), \ldots, X_C(N)\}$

For $n = 1, \ldots, N$
$M_C(n)$:   Model of the central subsystem with fixed load n.
$P_C(n)$: $\{D_i, J\}$
$Q_C(n)$: $\{X_n\}$

$\mathbf{F}_n$: $J = n$.

$\mathbf{R}_n$: $X_C(n) = X_n$.

SOLVE$(M_C(n), P_C(n))$:Product form algorithms: Convolution, MVA, etc.

Iteration: Not Required.

M_{TE}: Model of system with terminals, T, and a load dependent
flow equivalent server, E, for central subsystem
P_{TE}: $\{T, Z, S(n)\}$
Q_{TE}: $\{X\}$

$\mathbf{F}$: $S(n) = 1/X_C(n)$, $n = 1, \ldots, N$.

$\mathbf{R}$:   Identity. $X_0 = X$.

SOLVE(M_{TE}, P_{TE}):   Product form algorithms: Convolution, MVA, etc.

Iteration: Not Required.

Box 2.4: Memory queueing:
An example of multiple refinements without iteration.

Example 5: Computer System with Limited Degree of Multiprogramming
(*with fixed rate flow equivalent server*);
(*Compare with Box 2.4*).

M_{TC}: Single class queueing network model of an interactive system
      with terminals, CPU, disks and memory queue.

P_{TC}: $\{D_i, N, T, Z\}$.

Q_{TC}: $\{X_0, X_C(1), \ldots, X_C(N), p(n)\}$.

For $n = 1, \ldots, N$

$M_C(n)$:   Model of the central subsystem

$P_C(n)$: $\{D_i, J\}$

$Q_C(n)$: $\{X_n\}$

$\mathbf{F}_n$: $J = n$.

$\mathbf{R}_n$: $X_C(n) = X_n$.

SOLVE$(M_C(n), P_C(n))$: Product form algorithms: Convolution, MVA, etc.

Iteration: Not Required.

M_{TF}: Model of system with terminals and a fixed rate flow equivalent
      server for central subsystem.

P_{TF}: $\{T, Z, S_F\}$.

Q_{TF}: $\{X, \hat{p}(n)\}$; $(\hat{p}(n) = \Pr[n_F = n])$.

F: Homogeneous service time function (see example 1)

$$S_F = \frac{\sum_{n>0} p(n)}{\sum_{n>0}^{N} p(n)X_C(n) + p(n > N)X_C(N)}.$$

R: Identity: $X_0 = X$, $p(n) = \hat{p}(n)$.

SOLVE(M_{TF}, P_{TF}): Product form algorithms: Convolution, MVA, etc.

Iteration: Required.

Box 2.5: Memory queueing:
An example of multiple refinements with iteration.

Table 2.1: A simple instance of Example (5) illustrating
trade-off between cost and complexity.

T	Throughput (X)[1]		% DIFF[2]	No. Iter.	Cost[3]	
	LD	Fixed			LD	Fixed
6	1.06	1.04	-1.9	3	36	108
10	1.73	1.66	-4.0	3	100	126
15	2.51	2.37	-5.6	3	225	162

[1] LD (Ex. 4) employs a load dependent flow equivalent server.
  Fixed (Ex. 5) uses a equivalent fixed rate flow equivalent server.
[2] $(X_4 - X_3)/X_3 * 100$.
[3] Total number of additions and multiplications for solving M.
  It includes the cost of the last iteration for verification.

Demands: CPU = 0.2, Disk1 = 0.16, Disk2 = 0.2.
Think Time = 5.0, Number of terminals = T,
Maximum degree of multiprogramming = 6.

Another use for decomposition with iteration could be in modeling
memory constrained systems with multiple classes; decomposition without
iteration cannot be used for such systems because an application of
decomposition transformation leads to a flow-equivalent server whose service
rate at any time is dependent on the current multiprogramming mix, i.e., on
$(n_1(t), \cdots, n_R(t))$ where $n_r(t)$ is the number of class r customers present in
the subsystem at time t. A queueing network containing such a server does
not have a product form solution. However, if the service rates of this server
are averaged so that it depends only on the total queue length, i.e., on
$n = n_1 + \cdots + n_R$, rather than on $(n_1(t), \ldots, n_R(t))$, the resulting model
will have a product form solution.

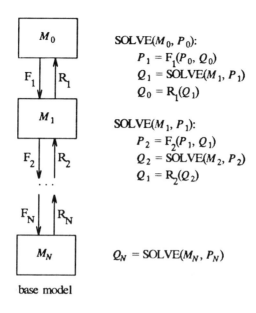

SOLVE(M_0, P_0):
$$P_1 = F_1(P_0, Q_0)$$
$$Q_1 = \text{SOLVE}(M_1, P_1)$$
$$Q_0 = R_1(Q_1)$$

SOLVE(M_1, P_1):
$$P_2 = F_2(P_1, Q_1)$$
$$Q_2 = \text{SOLVE}(M_2, P_2)$$
$$Q_1 = R_2(Q_2)$$

$$Q_N = \text{SOLVE}(M_N, P_N)$$

Figure 2.4: Recursion in SOLVE.

2.8 Example 6: Models Using Recursion

A recursive function definition is specified in the form

$$f(n) = \begin{cases} f_0, & n = 0 \\ g(f(n-1)), & n > 0 \end{cases}$$

where n is an index, f_0 is an initial condition, and g is some function.
Recursion is a powerful technique because it allows us to evaluate a function
with index n in terms of simpler evaluation of the function with lower index
$n-1$.

This concept is quite useful in the modeling process; see Figure 2.4.
Note that SOLVE(M_0, P_0) calls SOLVE recursively with new parameters
(M_1, P_1). Further note that SOLVE(M_1, P_1) can again recursively call

SOLVE for its own submodels. The base model M_N uses a different SOLVE procedure that computes Q_N with no further level of recursion. Note that it is possible to express the solution procedure as a composition of transformations:

$$\text{SOLVE}(M_0, P_0):$$
$$P_N = F_N(F_{N-1}(\cdots(F_1(P_0, Q_0), Q_1), \cdots), Q_{N-1})$$
$$Q_N = \text{SOLVE}(M_N, P_N)$$
$$Q_0 = R_1(R_2(\cdots(R_N(Q_N)))),$$

or equivalently,

$$Q_0 = R_1(\cdots(R_N(\text{SOLVE}(M_N, F_N(\cdots(F_1(P_0, Q_0), Q_1), \cdots), Q_{N-1}))))).$$

Thus, SOLVE need appear only once in the program.

Iteration and recursion should not be confused. Iteration as defined here is a technique to solve the equations of a model for unknown performance metrics. Recursion as defined here is a technique to transform a model into simpler models of same or different type. Iteration may be required to solve for unknowns in the set of equations arising from a recursive model.

As examples of recursion, we will consider the Convolution, the Mean Value Analysis and the Performance Bound Hierarchy algorithms for product form networks. Convolution [BRUE80, BUZE73] and Mean Value Analysis (MVA) [REIS80] are the most common algorithms used for solving product form queueing networks. The Performance Bound Hierarchy (PBH) [EAGE83] is a technique to obtain upper and lower bounds on throughput and response times of product form networks. An interesting characteristic of the PBH technique is a trade-off between the tightness of the bounds and computational cost of obtaining them.

The starting model, M_0, is a single-class product form queueing network model with K servers and N customers. For notational simplicity, we will consider networks of fixed-rate servers; the modeling process description can be extended to variable-rate servers and multi-class networks.

In the examples, the indices of recursion and, hence, the notation, differs among the models. Convolution uses recursion over the number of servers; hence $M(k)$ denotes an instance of model M_0 with only the servers $1, \ldots, k$ included. (Thus, $M(K)$ is the original model.) The MVA and PBH algorithms use recursion over the number of customers in the system; hence $M(n)$ denotes an instance of M_0 with n customers. (Thus, $M(N)$ is the original model). Figure 2.5 and Table 2.1 show the recursive schemata for these algorithms. We assume the reader is already familiar with these algorithms; the only new aspect is the interpretation as a recursive model.[1]

2.9 Hierarchy of Models and Its Solution

Three basic structural concepts have been discussed and illustrated in the preceding sections: *Transformation* of M_0 into one or more submodels; *Iteration* to solve systems of equations arising from models; and *Recursion* for expressing a model in terms of simpler versions of itself. In combination, these concepts allow for a hierarchy of models as illustrated in Figure 2.6.

The solution procedure for the hierarchy, i.e., SOLVE(M_0, P_0), is achieved by a sequence of traversals through the tree. On each traversal, each subtree is solved recursively. The tree traversal order may be important. The

---

1. We are grateful to Ken Sevcik for pointing out that these algorithms can be expressed in the modeling framework of Figure 2.4.

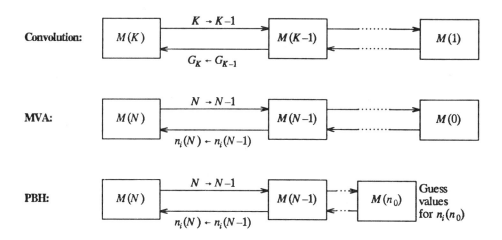

Please see Table 2.1 for reverse mappings.

Figure 2.5: Model transformations in the Convolution,
MVA and PBH algorithms.

Table 2.1: Summary of transformations for
the Convolution, MVA and PBH algorithms.

Single class, K server, N customer queueing network			
Algorithm	F^1	R	Base Condition and SOLVE
Convolution[2]	$k \to k-1$	$G_k(0) = 1$ $G_k(n) = G_{k-1}(n) +$ $\quad\quad G_k(n-1) \cdot V_k S_k$	$k = 1$ $G_1(0) = 1$ $G_1(n) = (V_1 S_1)^n$
MVA	$n \to n-1$	$R_i(n) = S_i(1 + \bar{n}_i(n-1))$ $X_0(n) = n/(\sum V_i R_i(n))$ $\bar{n}_i(n) = V_i R_i(n) X_0(n)$	$n = 0$ $\bar{n}_i(0) = 0$
PBH	$n \to n-1$	same as in MVA for both upper and lower bounds	some $n = n_0$ upper and lower bounds for $\bar{n}_i(n_0)$

[1] k: number of servers, n: number of customers.
[2] Other performance measures can be obtained in terms of $G_K(\cdot)$.

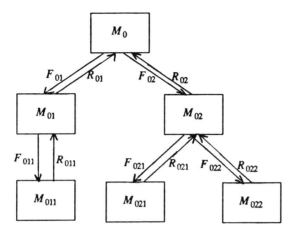

Figure 2.6: An example of hierarchy of models.

basic principle behind the order of traversal is that a submodel should be solved as soon as its parameters are available. Moreover, an iteration will require multiple traversals of the tree; only the subtrees involved in the iteration need to be traversed again. Because of multiple traversals, the cost of one traversal becomes important. There are two extremes at which a traversal (a cycle of an iteration) can be implemented.

1. *Full interleaving of recursion and iteration:* Each node of the tree denotes a call on SOLVE for that node. A traversal of tree for SOLVE(M_0, P_0) invokes a complete set of iterations for subtrees of M_0. This procedure is rather expensive. For example, in the example of Figure 2.6, if M_0 requires r_1 iterations between M_{01} and itself, and M_{01} requires r_2 iterations between itself and M_{011}, solution of M_0 will require $r_1 \cdot r_2$ invocations of M_{011}.

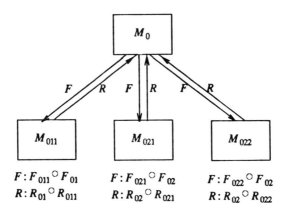

Figure 2.7: Fully expanded tree for the hierarchy in Figure 2.6.

2. *Full expansion of the tree:* The tree is "preprocessed" into a two level hierarchy by removing all interior nodes leaving only M_0 (root) and the original leaves (level 1 in the new tree). The forward and reverse maps are compositions of the maps along the paths in the original tree. For example, as a result of the preprocessing, the tree in Figure 2.6 is converted into the tree in Figure 2.7. A traversal in this tree will be *much* faster, i.e., the cost per iteration will be much lower. But more iterations may be required because some of the intermediate values of forward mappings (at internal nodes of original tree) will be less accurate. There is also a possibility of encountering extreme values of parameters leading to divergence or convergence to some other answer.

An intermediate approach would be to reduce the computational costs initially starting with a loose convergence criteria (large ϵ) for lower level iterations and tightening it up (i.e., reducing ϵ) as the iteration at a higher level approaches its fixed point.

2.10   Comparison With Examples of Hierarchical Modeling in Literature

Browne *et al.* [BROW75] present a "hierarchical" model for a large data management system based on CDC Cyber 70 equipment. At the top level, they use a gross or *macro* model in which major hardware subsystems are represented as single servers. Parameters of these servers are determined by analysis of *micro* models for corresponding subsystems. In the metamodeling framework, the hierarchy is similar to the one shown in Figure 2.3. M_0 is the system itself and models $M_1, \ldots, M_4$ represent micro models, namely, DMS Activity Model, CPU-CM-ECS Activity Model, CPU-ECS Interference Model and the System/Scratch Disk System Model. The macro model is the remaining model, M, at the *same* level in the hierarchy.

Courtois [COUR77] develops a linear, L level "hierarchical" model of a system of $L+1$ resources $R_0, \ldots, R_L$ by aggregating resources. The aggregate model at level l, $l = 0, \ldots, L-1$ is obtained by aggregating R_l with the aggregate resource for $R_0, \ldots, R_{l-1}$ constructed at level $l-1$. This aggregate resource is nothing but the flow-equivalent server for resources $R_0, \ldots, R_l$ [CHAN75b, DENN78]. In terms of the metamodeling framework, M_0 is the model of the system with $L+1$ resources. M_{01} aggregates resources R_0 and R_1 into an aggregate resource, say A_1. M_{02} has $A_1, R_2, \ldots, R_L$. At M_{02}, the method is recursively applied by aggregating A_1 with R_2 to obtain A_2 in M_{021} and then constructing M_{022}. Figure 2.6 can be viewed as the hierarchy for a 4 resource network.

Kumar and Davidson [KUMA80] use a "hierarchy" of models for optimum system design. Their hierarchy is organized according to the cost of solution and accuracy of a model. Models at higher levels in the hierarchy have:

"1) less structural validity;
2) more limited range of validity;
3) less detailed performance information;
4) less accurate information;
5) lower computational requirements" [KUMA80].

They try to obtain an optimal design by solving the higher level models for different configuration parameters and every time ensuring that lower level models are valid for the parameter values. Lower level models have to be solved again ("calibrated") when the parameter values lie outside the range of model validity. In the metamodeling hierarchy, these different models appear at the same level with detailed models characterizing the parameters for less detailed models. The hierarchy for this model is similar to the one in Figure 2.3. Recalibration of a detailed model amounts to iteration between different models.

The hierarchy of models, as presented here, differs from the hierarchies considered by Browne *et al.*, Courtois, and Kumar and Davidson. Their hierarchies were based on the amount of detail incorporated in the model at a level; higher levels have less detail. Moreover, higher levels are associated with larger sets of physical resources. Our hierarchies have the most detail at the highest level but derive performance measures from less detailed models at lower levels. Moreover, our hierarchies need not associate models with sets of resources in the physical system.

The hierarchies defined here correspond to the following reasoning process used by an analyst. The analyst constructs an accurate model M_0 for the system and finds a solvable approximation M of M_0. If the parameters for M cannot be readily obtained, then the analyst constructs submodels M_n of M_0 with the objective of obtaining information for parameterizing M. The process can, of course, be recursively repeated. No physical nesting of resources is required. No restriction is placed on the relative complexity of models at the same or different levels. The metamodeling framework permits hierarchical representation of modeling processes that are not hierarchical in the traditional sense (e.g., see the method of surrogates for analyzing simultaneous resource possession in Chapter 3). This view of hierarchical modeling is a more general and natural representation of the modeling process. The traditional view is restricted. It can, in many cases, somewhat informally describe the model, but it does not represent the modeling process well.

An example of a hierarchical modeling process following the structure presented here, and which cannot be considered hierarchical in the traditional sense, is Schwetman's analysis of long term scheduling via hybrid simulation [SCHW78]. Starting with a detailed simulator (e.g., its description) M_0 of a system, he constructed a hybrid simulation model (M) for the long term behavior of the system. In this model, the short term behavior, i.e., the the central subsystem, was represented as a single server whose service time, i.e., the time till next departure, was determined by a table lookup. These table entries (service times) were obtained by analyzing an analytical model, M_1, of the central subsystem for all possible central subsystem populations only once.[2] This approach, called *hybrid simulation*, reduced the cost of simulating M_0 significantly without significant loss of accuracy. The hierarchical structure of this model is shown in Figure 2.8.

As another example, consider the *isolation method* introduced by Labetoulle and Pujolle [LABE80]. In this method, the original model is partitioned in N subnetworks that possess known solutions. The interaction of

---

2. To be more precise, we need to develop a number of submodels for the central subsystem, one for each possible configuration of total number of customers in different classes in central subsystem. However, remembering Occam's rajor, we will represent them by M_1 alone.

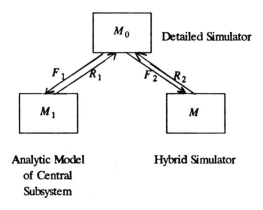

Figure 2.8: Hierarchical structure of hybrid simulation.

a subnetwork with its environment is specified by determining the characteristics of the input flows (input interface function) and the characteristics of the service times (output interface functions). The metrics of these subsystems (not physical outputs) constitute the metrics of the original model. When computation of the input flows and service times for a subnetwork require values of the metrics of other subnetworks, an iteration between these models will be necessary. A two level hierarchy similar to Figure 2.2 represents this process correctly.

2.11 Equation Oriented Approximations

The preceding discussion was illustrated with model transformations that can be interpreted as changes or additions to the physical structure of the original queueing system. The framework is, however, more general. We will apply it to system descriptions made up of state equations: Courtois's method of aggregation and to the Diffusion Approximation.

2.11.1 Courtois's Method of Aggregation

In his discussion of *aggregation* [COUR77], Courtois assumes that a set of n state flow balance equations constitute the original model M_0. The solution of the model is expressed as the column probability vector y, where

$$\tilde{y}(t+1) = \tilde{y}(t)Q$$

and Q is an $n \times n$ stochastic, single-step transition probability matrix where q_{kl} is the conditional probability that the system is in state l at time $t+1$ given that it was in state k at time t; and the symbol $"\tilde{\ }"$ denotes transpose. These equations are then mapped into another model M with fewer equations (N) by aggregating states. The solution of M is $\underline{Y}$, where

$$\tilde{\underline{Y}}(t+1) = \tilde{\underline{Y}}(t)\underline{P}$$

and $\underline{P}$ is an $N \times N$ stochastic, single-step transition probability matrix where p_{kl} is the conditional probability that the system M is in state l at time $t+1$ given that it was in state k at time t. The general structure of the transformation is summarized in Box 2.6.

The idea of the transformation is to lump specific sets of states of M_0 to form states of M. The probability $Y_I(t)$ of being in state I of M is the sum of the probabilities y_i of M_0 for $i \in I$, i.e.,

$$Y_I(t) = \sum_{i \in I} y_i(t).$$

The transition probability p_{IJ} in M is the weighted sum of transition probabilities q_{ij} of M_0 for $i \in I$ and $j \in J$:

$$p_{IJ} = \sum_{\substack{i \in I \\ j \in J}} q_{ij} \frac{y_i}{Y_I}$$

The disaggregating function estimates y_i for each $i \in I$ from Y_I (e.g., $\hat{y}_i = Y_I / |I|$).

Example: General State Aggregation [COUR77]

M_0:   Global balance equations for an n state model.
P_0: $\{\underline{Q}\}$
Q_0: $\{\underline{y}(t)\}$

M :   Simpler aggregate model with N states.
P : $\{\underline{P}\}$
Q : $\{\underline{Y}(t)\}$

F: Aggregate states using aggregation functions **A**
      $Y_I(t) = \mathbf{A}_I(y_i(t)),\ I = 1, \ldots, N.$

      Map $\underline{Q}$ into $\underline{P}$ using the methods described in [COUR77, Ch. 1].

R: Disaggregating functions **D**
      $y_i(t) = \mathbf{D}_i(Y_I(t)),\ i = 1, \ldots, n.$

SOLVE(M,P):   Solve $\underline{\bar{Y}}(t+1) = \underline{\bar{Y}}(t)\underline{P}$ using numerical techniques.

Iteration: Depends on **A** and **D**.
            (Note that we are talking about iteration between M_0 and M, and not about numerical techniques to solve M.)

Box 2.6: General structure for state aggregation.

Courtois applied this to systems of nearly-decomposable sets of states. The lumps are subsystems containing many internal transitions relative to transitions between lumps. For this case, the disaggregating function sets

$$\hat{y}_i = \pi_{Ii} Y_I$$

where π_{Ii} is the steady state probability of state $i \in I$ given that there are no exits from lump I. Courtois was able to characterize the error $|y_i - \hat{y}_i|$ arising from this method. The transformation is summarized in Box 2.7.

2.11.2 Diffusion Approximation

As another example, consider the *diffusion approximation* for obtaining an approximate solution for a *GI /G /*1 queue [CHAN78, GAVE68]. In this approximation, the changes in the queue length are approximated by the continuous motion of an imaginary particle. The movement of the particle from interval $[n, n+1)$ to $[n+1, n+2)$ can be mapped into a queue length change from n to $n+1$. The problem of finding the queue length distribution is thereby reduced to that of finding the probability density function, $p(x_0, x, t)$, for the particle position x on the non-negative real axis. The p.d.f. is given by

$$p(x_0, x, t)\, dx = \Pr[x \leq x(t) < x + dx \mid x(0) = x_0]$$

The displacement of particle $dx(t)$ in interval t, $t + dt$, $dx(t) = x(t + dt) - x(t)$, is normally distributed with mean $\beta \cdot dt$ and variance $\alpha \cdot dt$. Cox and Miller show that the particle's position at time t, $x(t)$, satisfies the Fokker-Planck diffusion equation

$$\frac{1}{2} \alpha \frac{d^2 p}{dx^2} - \beta \frac{dp}{dx} = \frac{dp}{dt} \quad (x > 0)$$

for appropriate choices of the parameters α and β [COX65]. The cumulative

Example: State Aggregation [COUR77]

M_0: Global balance equations for an n state model.
P_0: $\{Q\}$
Q_0: $\{\underline{y}, \underline{\pi}_I\}$

For $I = 1, \ldots, N$:
M_I: Global balance equations for lumped state model I.
P_I: $\{Q_I^{\bullet}\}$
Q_I: $\{\underline{y}^{\bullet}\}$

F_I: $Q_I^{\bullet}$ is the Ith principle submatrix of $Q^{\bullet}$ where $Q^{\bullet}$ is an $n \times n$ matrix such that $Q_I^{\bullet}$ are square matrices and other elements are zero.

$$Q = Q^{\bullet} + \epsilon \underline{C}$$

where $\underline{C}$ is an $n \times n$ matrix which has the property of keeping both Q and $Q^{\bullet}$ stochastic; $\epsilon > 0$.

R_I: Identity: $\underline{\pi}_I = \underline{y}^{\bullet}$.

SOLVE(M_I, P_I): Solve $\bar{y}^{\bullet} = \bar{y}^{\bullet} Q_I$ using numerical techniques [STEW78].

Iteration: Not required between M_0 and M_I.

M: Simpler aggregate model with N states
P: $\{\underline{P}, \underline{\pi}_I\}$
Q: $\{\underline{Y}\}$

F:
$$p_{IJ} = \sum_{\substack{i \in I \\ j \in J}} q_{ij} \, \pi_{Ii}$$
Other parameters same

R: $y_i = \pi_{Ii} Y_I$

SOLVE(M, P): Solve $\underline{\bar{Y}} = \underline{\bar{Y}} \, \underline{P}$ using numerical techniques.

Iteration: Not required between M_0 and M.

Box 2.7: State aggregation.

density function of the particle position has a closed form solution that is easily evaluated and serves as an approximation for the queue length.

The transformation has been summarized in Box 2.8. Since we are interested only in the steady state solution for the queue, the initial condition, x_0 ($n_0 \leq x_0 < n_0 + 1$), does not matter. In the box, the additional parameters are: λ is the arrival rate; μ is the service rate; and c_a and c_s are coefficient of variance squares for interarrival and service times.

For more details and additional references, see [CHAN78].

2.12 Conclusion

In this chapter we have discussed the structure of the modeling process. The basic principle is that a model is transformed into a simpler model by mapping parameters forward and results backward. This principle is extended by allowing more than one model to be refinements of a given model; by allowing iteration to solve for unknowns arising from equations defined by modeling structures; and by allowing recursion. The combinations of these extensions leads to a description of the modeling process as a scheme for constructing a hierarchy of models; this hierarchy may be solved iteratively. The generality of this scheme was illustrated by showing how a variety of common modeling processes fit into the single framework and by showing the metamodeling concept of hierarchy of models to be more general and comprehensive than the hierarchy concept used by other researchers.

The following chapters take up the semantics of the transformations. Several important questions will be considered: How do we represent a transformation succinctly? How do we find a good transformation? What are

Example: Diffusion Approximation for a *GI/G/*1 **Queue**

M_0:   A *GI/G/*1 queue.
P_0: $\{\lambda, c_a, \mu, c_s\}$
Q_0: $\{p(n)\}$

M :   (Differential equation of) motion of a particle.
P : $\{\alpha, \beta\}$
Q : $\{p(x_0, x; t)\}$

F: Compute parameters for the particle motion

$$\beta = \lambda - \mu,$$

$$\alpha = c_a \lambda + c_s \mu.$$

R: Map particle positions in $[n, n+1)$ into queue length n.

$$p(n) = \lim_{t \to \infty} \int_n^{n+1} p(x_0, x; t) \, dx$$

$$= (1 - \hat{\rho})\hat{\rho}^n$$

where $\hat{\rho} = \exp(-2(1 - \lambda/\mu)/(c_s + c_a\lambda/\mu))$.

SOLVE(M, P):   Solution of the Fokker-Planck diffusion equation
with the *reflective barrier* boundary condition
$$\int_0^\infty p(x_0, x; t)dx = 1.$$

Iteration: Not Required.

Box 2.8: Diffusion approximation for a *GI/G/*1 queue.

the properties of a good transformation? Will an iterative procedure ever converge, and if so, will it yield a unique solution?

CHAPTER 3

BEHAVIOR SEQUENCE TRANSFORMATIONS

AND MODELS WITH SHADOW SERVERS

In Chapter 2 we discussed some examples in which it was easy to visualize the nature of the transformations. Many systems, however, contain servers whose scheduling and service decisions depend on the queues at other servers or on the types of job present. In such cases, it is difficult to visualize the required transformations. In this chapter, we will study a class of transformations based on adding shadow servers to the network to account for additional queueing delays caused by interference from other devices or job-classes. The technique of behavior sequence transformations gives a pictorial aid for finding the parameters of the shadow servers.

We first review some background material to explain the idea of behavior sequence transformation. Using this idea, we provide the reasoning by which two well-known approximations -- the shadow CPU for preemptive priority discussed in Chapter 2, and the surrogate servers for simultaneous resource possession [JACO82] -- can be derived. We conclude the chapter by describing the aggregate server model [AGRA83], a new approximation developed with this technique.

3.1 Background

Product form queueing network models correspond in a natural way to systems composed of only autonomous, fair servers. An *autonomous server* uses only local information, such as local queue length, in its scheduling and service decisions. It does not use any global system state information such as queue length at other servers or the availability of resources elsewhere in the system. A *fair server* does not use job classes or job sizes to make its scheduling decisions. In queueing network models, these properties are manifested as the local balance conditions [CHAN77]; they lead to an efficiently computable product form solution [BRUE80, BUZE73, REIS80].

Many real systems, unfortunately, have servers that are either nonautonomous or unfair. These behaviors are generically termed *nonhomogeneous*. Product form networks tend to give poor results for nonhomogeneous systems. Examples of these behaviors are:

1. *Blocking:* a node in a computer network cannot transmit message if the destination node's memory is full. Blocking causes additional delays for the messages at the transmitting nodes.

2. *Simultaneous Resource Possession:* a disk I/O request has to acquire both a channel as well as the disk before data transfer can begin. Additional delay is experienced in waiting for the channel to become free.

3. *Memory-Constrained Systems:* a job has to wait for entry into the multiprogramming mix when the maximum multiprogramming level has been reached. A customer cannot use a device unless it has been granted required memory or a scheduling token.

4. *Critical Sections:* a program has to acquire a semaphore or a lock before it can enter critical section for serialized processing. Waiting for the semaphore results in additional delays.

5. *Priority scheduling:* low priority customers have to suffer additional delays due to preemption as well as the service of high priority customers arriving after them.

Behaviors 1-4 illustrate nonautonomous servers. Behavior 5 illustrates an unfair server. A given, nonhomogeneous system may contain combinations of these behaviors.

An exact solution of nonhomogeneous networks is usually prohibitively expensive. Therefore, we try to obtain an approximate solution for such systems by transforming an accurate model of such a system into an approximate product form model. The approach studied in this chapter is to include *shadow servers* in the transformed model that stand as surrogates for the additional delays caused by nonhomogeneous behaviors. The *behavior sequence transformation* technique to be described provides a pictorial aid for visualizing necessary transformations and obtaining the parameters of shadow servers from those of the original model. Examples are provided after a general description of the technique.

The idea behind behavior sequence transformation technique is straightforward. Begin with a diagram depicting the assignment of a given job to servers in a nonhomogeneous portion of the system. (This diagram is called a behavior sequence.) Identify delays at each server due to interference from other servers or other job classes. Then create one or more shadow servers whose service times account for these interference delays; adjust remaining service times and visit ratios so that overall delay in the nonhomogeneous subsystem is unchanged. Finally, construct a homogeneous queueing network, including the shadow servers, that could have generated the new, resultant behavior sequence.

In making these transformations, the performance quantities of interest -- e.g., total length of the behavior sequence or number of customers served in the interval -- are either held constant or transformed explicitly. Without these constraints, the solution of the transformed model may not be sufficiently close to the solution of the original model. The complete model transformation will be composed as a sequence of simple transformations, some of which remove only one part of the nonhomogeneous behavior and others rearrange the segments of the behavior sequence to aid in visualizing subsequent transformations.

3.2   Example 1: Preemptive Priority Scheduling

Sevcik's model [SEVC77] for dealing with a system employing preemptive priority at one or more servers was presented in Chapter 2. We will now give a more careful derivation of Sevcik's model using the idea of behavior sequence transformation. This analysis reveals a new result.

Systems with preemptive priority violate the fair service property at the server with priority scheduling. This behavior can be modeled by splitting the priority server into a set of shadow servers, one for each priority class at that server. Each shadow server's processing rate is degraded to reflect the contention due to customers at higher priority levels.

As before, we illustrate the concept by considering a system of two servers, CPU and DISK, and two classes H (high) and L (low). Class H customers have preemptive priority over class L customers at the CPU. A First Come First Served service (FCFS) discipline is used at the DISK and within each class at the CPU. The preemptive priority discipline at the CPU is the only form of nonhomogeneity in the network.

3.2.1 Class L Customer's Behavior Sequence

A portion of the behavior sequence of a class L customer is depicted in Figure 3.1. We have distinguished between two states of a class L customer at CPU, according to whether it is, or is not, at the head of the class L queue. In the first case, the customer may either be receiving service at CPU (s) or may be blocked because a class H customer is receiving service (q''). In the second case, the customer cannot receive service at the CPU because other class L customers precede it (q'). We make no such distinction at DISK because its operation is autonomous and fair. In rest of the discussion, we will focus on the CPU only.

Parameters of the model can be expressed as derived variables of this behavior sequence. In particular, class L CPU service demand is

$$S_{CPU,L} = \frac{T(n_{CPU,L} \geq 1, n_{CPU,H} = 0)}{C_L}$$

$$= \frac{p(n_{CPU,L} \geq 1, n_{CPU,H} = 0)}{X_L} , \tag{3.1}$$

where $T(\cdot)$ denotes the total time during which a condition holds and C_L is the number of customers in class L completing service.

The unfair scheduling discipline at the CPU introduces additional delays (q'') due to the interference from class H jobs at the CPU. These delays cannot be modeled as normal queueing delays behind other jobs in the queue. They can, however, be modeled by introducing a shadow CPU for class L, denoted CPU-L, whose service time includes both the original class L service, $S_{CPU,L}$, and the preemption delay (q''). Class H customers do not visit CPU-L.

A class L customer is at the head of CPU-L queue exactly when it was at the head of class L queue at the original CPU. In the transformed model,

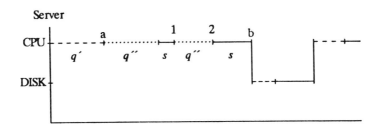

Legend

————	customer is receiving service
- - - -	customer is not at the head of class L queue: waiting
··········	customer at the head of class L queue: waiting or preempted
1	preemption occurs
2	service resumes
a	customer reaches head of queue
b	customer finishes CPU service

Figure 3.1: Behavior sequence of a class L customer.

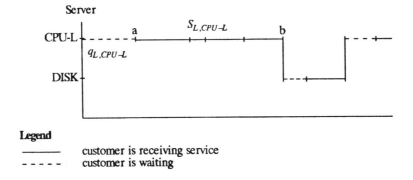

Legend

————	customer is receiving service
- - - -	customer is waiting

Figure 3.2: Transformed behavior sequence of a class L customer.

we have a shadow class L CPU, CPU-L which is visited by only class L jobs; see Figure 3.2. Thus $n_{CPU,L} \geq 1$ implies CPU-L is serving class L customers. Hence

$$S_{CPU-L,L} = \frac{T(n_{CPU,L} \geq 1)}{C_L}$$

$$= \frac{p(n_{CPU,L} \geq 1)}{X_L} \tag{3.2}$$

$$= \frac{p(n_{CPU,L} \geq 1)}{p(n_{CPU,L} \geq 1, n_{CPU,H} = 0)} S_{CPU,L}. \tag{3.3}$$

Eq. (3.1) has been used to replace X_L in eq. (3.2).

3.2.2 Class H Customer's Behavior Sequence

A portion of a class H customer's behavior sequence is shown in Figure 3.3. Class H customers are not delayed at the CPU by low priority class L customers. Class H CPU service time is

$$S_{CPU,H} = \frac{T(n_{CPU,H} \geq 1)}{C_H}$$

$$= \frac{p(n_{CPU,H} \geq 1)}{X_H}. \tag{3.4}$$

In the transformed model, class H jobs visit their own shadow CPU, denoted CPU-H. The behavior of CPU-H is identical to that of the CPU because class L jobs do not interfere with class H (Figure 3.4). In particular,

$$S_{CPU-H,H} = S_{CPU,H}. \tag{3.5}$$

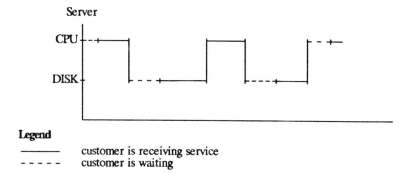

Figure 3.3: Behavior sequence of a class *H* customer.

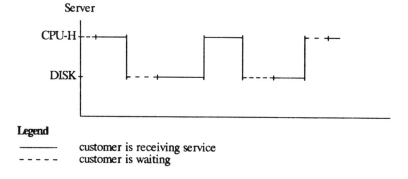

Figure 3.4: Transformed behavior sequence of a class *H* customer.

3.2.3 Transformed Model

Neither of the transformed behavior sequences (Figures 3.2 and 3.4) contains unfair operation at any server; the major causes of nonhomogeneity have been removed. The transformed behaviors can be realized by a product form network comprising the DISK and the two shadow servers, CPU-H and CPU-L, each of which serves only one class of jobs. The service demands at these shadow servers are given by Eqns. (3.3) and (3.5). The service times for the DISK are the same as in the original model. The reverse mapping is an identity function, i.e., $X_L = X_L'$, $X_H = X_H'$, $p(x) = p(x)$ for every state x.

As indicated in Chapter 2, the solution of this model requires iteration. The complete transformation is summarized in Box 3.1.

3.2.4 Comparison with Sevcik's Shadow CPU Algorithm

The service time elongation factor given by equation (3.3) is

$$F = \frac{S_{CPU-L,L}}{S_{CPU,L}}$$

$$= \frac{p(n_{CPU,L} \geq 1)}{p(n_{CPU,H} = 0, n_{CPU,L} \geq 1)}$$

$$= \frac{p(n_{CPU,L} \geq 1)}{p(n_{CPU,L} \geq 1) - p(n_{CPU,H} \geq 1, n_{CPU,L} \geq 1)}. \tag{3.6}$$

$$= \frac{1}{1 - p(n_{CPU,H} \geq 1 \mid n_{CPU,L} \geq 1)}. \tag{3.7}$$

If the random variables $n_{CPU,L}$ and $n_{CPU,H}$ are independent, then

$$p(n_{CPU,H} \geq 1 \mid n_{CPU,L} \geq 1) = p(n_{CPU,H} \geq 1) \tag{3.8}$$

whereupon the elongation factor becomes

$$F = \frac{1}{1 - p(n_{CPU,H} \geq 1)} = \frac{1}{1 - U_{CPU,H}}. \tag{3.9}$$

Example: New Shadow CPU Algorithm for Preemptive Priority at CPU

M_0: Two class queueing network model of system; two
queues at CPU with class H having preemptive priority on class L.

P_0: $\{S_{ir}, V_{ir}, N_r\}$

Q_0: $\{X_r, p(n_{CPU,L} \geq 1), p(n_{CPU,L} \geq 1, n_{CPU,H} \geq 1)\}$

M: Same queueing network as in M_0 except that CPU is split into two
CPU's - CPU-H and CPU-L visited by classes H and L respectively.

P: $\{S_{CPU-H,H}, S_{CPU-L,L}, S_{ir}, V_{ir}, N_r\}$

Q: $\{X_r', p(n_{CPU-L,L} \geq 1), p(n_{CPU-L,L} \geq 1, n_{CPU-H,H} \geq 1)\}$

F:

$$S_{CPU-L,L} = \frac{p(n_{CPU,L} \geq 1)}{p(n_{CPU,L} \geq 1) - p(n_{CPU,L} \geq 1, n_{CPU,H} \geq 1)} \cdot S_{CPU,L},$$

$$S_{CPU-H,H} = S_{CPU,H}, \text{ all other parameters same}$$

R: Identity

$$X_r = X_r',$$

$$p(n_{CPU,L} \geq 1) = p(n_{CPU-L,L} \geq 1),$$

$$p(n_{CPU,L} \geq 1, n_{CPU,H} \geq 1) = p(n_{CPU-L,L} \geq 1, n_{CPU-H,H} \geq 1).$$

SOLVE(M, P):Product form algorithm: Convolution, MVA, etc.

Iteration: Required.

Box 3.1: New shadow CPU algorithm for preemptive priority scheduling.

This is the elongation factor proposed by Sevcik. In other words, Sevcik's model implicitly assumes independence between $n_{CPU,L}$ and $n_{CPU,H}$ in the original model, as well as in the transformed model. This assumption does not hold in the network under consideration. It will hold, however, if either class H is an open class and does not loop back to CPU, or class H has preemptive priority over class L at DISK as well. The error is maximum when $N_L = 1$. Experimental results reported in Appendix A show that the factor in (3.7) gives smaller error than the one in (3.9).

3.3   Example 2: Simultaneous Resource Possession

Simultaneous resource possession is common in computer systems. It occurs in an I/O subsystem when a job must hold both a disk and a channel to perform data transfer, in multiprogrammed central subsystems when a job must hold both main memory and CPU/IO devices, and in terminal systems when a user must hold both a terminal and a port before logging in. In these and many other examples, the homogeneity conditions fail. No product form solution exists for an exact model of the system.

Jacobson and Lazowska developed an approach for this problem [JACO82]. They use two interacting, complementary models, M_1 and M_2, that include surrogate servers to account for the delays caused by simultaneous resource possession. The two models are solved iteratively because the solution of M_1 provides parameters for M_2, and vice versa.

We now provide an overview of the Jacobson-Lazowska method. It is followed by a reasoning by which the method can be derived.

3.3.1 Overview of the Jacobson-Lazowska Method

The Jacobson-Lazowska approach is applicable to systems in which resources can be partitioned into three disjoint sets:

P - the set of primary resources,

Q - the set of secondary resources, and

R - the remaining resources or rest of the system,[1]

where P and Q constitute the set of simultaneously held resources (see Figure 3.5). We assume that the homogeneity assumptions are satisfied in R.

Consider the behavior of a job in the PQ subsystem. A job must obtain a primary resource, say P_i, before requesting any secondary resource; P_i is held continuously while the job requests, obtains, and releases components of the secondary resource subsystem, Q.[2] Upon completion of the subsystem request, the job releases P_i and any secondary resource it may be holding. It can then request a resource from R, the rest of the system.

A request to the PQ subsystem has two components: the primary resource service and the secondary resource service. Let S_P denote the total active primary resource service that is not overlapped with the secondary resource service. Let S_Q denote the total service among all visits to secondary devices by one job.

A request to the PQ subsystem results in simultaneous possession of primary (P) and secondary (Q) resources. Such a request encounters two kinds of delays:

---

1. This partitioning applies to one subsystem in which simultaneous resource possession occurs. In a real system there can be multiple such subsystems: e.g., two sets of disks with a dedicated channel for each set. The Jacobson-Lazowska method is applicable in this situation as well.

2. There need not be any processing time associated with the primary resource. If some active processing time is associated with the primary resource, it may overlap with service times of secondary servers.

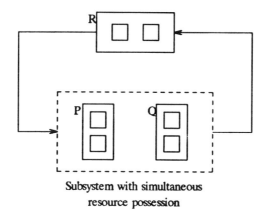

Subsystem with simultaneous
resource possession

Figure 3.5: General resource structure for the Jacobson-Lazowska
approach for analyzing simultaneous resource possession.

1. Queueing for access to a primary resource denoted as q_P, and

2. Queueing for service at secondary resources after the primary resource
   has been acquired; it is denoted as q_Q.

Jacobson and Lazowska further divide the delay q_P into the delay due to
primary resource congestion and the delay due to secondary subsystem
congestion. The *delay due to primary resource congestion* is the component of
the delay during which the customer holding the primary resource is receiving
service(from P or Q); it is denoted as q_{PP}. The *delay due to secondary
subsystem congestion* is the component of the delay during which the customer
holding the primary resource is receiving no service and is enqueued in Q; it
is denoted as q_{PQ}.[3]

---

3. These definitions for the delays due to congestion in the primary and the secondary
subsystem clarify the definitions presented in [JACO82]. Jacobson and Lazowska
agree that these are the definitions they had intended. The analysis presented in this
section helped us discover ambiguity in their description.

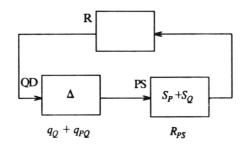

Figure 3.6: Model M_1 - primary resource congestion model.

Jacobson and Lazowska's two models, M_1 and M_2, compute these delays. Model M_1 replaces the PQ subsystem by two shadow servers, QD and PS (see Figure 3.6). The delays caused by secondary resource queueing, $q_Q + q_{PQ}$, are embodied in the delay server, QD. The active service of length $S_P + S_Q$ is represented as service at server PS. The delay due to primary resource congestion is computed from M_1's solution by

$$q_{PP} = R_{PS} - (S_P + S_Q),$$

where R_{PS} is the response time of the server PS.

Model M_2 replaces the PQ subsystem by two shadow servers, PD and QS (see Figure 3.7). The delay due to primary resource congestion, q_{PP}, is represented by delay server PD, and the active service and the secondary resource congestion delay is represented by flow-equivalent server QS. As shown in Figure 3.7 (a), the primary resources are represented as delay servers in QS. This representation is valid because QS is constructed by assuming that the primary resource has already been acquired by a request. From the solution of M_2 we compute the delay due to secondary subsystem congestion as

$$q_Q + q_{PQ} = R_{QS} - (S_P + S_Q),$$

where R_{QS} is the response time of the server QS.

The solution of M_1 provides the unknown parameter of M_2, q_{PP}. The solution of M_2 provides an estimate for the unknown parameter of M_1, $q_Q + q_{PQ}$. Starting from initial guesses for q_{PP} and $q_{PQ} + q_Q$, the two models are iteratively solved to obtain the final solution. Figure 3.8 shows the interaction between the two models.

3.3.2 Behavior Sequence Approach

Figure 3.9 interprets the models M_1 and M_2 in terms of their behavior sequences. Figure 3.9 (a) illustrates the behavior of a job during its sojourn in the PQ subsystem of the original model. The delay until the start of the P-service (period H) is partitioned into a normal part (q_{PP}), during which job holding P is receiving service (in P or Q), and an interference part (q_{PQ}), during which the job holding P is receiving no service because it is enqueued in Q. Some of the P-service overlaps with the Q-service (e.g., intervals b and c). This sequence is nonhomogeneous because of the interference queueing and the service overlap. Figure 3.9 (b) is a rearrangement of Figure 3.9 (a) with the normal P-queueing (q_{PP}), all non-overlapped P service, and all Q service attributed to the shadow server PS. All Q-queueing is attributed to the delay server QD. The holding time (H) in the PQ subsystem is unchanged. Figure 3.9 (c) is a rearrangement of Figure 3.9 (a) with the P-queueing (q_{PP}) attributed to the delay server PD, and all the Q-queueing and the PQ-service attributed to the shadow server QS. In this case the shadow

(a) Flow-equivalent server for *PQ* subsystem.

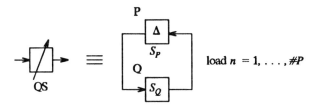

(b) Model M_2 with load-dependent flow-equivalent shadow server *QS*.

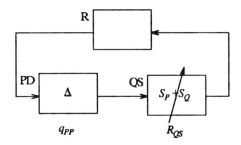

Figure 3.7: Model M_2 - secondary resource congestion model.

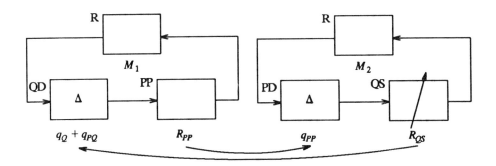

Figure 3.8: Interaction between primary (M_1) and

secondary (M_2) resource congestion models.

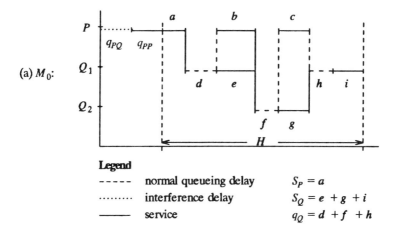

(a) M_0:

Legend

- - - - - normal queueing delay $S_P = a$

.... interference delay $S_Q = e + g + i$

——— service $q_Q = d + f + h$

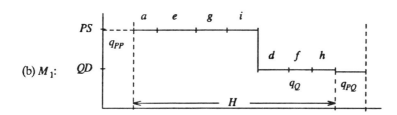

(b) M_1:

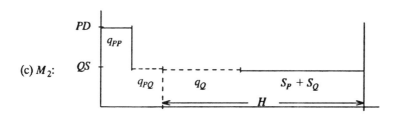

(c) M_2:

Figure 3.9: Overview of behavior sequences for models in the Jacobson-Lazowska Approach.

server is a flow-equivalent simulation of the portion of Figure 3.9 (a) within the intervals of q_{PQ} and H.

In the following sections, we review in detail the behavior sequence transformations suggested in Figure 3.9. In the process, we obtain a general formulation of the Jacobson-Lazowska approach. To fix ideas, we use as a running example a single class system with two primary resources P_1 and P_2, two secondary resources Q_1 and Q_2, and one additional resource R_1 (the rest of the system). In the following discussion, we first assume that P_1 and P_2 are statistically identical. We further assume that they are specifically identified in a request and are visited with equal frequency. (These conditions are relaxed later.)

3.3.3 Original Behavior Sequence

The key observation underlying the Jacobson-Lazowska method concerns the queueing delays associated with a request to hold two resources simultaneously. Specifically, they are the delays associated with acquiring a primary resource P_i, and acquiring a secondary resource Q_j; they are denoted by q_{Pi} and q_{qij}, respectively. The delay q_{Pi} is further classified into two categories depending upon the status of the job presently holding P_i. A portion of a job behavior sequence showing these service and delay intervals is drawn in Figure 3.10. The labels for these intervals are defined in Table 3.1. Table 3.2 provides definitions for total service times and queueing delays in terms of these basic intervals.

SYMBOL	DEFINITION
q_{pqi}	Tagged job waits for P_i when the holder of P_i is receiving no service and waiting for a secondary resource
q_{pp_i}	Tagged job waits for P_i when the holder of P_i is actively using some resource (in P or Q)
s_{pi}	Tagged job receives service from P_i but not overlapped with any service from a secondary resource
s_{qij}	Tagged job receives service from Q_j while holding P_i
q_{qij}	Tagged job waits for Q_j while holding P_i

Table 3.1: Definitions for time intervals for
the simultaneous resource possession example.

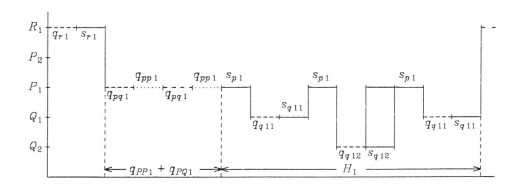

Legend

—— service

········· delay when the holder of P_i is in active service

- - - - - other delay (e.g., secondary subsystem congestion)

Figure 3.10: Original behavior sequence for
the simultaneous resource possession example.

Table 3.2: Derived variable definitions for
the simultaneous resource possession example.

SYMBOL	QUANTITY	DEFINITION[1]
S_{Qij}	Total secondary resource Q_j service while holding P_i	$\sum_l s_{qij}(l)$
S_{Qj}	Total secondary resource Q_j service	$\sum_i S_{Qij}$
S_{QPi}	Total secondary resource service while P_i is being held	$\sum_j S_{Qij}$
S_Q	Total secondary resource service	$\sum_j S_{Qj}$
S_{Pi}	Total service at P_i not overlapped with any secondary service	$\sum_l s_{pi}(l)$
S_P	Total non-overlapped primary resource service	$\sum_i S_{Pi}$
H_i	Holding period for P_i	$S_{Pi} + S_{QPi} + q_{Qi}$
S_{Hi}	Total service in the holding period H_i	$S_{Pi} + S_{QPi}$
q_{Qi}	Total wait in the holding period H_i	$\sum_l \sum_j q_{qij}(l)$
q_{PQi}	Delay due to congestion in secondary system while waiting for P_i	$\sum_l q_{pqi}(l)$
q_{PPi}	Delay due to congestion in primary system while waiting for P_i	$\sum_l q_{ppi}(l)$
q_{Pi}	Total wait for primary resource P_i	$q_{PPi} + q_{PQi}$

[1.] (l) indicates a segment of the delay or service.

3.3.4 Transformations Leading to Model M_1

We now specify the steps that transform the behavior sequence shown in Figure 3.11 into one generable by a product form model M_1. In Figure 3.11, the q_{pqi} segments of Figure 3.10 have been grouped together into a single segment q_{PQi} and the q_{ppi} segments of Figure 3.10 have been grouped together into a single segment q_{PPi}.

Transformation 1: Separation of Queueing and Service

Since q_{Qi} is known, we can dissociate the secondary subsystem queueing delay segments (q_{qij}) and move them to the end of the holding period. The resulting behavior sequence is shown in Figure 3.12.

Transformation 2: Introduction of a Delay Server

In Figure 3.12, the delay segments q_{qij} can be viewed as service time at a delay server, QD. The delay segment q_{PQi} can also be represented as service at QD. This transformation leads to the behavior sequence shown in Figure 3.13. Note that to parameterize QD, we only need the value of the sum $q_{PQi} + q_{Qi}$; the lengths of the individual components are not required.

Transformation 3: Server Aggregation

Let us now consider the active PQ service segment in the behavior sequence displayed in Figure 3.13. (The length of this segment is $S_{P1} + S_{QP1}$.) This segment can be viewed as the service at the shadow server $PS1$ (see Figure 3.14). In general, the active service associated with P_i is represented as the service time at the shadow server, PS_i. The service time for server PS_i is equal to the duration of the active service, i.e.,

$$S_{PSi} = S_{Pi} + S_{QPi}.$$

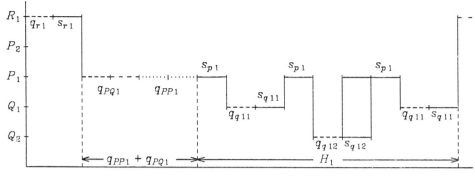

Legend

——— service

········· delay due to primary subsystem congestion

- - - - other delay (e.g., delay due to secondary subsystem congestion)

Figure 3.11: Figure 3.10 behavior sequence after rearrangement of primary resource acquisition delays (q_{pp} and q_{pq}).

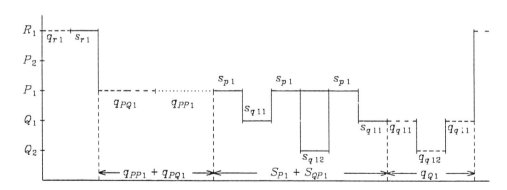

Legend

——— service

········· delay due to primary subsystem congestion

- - - - other delay (e.g., delay due to secondary subsystem congestion)

Figure 3.12: Figure 3.11 behavior sequence after transformation 1: separation of queueing and service.

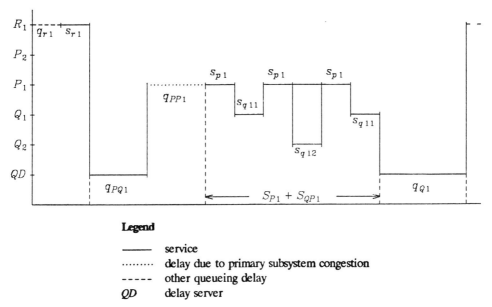

Figure 3.13: Figure 3.12 behavior sequence after delay server QD's introduction.

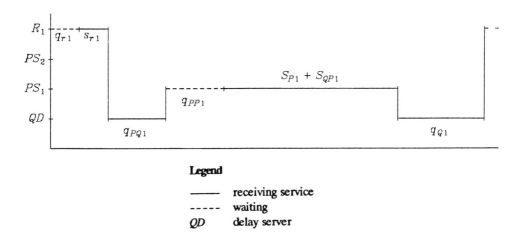

Figure 3.14: Model 1 behavior sequence.

The reverse mapping is an identity and the delay q_{PPi} is computed by

$$q_{PPi} = R_{PSi} - S_{PSi}.$$

Model M_1

The behavior sequence shown in Figure 3.14 exhibits fair and autonomous behavior at every server; this sequence, therefore, can be generated by a product form model, M_1. In M_1, the PQ subsystem is replaced by shadow servers QD and PSi. QD is a delay server and represents the delay due to secondary subsystem congestion $(q_{PQi} + q_{Qi})$ per visit to the PQ subsystem. PSi stands as a surrogate for P_i in the PQ subsystem.

3.3.5 Transformations Leading to Model M_2

Starting with the behavior sequence shown in Figure 3.15, we develop transformations which lead to a behavior sequence that can be generated by the product form model, M_2. This starting behavior sequence is the same as the one exhibited in Figure 3.11 except that the order of the segments q_{PPi} and q_{PQi} has been reversed.

Transformation 1: Delay Server Introduction

Since the delay q_{PP1} is known, we represent it as service at a delay server, PD. This transforms Figure 3.15 into Figure 3.16.

Transformation 2: Service Overlap Removal

At the beginning of the holding period H_1, P_1 has already been acquired (see Figure 3.16). Except for the overlap between P_1 service and Q_2 service, the portion of the behavior sequence during the holding period H_1 is generable by a product form network. Hence, we delete the P_1 service period

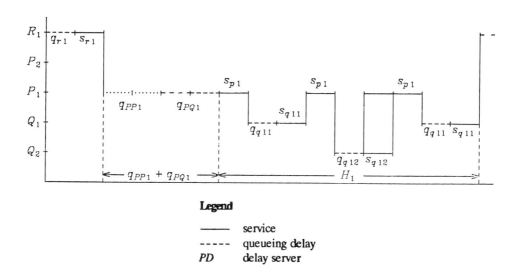

Legend

—————— service

- - - - - queueing delay

PD   delay server

Figure 3.15: Figure 3.10 behavior sequence after transformation 0: rearrangement of delays (order of q_{PPi} and q_{PQi} different from Figure 3.11).

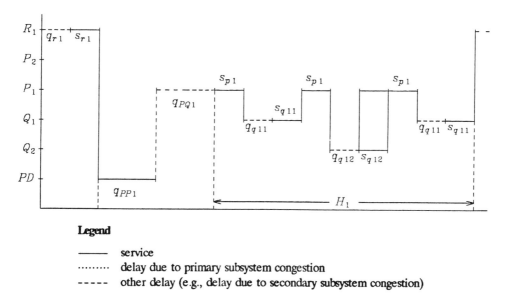

Legend

—————— service

········· delay due to primary subsystem congestion

- - - - - other delay (e.g., delay due to secondary subsystem congestion)

Figure 3.16: Figure 3.15 behavior sequence after transformation 1: *PD* introduced.

that overlaps with the Q_2 service and obtain the behavior sequence drawn in Figure 3.17. The length of the holding period has been preserved.

Transformation 3: Decomposition

To determine next transformation, consider the wait and service periods observed by the job during the holding period H_1 (see Figure 3.17). This interval of behavior could be generated by a product form model M_{En} that represents the PQ-subsystem behavior, as per Figure 3.17, under fixed load n. M_{En} has a delay server to model delay S_{P1}, secondary subsystem resources to model the the service in the Q subsystem and n customers; see Figure 3.7 (a).

In the transformed model, we represent the H_1 interval as service at a flow-equivalent server QS. QS is constructed ' by equating the "on-line" behavior of the model M_{En} to its "off-line" behavior [DENN78]. The service function $S_{QS}(n)$ for QS is

$$S_{QS}(n) = \frac{1}{X_{En}}, \quad n = 1, \cdots, \#P,$$

where X_{En} is the throughput of M_{En}, and $\#P$ is the number of primary resources. (Because $S_{P1} = S_{P2}$ and $S_{QP1j} = S_{QP2j}$, all customers in the PQ subsystem are alike and M_{En} is a single class model.)

From the response time of QS, R_{QS}, we can easily compute the delay due to secondary subsystem congestion:

$$q_{PQi} + q_{Qi} = q_{QS} = R_{QS} - (S_{Pi} + S_{QPi}).$$

Model M_2

The behavior sequence pictured in Figure 3.18 exhibits fair and autonomous behavior at each server; therefore, it can be produced by a product form network named M_2. M_2 represents the primary resource congestion as service at the delay server PD. The service at the PQ subsystem

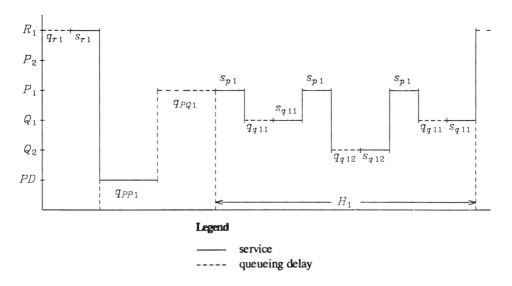

Figure 3.17: Figure 3.16 behavior sequence after transformation 2: service overlap between P_1 and Q_2 removed.

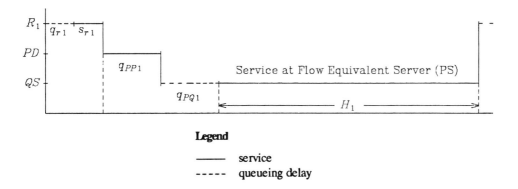

Figure 3.18: Figure 3.17 behavior sequence after transformation 3: flow-equivalent server QS introduced.

and the delay due to secondary subsystem congestion is included via the flow-equivalent server QS that is constructed by assuming that the required primary resources have already been allocated to the jobs in the PQ subsystem. The rest of the system is represented as is.

On the Validity of the Decomposition Transformation

We have used two shadow servers, PD and QS, to represent the PQ subsystem in M_2. The queueing delay q_{PQ} is underestimated or overestimated at QS depending on n_A, the queue length seen by an arriving customer. Below we discuss these two problems.

1. *Underestimation of q_{PQ} ($n_A < \#P$):*

   QS was constructed with the assumption that if an arriving customer sees less than $\#P$ customers upon arrival, a primary resource is available for it. In this situation, the response time at QS includes only the delays for the secondary resources (q_Q); estimated q_{PQ} is zero which is an underestimate when a primary resource is preselected by a request.

2. *Overestimation of q_{PQ} ($n_A \geq \#P$):*

   When $n_A \geq \#P$, R_{QS} includes the queueing delay due to active service of the customer holding the primary resource. To see this, consider a degenerate system with only one primary resource with service time S_P, no secondary resources and $N > 1$ customers (note that this system has a product form solution). QS is a single, load independent server with service time S_P. It is easy to see that $R_{QS} > S_P$, i.e., $q_{QS} = R_{QS} - S_P > 0$ because $q_Q = 0$. But in the real system $q_{PQ} = 0$ because there is no queueing for secondary resources.

These two errors in the estimates compensate for each other.

3.3.6 Generalization

We have so far assumed that: 1) primary resources are distinguished, i.e., a request specifies a particular P_i (e.g., request for a particular disk), and 2) primary resources are statistically identical. When primary resources are not distinguished, they are represented as a mult-server in model M_1; in effect, M_1 preserves the queueing structure of primary resources. M_2 is not affected. When primary resources are not identical, as an approximation, we use average values of service times for constructing the flow-equivalent server QS used in M_2; no approximation is needed for M_1 because each primary resource can be separately represented in M_1 with correct value of the service time $(S_{Pi} + S_{QPi})$.

Though we have explained the transformations by considering only one visit to the PQ subsystem, the transformations can be easily written in terms of the total service demands D rather than service time per visit; see the summary in Box 3.2.

Since neither delay q_{PP} nor $q_{PQ} + q_Q$ $(= q)$ is known *a priori*, we solve the models iteratively:

> SOLVE(M_0, P_0):
>> SOLVE(M_{En}, P_{En}), $n = 1, \cdots, \#P$.
>> Initially assume $\hat{q} = 0$.
>> **repeat**
>>> $q_{PQ} + q_Q = \hat{q}$
>>> $q_{PP} = $ SOLVE(M_1, $q_{PQ} + q_Q$)
>>> $\hat{q} = $ SOLVE(M_2, q_{PP})
>> **until** $(\hat{q} - (q_{PP} + q_Q)) < \epsilon$

In the above outline, we have explicitly shown the variables directly involved in the iteration; other variables are not shown for clarity. The proofs of convergence can be found in Chapter 5 and [JACO82].

3.4 Example 3: Serialization

In multiprogrammed computer systems jobs are normally processed concurrently to improve device utilization and system throughput. However, there are some shared logical resources which must be accessed serially because concurrent use can lead to inconsistent results. Because only one job at a time can use such a resource, this kind of processing is usually called "serialization" of requests for that resource. Serialization leads to nonautonomous behavior because a job has to first acquire a "token" granting access to the logical resource before it can request service at physical devices. Examples include critical sections guarded by semaphores and records guarded by database locks. In the following discussion, we will generically refer to all serialized resources as critical sections; a job in a critical section is within a *serialized phase* and is called a *serialized job*.

Although serialization is a case of simultaneous resource possession, the Jacobson-Lazowska method is not applicable because the physical devices cannot be partitioned in the three disjoint sets, P, Q and R. For example, the resources Q and R overlap because a job in the critical section shares the CPU with the jobs outside the critical section.

3.4.1 Overview of the Aggregate Server Method

We developed the *aggregate server method* for analyzing serialization [AGRA83]. The concept of behavior sequence transformation played a central role in the development of the technique. The underlying idea is straightforward. In the initial (accurate) model, physical devices are

---

Example: Jacobson-Lazowska Model of Simultaneous Resource Possession

M_0: Set of primary (P), secondary (Q) and remaining (R) resources single class model.

P_0: $\{D_{Pi}, D_{PQij}, D_{Ri}, N\}$; D's are TOTAL demands.

Q_0: $\{X_0, q_{PP}, q_Q + q_{PQ}, X_{QS}(n)\}$.

M_1: Primary resource congestion model with set of servers PS, QD, R. If P_i's belong to a pool (non-distinguishable), PS is a mult-server.

P_1: $\{D_{Ri}, D_{PSi}, D_{QD}, N_r\}$.

Q_1: $\{X_1, R_{PSi}\}$.

$\mathbf{F_1}$: $D_{PSi} = D_{Pi} + \sum_j D_{PQij}$; $D_{QD} = q_Q + q_{PQ}$; all other parameters same.

$\mathbf{R_1}$: Identity: $X_0 = X_1$;
$$q_{PP} = \sum_i q_{PPi} = \sum_i [R_{PSi} - D_{PSi}].$$

SOLVE(M_1, P_1):Product form algorithm: Convolution, MVA, etc.

M_2: Secondary resource congestion model with set of servers PD, QS, R. QS is load-dependent.

P_2: $\{D_{Ri}, D_{PD}, D_{QS}(n), N\}$.

Q_2: $\{X_2, R_{QS}\}$.

$\mathbf{F_2}$: $D_{QS}(n) = \dfrac{1}{X_{QS}(n)}$, $n = 1, \cdots, \#P$.

$\qquad D_{PD} = q_{PP}$; all other parameters same.

$\mathbf{R_2}$: Identity: $X_0 = X_2$;
$$q_Q + q_{PQ} = q_{QS} = R_{QS} - \sum_i [D_{Pi} + \sum_j D_{PQij}].$$

SOLVE(M_2, P_2):Product form algorithm: Convolution, MVA, etc.

(Summary Continued)

Box 3.2: The Jacobson-Lazowska model of simultaneous resource possession.

Example (Cont'd.):
     Jacobson-Lazowska Model of Simultaneous Resource Possession

M_{En}: Auxiliary model for flow equivalent serve, QS. $n = 1, \cdots, \#P$
     P for primary resources (delay server),
     Q secondary resource servers.
P_{En}: $\{D_P, D_{Qj}, n\}$.
Q_{En}: $\{X_{En}\}$.

$\mathbf{F_{En}}$: $D_P = \sum_i D_{Pi}$,

     $D_{Qj} = \sum_i D_{PQij}$; all other parameters same.

$\mathbf{R_{En}}$: Identity
     $X_{QS}(n) = X_{En}$.

SOLVE(M_{En}, P_{En}): Product form algorithm: Convolution, MVA, etc.

Iteration: Required. Between models M_1 and M_2 via M_0.
     Models M_{En} have to be solved only once.
     Solving M_{EN} alone gives solution for all M_{En}.

Box 3.2: (Continued).

represented as servers and a queue is maintained for each critical section (serialized phase). A job is tagged with its present phase index, z, ($z = 0$ means nonserialized). At no time more than can one job be tagged with the same serialized phase index ($z \neq 0$). When a job exits a critical section, its tag is changed to indicate noncritical section processing ($z = 0$), and a waiting job may now enter the just released critical section.

In the transformed model, each critical section is viewed as a single shadow server whose service time is the critical section residency time (the time from critical section entry to exit). When a job requests a critical section, it visits the corresponding shadow server.

When a job is in a critical section, it delays other jobs because it still contends for physical devices. In the transformed model, therefore, the physical devices must also be replaced by slower shadow servers. Their speeds reflect the capacity lost to serialized jobs.

The approximate model is constructed in two steps. First we construct a shadow device for each physical device and each phase. Then we aggregate the shadow devices for each serialized phase into a single shadow critical section server. Below we illustrate the model development by considering a behavior sequence that can be generated by a network with two devices, CPU and DISK, and one critical section, CS. We assume that the devices and the critical section are scheduled according to a FCFS discipline. (Expressions for the processor sharing discipline at the physical servers and random selection at the critical sections can be easily written. These expressions are the same as the expressions for FCFS scheduling.)

In the following discussion, the state of server i is written as $(\underline{n}_i ; z)$; $\underline{n}_i = (n_{0i}, n_{1i})$, and $z = 0, 1$; n_{0i} and n_{1i} are the number of customers in phase 0 (non-critical section) and phase 1 (critical section) at server i; z is the phase index of the customer in service at i.

3.4.2 Transformations Leading to the Aggregate Server Model

A job behavior sequence that exhibits serialization and sharing of devices among customers in different phases is shown in Figure 3.19. Serialization is shown by the delay for critical section entry. There are three states of a customer at a device:

1. The tagged customer is not at the head of the queue of customers of its own phase;

2. The tagged customer is at the head of the queue of customers in the same phase and is receiving service; and

3. The tagged customer is at the head of the queue of customers in the same phase, but is waiting because a customer in the other phase is receiving service.

The third type of delay is a form of interference among job-classes; it cannot be represented by a product-form model.

The service times at various devices in different phases in M_0 can be derived from the behavior sequence. The service time per visit to device i when the customer is not in the critical section is:

$$S_{0i} = \frac{T(n_{0i} \geq 1, n_{1i} \geq 0; 0)}{C_{0i}}$$

$$= \frac{p(n_{0i} \geq 1, n_{1i} \geq 0; 0)}{X_{0i}}, \tag{3.10}$$

and when the job is in the critical section, the service time is:

$$S_{1i} = \frac{T(n_{0i} \geq 0, n_{1i} = 1; 1)}{C_{1i}}$$

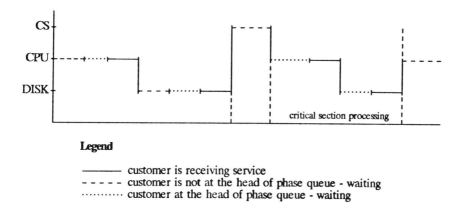

Legend

—————— customer is receiving service
- - - - - customer is not at the head of phase queue - waiting
············ customer at the head of phase queue - waiting

Figure 3.19: Behavior sequence of a customer requesting a critical section.

$$= \frac{p(n_{0i} \geq 0, n_{1i} = 1; 1)}{X_{1i}}, \tag{3.11}$$

where $T(\cdot)$ is the total time a condition holds, C is the number of completions at a device, $p(\cdot)$ denotes an occupancy probability, and X is the throughput.

Now let us discuss the transformations which eliminate the sharing of physical devices between jobs in different phases while representing the degradation due to serialization.

Transformation 1: Load Concealment Transformation

The sharing of physical devices is eliminated by constructing a shadow server for each physical device for each phase; see Figure 3.20. This mapping transforms the original model M_0 into a model M_1 that consists of two isomorphic networks, one for each phase, and a critical section queue. Job movement between these networks is administered by serialization controllers;

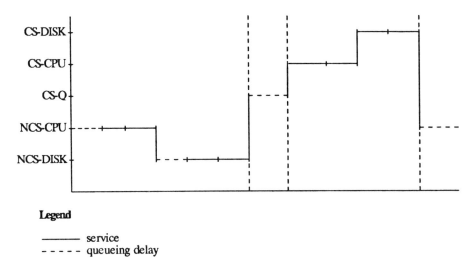

Figure 3.20: Behavior sequence after load concealment.

a customer going from the nonserialized network (index 0) to the serialized network (index 1) may have to wait in the critical section queue.

Parameters of M_1 are determined in a straightforward manner. By construction of M_1, whenever a job is at the head of a queue for its phase in M_0 (Figure 3.19), it receives service at the corresponding shadow server in M_1 (Figure 3.20). Therefore, the service times at the shadow servers (for phase z's server i) are given as:

$$S_{0i}' = \frac{T(n_{0i} \geq 1, n_{1i} \geq 0)}{C_{0i}}$$

$$= \frac{p(n_{0i} \geq 1)}{X_{0i}} \qquad (3.12)$$

$$= \frac{p(n_{0i} \geq 1)}{p(n_{0i} \geq 1, n_{1i} \geq 0;0)} S_{0i} , \qquad (3.13)$$

and

$$S'_{1i} = \frac{T(n_{0i} \geq 0, n_{1i} = 1)}{C_{1i}}$$

$$= \frac{p(n_{0i} \geq 0, n_{1i} = 1)}{X_{1i}} \tag{3.14}$$

$$= \frac{p(n_{0i} \geq 0, n_{1i} = 1)}{p(n_{0i} \geq 0, n_{1i} \geq 1; 1)} S_{1i}. \tag{3.15}$$

The reverse mapping is somewhat involved because there is no simple, exact way to estimate the probability that a phase z job is in service from the marginal and joint probability distributions in the transformed network. E.g., $p(n_{0i} \geq 1; 0)$ cannot be exactly estimated from $p(n_{0i} = 1)$, $p(n_{1i} \geq 1)$, and $p(n_{0i} \geq 1, n_{1i} = 1)$. However, with the independence assumption that a serialized job has an equal chance of being in service as any non-serialized job present at the server, we get:

$$p(n_{0i} = r, n_{1i} = k; 0) = \frac{r}{r+k} p(n_{0i} = r, n_{1i} = k), \ r \geq 1, k = 0, 1$$

$$p(n_{0i} = r, n_{1i} = 1; 1) = \frac{1}{r+1} p(n_{0i} = r, n_{1i} = 1), \ r \geq 0 \tag{3.16}$$

The above independence assumption is equivalent to assuming processor sharing scheduling.

Transformation 2: Server Aggregation (Decomposition)

The behavior sequence in Figure 3.20 is not generable by a product form network because of the nonautonomous behavior of NCS-CPU, NCS-DISK and CS-Q. This errant behavior is removed by *aggregating* NCS-CPU and NCS-DISK into a single server CS and associating CS-Q with this server (see Figure 3.21). (The method derives its name, *aggregate server method*, from this transformation.) The service time per visit for this shadow critical section server is simply the critical section residency time, i.e.,

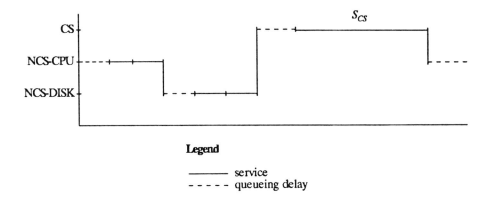

Figure 3.21: Behavior sequence after server aggregation (decomposition).

$$S_{CS} = \sum_{i=1}^{2} V_{1i} S'_{1i} \qquad (3.17)$$

where V_{1i} is the number of visits to device i per visit to the critical section.

The state probabilities for model M_1 are directly obtained from the solution of this model, called M_2, as follows:

$$p(n_{1i} = 1 \mid n_{CS} \geq 1) = \frac{V_{1i} S'_{1i}}{S_{CS}} \qquad (3.18)$$

or

$$p(n_{1i} = 1) = \frac{V_{1i} S'_{1i}}{S_{CS}} p(n_{CS} \geq 1). \qquad (3.19)$$

And as an approximation, we estimate the joint state probabilities as

$$p(n_{0i} = r, n_{1i} = 1) = p(n_{0i} = r, n_{1i} = 1, n_{CS} \geq 1)$$

$$= p(n_{1i} = 1 \mid n_{CS} \geq 1, n_{0i} = r) \cdot p(n_{0i} = r, n_{CS} \geq 1)$$

$$\approx p(n_{1i} = 1 \mid n_{CS} \geq 1) \cdot p(n_{0i} = r, n_{CS} \geq 1) . \qquad (3.20)$$

The above approximation, i.e.,

$$p(n_{1i} = 1 \mid n_{CS} \geq 1, n_{0i} = r) \approx p(n_{1i} = 1 \mid n_{CS} \geq 1) , \qquad (3.21)$$

is equivalent of saying that a job's whereabouts when inside the critical section are independent of other phase queue length at a device.

The Transformed Model

Servers $NCS - CPU$, $NCS - DISK$, and CS are fair and autonomous. The behavior sequence displayed in Figure 3.21 is, therefore, generable by product form network M_2. In general, M_2 consists of K shadow servers corresponding to noncritical section processing at K physical devices. It has Z additional aggregate servers to represent serialized processing in Z critical sections. The transformations for the general case of K devices and Z critical sections are summarized in Box 3.3. The hierarchy of models is displayed in Figure 3.22. These models are solved iteratively.

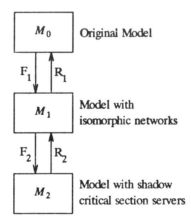

Figure 3.22: Model hierarchy for aggregate server method.

Example: The aggregate server method (Serialization Delays)

M_0: Single class network of K PS/FCFS devices, Z critical sections.
P_0: $\{S_{zi}, V_{zi}, V_z, N\}$.
Q_0: $\{X_0,$ state probabilities, e.g., $p(n_{0i}=r, n_{zi}=1)\}$.

M_1: network with $Z+1$ isomorphic networks.
P_1: $\{S_{zi}', V_{zi}, V_z, N\}$.
Q_1: $\{X_1,$ state probabilities $p'(n_{0i}=r, n_{zi}=1)\}$.

F_1:

$$S_{0i}' = \frac{p(n_{0i} \geq 1)}{\displaystyle\sum_{r=1}^{N} \sum_{k=0}^{min(N-r,Z)} \frac{r}{r+k} \, p\left(n_{0i}=r, \sum_{z=1}^{Z} n_{zi} = k\right)} \, S_{0i} \quad ;$$

For serialized phases z, $z = 1, \cdots, Z$

$$S_{zi}' = \frac{p(n_{zi} = 1)}{\displaystyle\sum_{r=0}^{N-1} \sum_{k=0}^{min(N-r-1,Z-1)} \frac{1}{1+r+k} \, p\left(n_{0i}=r, n_{zi}=1, \sum_{\substack{q=1 \\ q \neq z}}^{Z} n_{qi} = k\right)} \, S_{zi}$$

Note: Elongated service times are expressed for PS servers.
With the reverse mapping in (3.16), same
expression is obtained for FCFS servers.

R_1: Identity.
$X_0 = X_1$, $\quad p(\underline{n}) = p'(\underline{n})$.

SOLVE(M_1, P_1):SOLVE(M_2, P_2).

Iteration: Required.

(Summary continued)

Box 3.3: The aggregate server method for serialization delays.

Example: The aggregate server method (Serialization Delays)

M_2: Model with critical section network aggregated into a server
total $K + Z$ servers: $1, \cdots, K$ shadow physical servers,
$K + 1, \cdots, K + Z$ shadow critical section servers.

P_2: $\{S_i, V_i, N\}$.

Q_2: $\{X_2$, state probabilities $p^{'}(n_i = r, n_{K+z} \geq 1)\}$.

F_2:

$$S_i = S_{0i}^{'}, \quad V_i = V_{0i}, \quad i = 1, \cdots, K \; ;$$

$$S_{K+z} = \sum_{i=1}^{K} S_{zi}^{'} V_{zi}, \quad V_{K+z} = V_z, \quad z = 1, \cdots, Z.$$

R_2: Identity:

$$X_1 = X_2;$$

$$p^{'}(n_{zi} = 1) = \frac{S_{zi}^{'}}{S_{K+z}} \, p^{'}(n_{K+z} \geq 1), \quad z = 1, \cdots, Z \, ;$$

$$p^{'}(n_{0i} = r, n_{zi} = 1) = \frac{S_{zi}^{'}}{S_{K+z}} \, p^{'}(n_i = r, n_{K+z} \geq 1), \quad z = 1, \cdots, Z \, ;$$

etc.

SOLVE(M_2, P_2): Product form algorithm: Convolution, MVA, etc.

Iteration: Not Required.

Box 3.3 (Continued).

Agrawal and Buzen [AGRA83] furnish details on the simplification of expressions for elongated service times (see Box 3.3), and provide an efficient algorithm for their computation and extensive validation. In appendix B, we extend the aggregate server method to single class open networks as well as mixed networks in which two classes do not visit same critical section.

3.5 Conclusion

An important class of model transformations introduce shadow servers in the transformed models to account for the delays caused by nonhomogeneity. Behavior sequence transformations are proposed as a pictorial aid for determining the parameters of the transformed model and as an aid in developing transformations at the conceptual level. It is probable that behavior sequence transformation technique will be useful in specifying model transformations other than those involving shadow servers.

Because they are basically pictorial aids, behavior sequence diagrams are usually not very precise. Moreover, not all transformations can be conveniently pictured as behavior sequence transformations. A more general, formal, and concise way to specify the transformations is state space transformations. These transformation are discussed in Chapter 4.

CHAPTER 4

STATE SPACE TRANSFORMATIONS

Behavior sequence transformations were discussed in Chapter 3 as a pictorial aid for developing models with shadow servers. They are an instance of the more general state space transformations, which are the subject of this chapter. Several state space transformations occur so frequently that we have given them special names:

Load concealment transformation,

State aggregation transformation,

Server aggregation (decomposition) transformation,

Response time preservation transformation,

Load separation transformation,

Class aggregation transformation,

Load scaling transformation,

Response time modeling transformation, and

Delay server introduction transformation.

When applied to the running example of the system containing the preemptive-priority CPU, the state space transformation reveals a variable-rate low-priority shadow CPU model that is more accurate than the fixed-rate shadow CPU model discussed earlier.

4.1 State Space Transformations

The pictorial aid of behavior sequence transformation is a helpful guide to the intuition but is not sufficiently precise or powerful to deal with the full range of common approximate models. For example, service time distributions, variable service rates, and some scheduling disciplines (e.g., processor sharing) cannot be easily pictured. Behavior sequence diagrams must be augmented with state-space definitions for computing parameters. Once the intuition is understood, behavior sequence diagrams can become cumbersome for further understanding of the approximation.

State space transformations describe how the state space and the state transitions of the given model are mapped into the state space and the state transitions of the transformed model. These transformations are more compact and complete because, as shown below, a model's state space encodes all the information available about the system at the given level of abstraction [BUZE83].

The state-space is a model's full description. The state occupancy probabilities are the most detailed performance measures; other performance measures can be derived from them. The state space structure reflects the characteristics of servers, customers, customer classes, and service time distributions. An example is shown in Figure 4.1 for a two-class priority server with maximum of two jobs present. Figure 4.1 (a) is the state transition diagram when the server allows preemptive priority; Figure 4.1 (b) is the state transition diagram when the server allows non-preemptive priority. Homogeneous arrival and service assumptions are reflected as the simple labels $(\lambda_H, \mu_H, \lambda_L, \mu_L)$ on state transitions. The different assumptions about the scheduling discipline of the priority server result in different set of reachable

STATE: $(n_H, n_L; C)$: n_H - No. of class H customers, n_L - No. of class L customers, C - Class of the customer in service.

(a) Preemptive priority server.

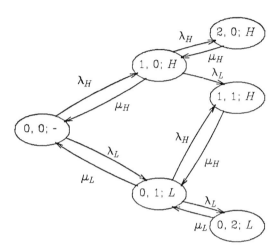

(a) Non-preemptive priority server.

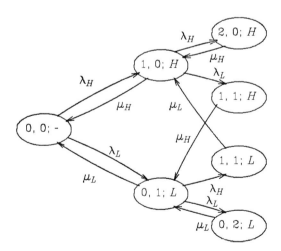

Figure 4.1: State transition diagram for priority servers.

states and in the transitions among them. In the same way, the image of the state space transformations will differ significantly from the original.

These concepts are formalized below. Examples follow in subsequent sections.

Model M, in its most detailed form, is described as a triplet (Σ, A, f), where

> Σ - is the state space,
>
> A - is the set of transition rate triplets (i, j, r_{ij}), where i and j are in Σ and r_{ij} is interpreted as
>
> > 1. The probability that the transition $i \rightarrow j$ occurs in a dt interval in a stochastic model given that the system is in state i; or
> >
> > 2. The flow rate between states $i \rightarrow j$ in a flow-balanced operational model.
>
> f - is a mapping for computing transition rates A from the model parameters P; $f : \Sigma \times \Sigma \times P \rightarrow A$.

The *parameters P* are a set of independently measurable quantities that describe the rates in set A.

Note that if the high level description of the model is a queueing network, then f will specify how to compute transition rates from visit ratios and service times. On the other hand, if the "high level model" itself is described in terms of states, f is an identity mapping and P is the set of transition rates.

The *solution procedure* SOLVE is a mapping from (M, P) to $Q = \{p(x), x \in \Sigma\}$, the state occupancy distribution. All other metrics can be calculated from this distribution.

In terms of these concepts, the basic modeling pattern is

$$
\begin{array}{ccc}
M_0 & & M \\
P_0 \times Q_0 & \xrightarrow{\;\;F\;\;} & P \\
& & \downarrow \text{SOLVE} \\
\hat{Q}_0 & \xleftarrow{\;\;R\;\;} & Q
\end{array}
$$

where

$Q_0 = \{p_0(y), y \in \Sigma_0\}$ are the metrics of M_0;

$\hat{Q}_0 = \{\hat{p}_0(y), y \in \Sigma_0\}$ are the estimates of Q_0 as obtained by the solution procedure;

$Q = \{p(x), x \in \Sigma\}$ are the metrics of M;

F: $P_0 \times Q_0 \rightarrow P$ is the forward mapping that maps the states of M_0 into the states of M, and computes state transition rates in M as follows. Let a and b be the states in M_0 that are mapped in the states i and j in M, respectively. Let r_{0ab} denote the transition rate from a to b. Then, the transition rate from i to j in M is

$$
r_{ij} = \frac{\displaystyle\sum_{\substack{a \in i \\ b \in j}} p_a r_{0ab}}{\displaystyle\sum_{a \in i} p_a} , \tag{4.1}
$$

where p_a is the proportion of time in state $a \in \Sigma_0$;

SOLVE: $(M, P) \rightarrow Q$; and

R: $Q \rightarrow \hat{Q}_0$ is the reverse mapping. If $a \in \Sigma_0$ is mapped into $i \in \Sigma$, and if $p(a \mid i)$ is the proportion of the time spent in state a given that system is in i,

$$
\hat{p}_0(a) = p(i) \cdot p(a \mid i).
$$

If F is not one to one, $p(a \mid i)$ may be estimated from some other model.

Note $\hat{p}_0(\cdot)$ are the new estimates of $p_0(\cdot)$ obtained from the composition of F, SOLVE and R. In iterative procedures, we usually assume that $p_0^{(i+1)}(y) = \hat{p}_0^{(i)}(y)$.

4.2   Example: Decomposition of Memory Queue

As an example, consider the decomposition transformation for modeling memory queueing (Section 2.6). The original model, M_0, has one single class of jobs, K devices, a memory queue, and T terminals. The state vector of M_0 is $(n_1, \ldots, n_K, m, t)$ where n_k is the number of customers at device k, m is the number of customers in the memory queue, and t is the number of customers thinking at terminals. Restrictions are, first, $n_1 + \cdots + n_K + m + t = T$, is the number of logged on terminals, second, $n = n_1 + \cdots + n_K \le N$, where N is the maximum level of multiprogramming, and third, $m = 0$ if $n < N$. A state transition diagram schematic is shown in Figure 4.2 (a). The transition rates are determined by model parameters.

The transformation replaces the central subsystem by its flow-equivalent server E and associates memory queue with E. The state space of the transformed model is (n_E, t), where $n_E = n_1 + \cdots + n_K + m$ is the number of customers queued at E. The state transformation is

$$(n_1, \ldots, n_K, m, t) \rightarrow (n_1 + \cdots + n_K + m, t).$$

The transformed state transition diagram is shown in Figure 4.2 (b). Observe that the transitions which do not change m or t in M_0 do not appear in M. The transition rate from state i to state j is given by Eqn. (4.1).

(a) Typical transitions in M_0.

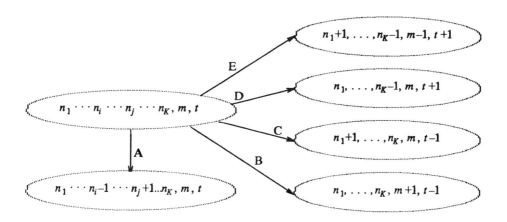

A - internal transition $(i \rightarrow j)$ inside the central subsystem
B - new request, $\sum n_i = N$, $m \geq 0$
C - new request, $\sum n_i < N$, $m = 0$; customer goes to device 1
D - completion, memory queue empty $(m = 0)$; customer leaves from device K
E - completion, memory queue nonempty $(m \geq 0)$

(b) Typical transitions in M.

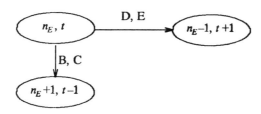

A - invisible
B - new request, $\sum n_i = N$
C - new request, $\sum n_i < N$
D - completion, memory queue empty
E - completion, memory queue nonempty

Figure 4.2: Memory example state transition structure.

4.3   Example: Shadow CPU Model for Preemptive Priority Scheduling

In this section, we once again consider the shadow CPU model for preemptive priority. The purpose is two-fold. First, we wish to illustrate the model development in terms of state space transformations. Second, a concept of variable-rate shadow servers emerges from this discussion (Section 4.4).

The model M_0 represents a two-class (H and L), closed queueing network with K fixed-rate servers. Class H customers preempt class L customers at the CPU (server K). Network populations are fixed at N_H and N_L for classes H and L respectively. The state vector is represented as $\underline{n} = ((n_{1H}, n_{1L}), \ldots, (n_{KH}, n_{KL}))$ where n_{ir} is the number of class r customers at server i. This state description is reasonable because we assume that the service times within a class are homogeneous. Service time parameters can be written in terms of the state probabilities $p(\underline{n})$ and device throughputs, X_{ir}. For servers $1, \ldots, K-1$,

$$S_{iH} = \frac{\displaystyle\sum_{l=1}^{N_H} \sum_{m=0}^{N_L} \frac{l}{l+m} \, p_0(n_{iH} = l, n_{iL} = m)}{X_{iH}}, \tag{4.2}$$

$$S_{iL} = \frac{\displaystyle\sum_{l=0}^{N_H} \sum_{m=1}^{N_L} \frac{m}{l+m} \, p_0(n_{iH} = l, n_{iL} = m)}{X_{iL}}. \tag{4.3}$$

The numerators of these expressions are the utilizations due to H and L classes, respectively. At the CPU,

$$S_{CPU,H} = \frac{p_0(n_{CPU,H} \geq 1)}{X_{CPU,H}}, \tag{4.4}$$

$$S_{CPU,L} = \frac{p_0(n_{CPU,H} = 0, n_{CPU,L} \geq 1)}{X_{CPU,L}}. \tag{4.5}$$

The other parameters of the model are visit ratios V_{ir}.

In the transformed model M, the priority-scheduled CPU is replaced by two fixed rate CPU's, CPU-H and CPU-L, for class H and class L, respectively. The state vector now has the form

$$\underline{n}' = ((n_{1H}, n_{1L}), \ldots, (n_{K-1,H}, n_{K-1,L}), (n_{CPU-H,H}, 0), (0, n_{CPU-L,L})).$$

The state transformation keeps the number of customers in each class at servers $1, \ldots, K-1$ unchanged, equates $n_{CPH-H,H}$ to $n_{CPU,H}$, and assigns $n_{CPU,L}$ to $n_{CPU-L,L}$. Because of the one to one correspondence between $\underline{n}$ and $\underline{n}'$, the measures of model M are given by

$$
\begin{aligned}
p(\underline{n}') &= p_0(\underline{n}), \\
X'_{ir} &= X_{ir}, \quad i = 1, \cdots, K-1, \\
X'_{CPU-H,H} &= X_{CPU,H}, \\
X'_{CPU-L,L} &= X_{CPU,L},
\end{aligned}
\tag{4.6}
$$

where primed quantities are the counterparts (in M) of the unprimed quantities (in M_0). In view of this forward transformation, we can now compute the service time parameters for the servers in M as follows. For $i = 1, \ldots, K-1$,

$$
\begin{aligned}
S'_{iH} &= \frac{\displaystyle\sum_{l=1}^{N_H} \sum_{m=0}^{N_L} \frac{l}{l+m} \, p(n_{iH} = l, n_{iL} = m)}{X'_{iH}} \\[2em]
&= \frac{\displaystyle\sum_{l=1}^{N_H} \sum_{m=0}^{N_L} \frac{l}{l+m} \, p_0(n_{iH} = l, n_{iL} = m)}{X_{iH}}
\end{aligned}
\tag{4.7}
$$

$$= S_{iH}, \qquad\qquad\qquad\qquad \text{[..by (4.2)]} \quad (4.8)$$

$$S'_{iL} = \frac{\displaystyle\sum_{l=0}^{N_H}\sum_{m=1}^{N_L}\frac{m}{l+m}\,p\,(n_{iH}=l,\,n_{iL}=m)}{X'_{iL}}$$

$$= \frac{\displaystyle\sum_{l=0}^{N_H}\sum_{m=1}^{N_L}\frac{m}{l+m}\,p_0(n_{iH}=l,\,n_{iL}=m)}{X_{iL}} \tag{4.9}$$

$$= S_{iL}, \qquad\qquad\qquad\qquad\qquad [..\text{by (4.3)}] \quad (4.10)$$

$$S'_{CPU-H,H} = \frac{p\,(n_{CPU-H,H} \ge 1)}{X'_{CPU-H,H}}$$

$$= \frac{p_0(n_{CPU,H} \ge 1)}{X_{CPU,H}} \tag{4.11}$$

$$= S_{CPU,H}, \qquad\qquad\qquad\qquad [..\text{by (4.4)}] \quad (4.12)$$

$$S'_{CPU-L,L} = \frac{p\,(n_{CPU-L,L} \ge 1)}{X'_{CPU-L,L}}$$

$$= \frac{p_0(n_{CPU,L} \ge 1)}{X_{CPU,L}} \tag{4.13}$$

$$= \frac{p_0(n_{CPU,L} \ge 1)}{p_0(n_{CPU,H}=0,\,n_{CPU,L} \ge 1)}\,S_{CPU,L}. \qquad [..\text{by (4.5)}] \quad (4.14)$$

The visit ratios are determined directly: $V'_{CPU-H,H} = V_{CPU,H}$, $V'_{CPU-L,L} = V_{CPU,L}$, $V'_{CPU,L-H} = 0$, $V'_{CPU,H-L} = 0$, and all other $V'_{ir} = V_{ir}$. The reverse mapping is given by

$$\hat{p}_0(\underline{n}) = \hat{p}\,(\underline{n}'),$$
$$\hat{X}_r = \hat{X}'_r. \tag{4.15}$$

These are the same as the transformations specified in Box 3.1.

The model M contains only fair and autonomous servers, and is thus, solvable by product form algorithms. Because the stretchout factor is not known initially, the model is solved iteratively. The convergence criterion is that the values of $S'_{CPU-L,L}$ do not change significantly on successive iterations.

4.4 Example: Load Dependent Shadow CPU Model for Preemptive Priority Scheduling

In the previous discussion of the priority CPU mdel, the elongated service time at CPU-L is computed by averaging the contention over the whole observation period. The averaging involves an implicit assumption that the CPU-L service function is homogeneous. (And, indeed, that the other device service functions are also homogeneous.) The following discussion shows how to remove this assumption and improve the accuracy of the approximate model. (The analysis for the devices other than CPU-L is similar to that given below.)

In M_0,

$$S_{CPU,L}(n) = \frac{T(n_{CPU,H} = 0, n_{CPU,L} = n)}{C_{CPU,L}(n)},$$

where $C_{CPU,L}(n)$ is the number class L completions at CPU which leave when the queue length is n. Dividing both numerator and denominator by $T(n_{CPU,L} = n)/T$ and applying Baye's rule of conditional probabilities yields

$$S_{CPU,L}(n) = \frac{p_0(n_{CPU,H} = 0 \mid n_{CPU,L} = n)}{X_{CPU,L}(n)}. \tag{4.16}$$

We assume that the service times in M_0 are homogeneous, i.e.,

$$S_{CPU,L}(n) = S_{CPU,L}. \tag{4.17}$$

In the transformed model M,

$$S'_{CPU-L,L}(n) = \frac{T(n_{CPU,L} = n)}{C_{CPU,L}(n)}$$

$$= \frac{1}{X_{CPU,L}(n)}$$

$$= \frac{1}{p_0(n_{CPU,H} = 0 \mid n_{CPU,L} = n)} S_{CPU,L} \qquad \text{[by (4.16) and (4.17)]}$$

$$= \frac{1}{1 - p_0(n_{CPU,H} \geq 1 \mid n_{CPU,L} = n)} S_{CPU,L}. \qquad (4.18)$$

where $p_0(n_{CPU,H} \geq 1 \mid n_{CPU,L} = n)$ is the class H CPU utilization in M_0 assuming that n class L customers are blocked at the CPU, i.e., assuming that $N_L - n$ class L customers are present in the rest of the network (servers $1, \ldots, K-1$). An estimate for $p_0(n_{CPU,H} \geq 1 \mid n_{CPU,L} = n)$ is given by the class H CPU utilization $U^*_{CPU,H}(k, N_H)$, $k = N_L - n$, in an auxiliary model M_k, which is the same as M_0 except that in M_k there are k class L customers, none of which visit CPU, i.e., $V_{CPU,L} = 0$.

Similar analysis shows that the other service functions in M are homogeneous provided that they were homogeneous in the original system. A model using these service functions is displayed in Box 4.1. Numerical comparison with other techniques is provided in Appendix A. Accuracy is improved.

The result that the service function of CPU-L may be load-dependent agrees with intuition. The intuition is that if class H does not have preemptive priority over class L at any server in the rest of the network, then a class H customer is delayed at that server by class L customers ahead of him. This delay increases as the number of class L customers in the rest of

Example: Variable-rate shadow CPU model for preemptive priority.

M_0: Two-class queueing network model of system; two queues at CPU with class H having preemptive priority on class L.

P_0: $\{S_{ir}, V_{ir}, N_r\}$.

Q_0: $\{X_r, U_{CPU,H}, U^{\bullet}_{CPU,H}(k,N_H)\}$.

For $k = 0, 1, \ldots, N_L$

M_k: Same queueing network as in M_0 except that class L jobs do not visit CPU, i.e., $V_{CPU,L} = 0$.'

P_k: $\{S_{ir}, V_{ir}, N_H, k\}$.

Q_k: $\{U_{CPU,H}\}$.

$\mathbf{F}_k$: $S_{CPU,L} = 0$, all other parameters same.

$\mathbf{R}_k$: Identity: $U^{\bullet}_{CPU,H}(k,N_H) = U_{CPU,H}$.

SOLVE(M_k, P_k):Product form algorithm: Convolution, MVA, etc.

Iteration: Not Required.

M : Same queueing network as in M_0 except that CPU is split into CPU-H and CPU-L visited by classes H and L respectively. CPU-L is load dependent.

P : $\{S_{CPU-H,H}, S_{CPU-L,L}(n), S_{ir}, V_{ir}, N_r\}$.

Q : $\{X_r, U_{CPU-H,H}\}$.

F: (Load Concealment Transformation)

$$S_{CPU-L,L}(n) = \frac{1}{1 - U^{\bullet}_{CPU,H}(N_L-n, N_H)} \cdot S_{CPU,L},$$

(or, Rate function $r_{CPU-L}(n) = 1 - U^{\bullet}_{CPU,H}(N_L-n, N_H)$.)

$S_{CPU-H,H} = S_{CPU,H}$, all other parameters same.

R: Identity:

$X_r = X_r^{\cdot}$, $U_{CPU,H} = U_{CPU-H,H}$.

SOLVE(M, P):Product form algorithm: Convolution, MVA, etc.

Iteration: Not Required.

Notes: If the Convolution algorithm is used, it is advisable to renumber devices such that CPU-H is the Kth and $CPU-L$ is the $K+1$st device. Then, server $K+1$ (i.e., CPU-L) can be convolved in the G vector obtained from solution of $M_1, \ldots, M_{NL}$.

Box 4.1: Variable-rate shadow CPU model for preemptive priority at CPU.

the network increases. As the delay increases, class H throughput of the rest of the network decreases, i.e., the preemption rate at CPU decreases.

4.5 A Catalog of General Transformations

The priority CPU and aggregate server models both use the concept of hiding one workload from another by slowing service rates to account for resources consumed by the hidden workload. This concept can be stated in a general way and called a *load concealment transformation*. The load concealment transformation can be used in many other situations besides the ones studied in detail here.

In fact, many of the transformations employed in our examples can be formulated for general application in the construction of approximate models. Other examples are:

- *State Aggregation*, in which states of M stand for sets of states in M_0. The memory queue decomposition model employed this principle.

- *Server Aggregation*, in which a subnetwork of devices is replaced by a single, flow-equivalent device. This is an important special case of state aggregation.

- *Response Time Preservation*, in which a subnetwork of devices is replaced by a set of equivalent servers.

- *Load Separation*, in which interacting classes are replaced with non-interacting classes.

- *Class Aggregation*, in which classes of jobs are lumped.

- *Load Scaling*, in which the number of jobs in the system is scaled down and service rates slowed accordingly.

- *Response Time Modeling*, in which Mean Value Analysis is used to combine separate models for the response times of non-homogeneous servers or subsystems.

- *Delay Server Introduction*, in which delay servers are used to model interference. The parameters of these servers are usually determined iteratively.

The above list constitutes a catalog of basic transformations that can be used as tools by analysts constructing approximate models. Each is discussed in detail below. Some of these tools have been discussed previously in [BUZE83].

4.5.1 Load Concealment Transformation

Load concealment transformation is one of the most common transformations. It was used in the preemptive priority example to create shadow CPU's for each class and in the aggregate server model to create a shadow server for each server and each processing phase. It removes the interference at a server between customers in different classes by creating separate shadow servers for each class; the effect of contention is represented by elongating the service time for a class in inverse proportion to the idleness remaining from other classes.

The load concealment transformation operates on an individual server, say k. In model M_0, the customers at server k are divided into two or more classes. In model M, at a shadow server corresponding to server k, all but one of the classes are concealed. Several shadow servers can be created by applying this transformation separately for each visible class. (The method can be extended to handle sets of visible classes.)

This transformation converts queueing delay accumulated while waiting for the concealed classes to extra service time for the visible class.

Suppose that R customer classes visit a processor-sharing (PS) server i in M_0 and one (say, class r) visits a shadow server ir in M. The transformation is defined as follows. In M_0, let

$n_{ir}(t)$ = the number of customers of class r at server i at time t.

In M, customers of classes $1, \cdots, r-1, r+1, \cdots, R$ are concealed at shadow server ir; let

$m_{ir}(t)$ = the total number of visible (class r)

customers at server ir at time t.

The transformation is simply

$$m_{ir}(t) = n_{ir}(t).$$

The implications of this transformation are straightforward. Let $T(\underline{n_i})$ denote the total time during which the customer class vector $\underline{n_i} = (n_{i1}, \ldots, n_{iR})$ is observed at server i in M_0. Let $T_{ir}(m)$ be the total time there are m visible (class r) customers at server ir in M. The transformation assigns:

$$T_{ir}(m) = \sum_{n_{ir}=m} T(\underline{n_i}).$$

Therefore, the state occupancies in M are

$$p_{ir}(m) = \sum_{n_{ir}=m} p(\underline{n_i}).$$

Also, the number of visible (class r) customer completions at ir, given $n_{ir} = n$, is $C_{ir}(n)$.

The service time per visit for a class r customer is

$$
S_{ir} = \frac{\displaystyle\sum_{\substack{\underline{n_i} \\ n_{ir} \geq 1}} \frac{n_{ir}}{n_{i1} + \cdots + n_{iR}} T(\underline{n_i})}{\displaystyle\sum_{n \geq 1} C_{ir}(n)}
$$

$$
= \frac{\displaystyle\sum_{\substack{\underline{n_i} \\ n_{ir} \geq 1}} \frac{n_{ir}}{n_{i1} + \cdots + n_{iR}} p_i(\underline{n_i})}{X_{ir}}. \tag{4.19}
$$

The contention due to invisible customers elongates the apparent demand of the visible customers. The stretched out service time is given by

$$
S_{ir}' = \frac{\displaystyle\sum_{m \geq 1} T_{ir}(m)}{\displaystyle\sum_{m \geq 1} C_{ir}(m)}
$$

$$
= \frac{\displaystyle\sum_{m \geq 1} p_{ir}(m)}{X_{ir}}. \tag{4.20}
$$

By Eqn. (4.19) and the state mapping,

$$
S_{ir}' = \frac{\displaystyle\sum_{n \geq 1} p_{ir}(n)}{\displaystyle\sum_{n_{ir} \geq 1} \frac{n_{ir}}{n_{i1} + \cdots + n_{iR}} p(\underline{n_i})} S_{ir}. \tag{4.21}
$$

The reverse transformation is

$$p(\underline{n}_i) = p(m_{i1} = n_{i1}, \ldots, m_{iR} = n_{iR})$$

$$X_{ir} = \frac{\displaystyle\sum_{\substack{\underline{n}_i \\ n_{ir} \geq 1}} \frac{n_{ir}}{n_{i1} + \cdots + n_{iR}} p(\underline{n}_i)}{S_{ir}} \qquad (4.22)$$

$$X_r = X_r'.$$

One common way to write the transformation is to specify service time elongation factor

$$F_{ir} = \frac{S_{ir}'}{S_{ir}}$$

$$= \frac{p_{ir}(n \geq 1)}{\displaystyle\sum_{n_{ir} \geq 1} \frac{n_{ir}}{n_{i1} + \cdots + n_{iR}} p_i(\underline{n}_i)}, \qquad (4.23)$$

where $p_{ir}(n \geq 1)$ is simply the portion of time there is at least 1 class r customer present at the server i.

Because of the averaging in the definition of stretched out service times (Eqns. (4.20) & (4.21)), this transformation is not exact even for product form networks. The error analysis of this transformation is not studied here.

4.5.2 State Aggregation Transformation

A state aggregation transformation (Section 2.10) seeks to reduce the complexity of the model by replacing a set of (strongly interacting) states with a single state. The justification that such transformations do not introduce much error is rooted in the theory of near-decomposability [SIMO61] and has been studied in detail by Courtois [COUR77]. The technique was directly applied by Brandwajn [BRAN74] to model virtual memory time-sharing systems and by Courtois [COUR75] to analyze the stability and saturation in multiprogrammed virtual memory systems.

Direct application of the state aggregation transformation can be tedious. One must first construct the whole state space and then identify the subsets to aggregate. Vantilborgh *et al.* [VANT80] point out that this will be straightforward when aggregate state subsets arise immediately from subnetworks whose internal transitions are high compared to their arrival and completion rates. These ideas are illustrated in the examples that follow.

Example 1: Heidelberger and Trivedi's State Aggregation Model
for FORK and JOIN

Heidelberger and Trivedi study systems in which processes are created (FORK) or deleted (JOIN) [HEID83]. They assume that state transitions corresponding to FORK and JOIN operations are much less frequent than the state transitions corresponding to completions of service at a device. Therefore, they aggregate the states in which the number of active (parent and child) processes is the same.

To illustrate the idea, consider an example. Let a type 0 main process, P_0, in M_0 have the following execution pattern:

$$P_0:$$
```
        DO Initial Processing
        FORK(P1, P2)
        JOIN
        DO Final Processing,
```

i.e., after initial processing, P_0 forks off two processes P_1 and P_2, waits for both of them to finish, and then ends after final processing. Child process P_i has the following execution pattern:

$P_i:$
      DO Processing Type i
      QUIT.

Now we aggregate states such that each component state has an equal number of active processes of each type, i.e., the state transformation is:

$$(\underline{n}_1, \ldots, \underline{n}_K) \rightarrow (a_0, a_1, a_2)$$

where

$\underline{n}_i = (n_{i0}, n_{i1}, n_{i2})$ and n_{ir} is the number of processes of type P_r at server i, and

$a_r = \sum_{i=1}^{K} n_{ir}$ is the number of active P_r processes.

The conditional state occupancies for constituent states in an aggregate, $p(\underline{n}_1, \ldots, \underline{n}_K \mid a_0, a_1, a_2)$, are determined by analyzing the original queueing network for the system with a_r class r jobs. Class throughputs provide the transition rates among aggregates, e.g.,

$$r((a_0, a_1, a_2) \rightarrow (a_0{-}1, a_1{+}1, a_2{+}1)) = X_0(a_0, a_1, a_2),$$

where $X_0(a_0, a_1, a_2)$ is the P_0 throughput, i.e., rate at which FORK is performed when a_0 type P_0, a_1 type P_1, and a_2 type P_2 jobs are active. For details, see [HEID83].

Example 2: Thomasian's Critical Section Model

Consider a system with Z critical sections. When a process is executing in critical section z ($z \geq 1$), the process is considered to be in phase z. Phase 0 processes are the ones executing outside the critical section.

Thomasian postulates that the critical section requests are much less frequent than device requests and that a process makes several device requests within a critical section [THOM83]. With these assumptions, all states with an equal number of active transactions in each phase can be aggregated:

$$(\underline{n}_1, \ldots, \underline{n}_K ; w_1, \ldots, w_Z) \rightarrow (\sum_i n_{i0}, \sum_i n_{i1} + w_1, \ldots, \sum_i n_{iZ} + w_Z),$$

where $\underline{n}_i = (n_{i1}, \ldots, n_{iR})$, n_{ir} is the number of phase r customers at device i (note $\sum n_{iz} \leq 1$ for $z \geq 1$), and w_z is the number of customers waiting for entry in the critical section z. Phase 0 customers are outside the critical sections.

The transition rate out of an aggregate state and the conditional state occupancies for the constituent states are determined by analyzing the system with n_r phase r customers where $n_r = \sum_i n_{ir}$. (In this model each processing phase is represented as a separate class; class 0 customers do not request critical sections.) As an example, for a two critical section system, one transition rate is

$$r((n_0, 1 + w_1, n_2 + w_2) \rightarrow (n_0 + 1, w_1, n_2 + w_2)) = X_1(n_0, 1, n_2),$$

where $X_1(n_0, 1, n_2)$ is class 1 throughput with n_0 class 0, one class 1 and n_2 class 2 customers active.

4.5.3 Server Aggregation Transformation

This is probably the most important state aggregation transformation; it has been commonly called *decomposition* in queueing network literature. It replaces a set of K strongly interacting servers by a flow-equivalent server E; the state transformation is:

$$(n_1, \ldots, n_K) \rightarrow (n_E = n_1 + \cdots + n_K).$$

To illustrate further, consider a subsystem containing devices $1, \ldots, K$. Let $\underline{n} = (n_1, \ldots, n_K)$ be a state of this subsystem. Let

$$\Sigma(N) = \{ \underline{n} \mid \sum_{i=1}^{K} n_i = N \},$$

and

$$\Sigma = \bigcup_{N \geq 0} \Sigma(N).$$

If the rate of interactions (transitions $\underline{m} \to \underline{n}$, for $\underline{n} \in \Sigma(N)$ and $\underline{m} \notin \Sigma(N)$) is small compared to internal transition rates ($\underline{n} \to \underline{k}$, for $\underline{k}, \underline{n} \in \Sigma(N)$), then the theory of decomposability says

$$p(\underline{n}) \approx p(\underline{n} \mid \underline{n} \in \Sigma(N)) \, p(N),$$

where $p(N)$ is the proportion of time the subsystem has N customers in it, and $p(\underline{n} \mid \underline{n} \in \Sigma(N))$ is the proportion of time state $\underline{n}$ is observed given that subsystem has fixed load N on it. To find $p(\underline{n} \mid \underline{n} \in \Sigma(N))$, we consider an off-line experiment, i.e., analyze the isolated subsystem under fixed load. To find $p(N)$, consider a new model whose states represent $\Sigma(N)$ for $N = 0, 1, \cdots$. The transition $N - 1 \to N$ occurs iff there is an arrival to the subsystem, which occurs with the rate

$$\lambda(N - 1) = \frac{\displaystyle\sum_{\substack{\underline{m} \in \Sigma(N-1) \\ \underline{n} \in \Sigma(N)}} r(\underline{m} \to \underline{n}) \, p(\underline{m})}{\displaystyle\sum_{\underline{m} \in \Sigma(N-1)} p(\underline{m})}.$$

Similarly the completion rate is

$$\mu(N) = \frac{\displaystyle\sum_{\substack{\underline{m} \in \Sigma(N-1) \\ \underline{n} \in \Sigma(N)}} r(\underline{n} \to \underline{m}) \, p(\underline{n})}{\displaystyle\sum_{\underline{n} \in \Sigma(N)} p(\underline{n})}.$$

Note that $\mu(N) = X_0(N)$, the throughput of the subnetwork with load N. The macro system satisfies the flow-balance equation

$$p(N - 1)\lambda(N - 1) = p(N)\mu(N).$$

This is the equation corresponding to a network in which devices $1, \ldots, K$ are replaced with a server E of rate

$$\mu_E(N) = X_0(N).$$

Thus the aggregation of servers and states is closely related.

Justification for the Validity of the Transformation

The justification lies in the theory of near-decomposability [COUR77], and in the complete-decomposability of product form networks [CHAN75b]. Chandy, Herzog and Woo have shown that *any* subset of servers in a product form network is replaceable by its flow-equivalent server, i.e., the transformation is exact for any arbitrary set of servers in a product form network [CHAN75b]. Drawing upon this analysis, they suggest that a subsystem can also be replaced by its flow-equivalent server in non-product form networks. Vantilborgh *et al.* have shown that if the transitions within the subset of servers are an order of magnitude stronger than the transitions to and from the rest of the network, the subsystem is nearly-decomposable and the transformation is quite accurate [VANT80].

Example 1: Sauer and Chandy's Priority Algorithm

Sauer and Chandy [SAUE75b] consider a system with three classes H, M, and L.[1] Class H has priority over class M, and class M, in turn, has priority over class L at CPU. The service at I/O devices is FCFS. To model this system, they replace the I/O subsystem by its flow equivalent server, E. The transformed network (CPU and E) is solved using global balance equations. The aggregation reduces the number of states, and therefore the cost of solution, considerably without significant loss of accuracy.

Example 2: Memory Queueing

The memory queueing example uses decomposition (server aggregation) twice: 1) to replace the central subsystem with its flow-equivalent server E, leading to the subsystem shown in Figure 4.3, and then 2) to replace the

---

1. This model is, in fact, used as a submodel for analyzing a system with more than 3 priority classes. See Example 2 in Section 4.5.6, Class Aggregation.

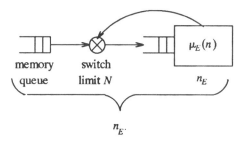

Figure 4.3: Flow-equivalent server for central subsystem and memory queue.

subsystem (memory queue, switch, and E) with $E\,'$, in which

$$\mu_{E\,'}(n_{E\,'}) = \begin{cases} \mu_E(n_{E\,'}), & n_{E\,'} \leq N \\ \mu_E(N), & \text{otherwise.} \end{cases}$$

This two step transformation is also used in the Jacobson-Lazowska model for simultaneous resource possession (Section 3.3), and in the aggregate server model (Section 3.4).

Example 3: Server Aggregation in Multiclass Networks

A straightforward application of the transformation yields following service function for class r

$$S_{Er}(n_1, \ldots, n_R) = \frac{1}{X_r(n_1, \ldots, n_R)},$$

where n_r is the number of class r customers in the subsystem and $X_r(\cdot)$ is the class r throughput for given population. When the server E with this service function is included in the network in lieu of the subsystem, the resulting network does not have a product form solution because the service function for class r at server E, S_{Er}, depends directly on the number of customers in other classes. To overcome this difficulty, we apply the *load concealment transformation* to create shadow equivalent servers for each class:

$$S_{Er}(n) = \frac{\displaystyle\sum_{\substack{\underline{n}\ s.t.\\ n_r=n}} T(\underline{n})}{\displaystyle\sum_{\substack{\underline{n}\ s.t.\\ n_r=n}} C_r(\underline{n})}$$

$$= \frac{\displaystyle\sum_{\substack{\underline{n}\ s.t.\\ n_r=n}} T(\underline{n})}{\displaystyle\sum_{\substack{\underline{n}\ s.t.\\ n_r=n}} \frac{C_r(\underline{n})}{T(\underline{n})}\, T(\underline{n})}$$

$$= \frac{\displaystyle\sum_{\substack{\underline{n}\ s.t.\\ n_r=n}} T(\underline{n})}{\displaystyle\sum_{\substack{\underline{n}\ s.t.\\ n_r=n}} X_r(\underline{n})\, T(\underline{n})}$$

$$\approx \frac{1}{X_r(\bar{\underline{n}}(n_r=n))}\ \frac{\displaystyle\sum_{\substack{\underline{n}\ s.t.\\ n_r=n}} T(\underline{n})}{\displaystyle\sum_{\substack{\underline{n}\ s.t.\\ n_r=n}} T(\underline{n})},$$

$$S_{Er}(n) \approx \frac{1}{X_r(\bar{\underline{n}}(n_r=n))},$$

where

$$\bar{\underline{n}}(n_r = n) = (\bar{n}_1(n_r = n), \ldots, \bar{n}_{r-1}(n_r = n), n, \bar{n}_{r+1}(n_r = n), \ldots, \bar{n}_R(n_r = n)),$$

and $\bar{n}_j(n_r = n)$ is the average number of class j customers in the subsystem given that n class r customers are present in the network.

If we also assume that average class j population in the subsystem is independent of the class r population in the subsystem, we get

$$S_{Er}(n) \approx \frac{1}{X_r(\bar{n}_1, \ldots, \bar{n}_{r-1}, n, \bar{n}_{r+1}, \ldots, \bar{n}_R)}.$$

This service function is used by Brandwajn [BRAN82], and by Lazowska and Zahorjan [LAZO82] in their model for multiclass memory constrained systems. Because the rest of the network consisted only of the terminals where there is no queueing, they treat each set of E_r and and class r terminals as a single class network. They obtain average customer populations by analyzing the set of single class networks iteratively.

4.5.4 Response Time Preservation Transformation

The response time preservation transformation replaces a subsystem by a set of equivalent servers. The service times at the equivalent servers are determined such that the customer response time at the subsystem under an assumed arrival process is same as that at the equivalent servers. This transformation yields a general method for developing approximate solutions for a wide class of problems including general service time distributions, priority scheduling, distributed systems. The details are presented in Appendix C.

4.5.5 Load Separation Transformation

This transformation removes non-autonomous (interdependent) behavior of customers by putting interacting customers in different, independent classes. The replacement normally accounts for the contention for physical resources but does not model synchronization delays. Synchronization delays can be modeled by adding shadow servers.

Example 1: Heidelberger and Trivedi's Model for Asynchronous Concurrency

Heidelberger and Trivedi present a model for a system in which processes are created (FORK) but the parent process does not wait for child processes to finish (no JOIN) in [HEID82]. They model the child processes as open classes.

To illustrate the idea, consider an example. Assume there are N_0 (fixed) main processes, denoted as P_0 (type 0), in M_0. P_0 has the following execution pattern:

P_0:
DO Initial Processing
FORK(P1, P2)
DO Final Processing.

Child process P_i has the following execution pattern:

P_i:
DO Processing Type i
QUIT.

In M, the set of type P_0 customers forms a closed class. But because the number of forked P_i jobs is not fixed, P_i's are represented as an open class i. By assuming that all classes are independent, we obtain a product form solution for M. Because each P_0 creates one P_i, the arrival rate of class i, λ_i, equals the class 0 throughput, X_0. As X_0 is not known initially, the model is solved iteratively. For details, see [HEID82].

Example 2: Heidelberger and Trivedi's Complementary Delay Model for Internal Program Concurrency

In the complementary delay model for analyzing process creation (FORK) and deletion (JOIN), Heidelberger and Trivedi replace forked jobs P_i's by closed class i and represent the main processes P_0's as class 0

[HEID83]. The synchronization delays between processes are accounted for by introducing additional delay servers.

To illustrate the principle, consider an example. Assume there are N_0 (fixed) main processes, denoted as P_0 (type 0), in M_0. P_0 has the following execution pattern:

P_0:
DO Initial Processing
FORK(P1, P2)
JOIN
DO Final Processing.

Child process P_r has the following execution pattern:

P_r:
DO Processing Type r
JOIN.

Also assume that there are $N_r = N_0$ processes reserved for P_r's. Now examine the time spent by each process.

1. After Initial Processing, P_0 creates P_1 and P_2 and waits for them to finish; let the time in this dormant state be denoted as D_0. Once both P_1 and P_2 are done, P_0 resumes active processing.

2. After having finished Type r processing, P_r waits for its sibling to finish; let D_{wr} denote this wait.

3. When both P_1 and P_2 are done, the processes are freed and remain free till next FORK. This idle time equals the time till next FORK, i.e., the elapsed time for the Initial Processing and the Final Processing of the parent job; let it be denoted as D_d.

In M, we represent P_r as a closed class r because N_r is fixed. To account for the whole period, P_0 suffers delay D_0. P_r, $r = 1, 2$, suffers delay D_{wr} and D_d. Clearly,

$$D_0 = \max \{R_1, R_2\},$$
$$D_d = R_0, \text{ and}$$
$$D_{wr} = D_0 - R_r,$$

where R_r denotes the *active* processing time. Because R_r are not known initially, they are computed iteratively.

4.5.6 Class Aggregation Transformation

The class aggregation transformation averages the customers in somewhat similar classes into the customers of a single aggregate class. As a state transformation, it can be written as

$$(n_{i1}, \ldots, n_{iR}) \rightarrow (n_i = \sum_{i=1}^{R} n_{ir}),$$

where n_{ir} is the number of class r customers at device i. This common transformation is really another instance of state aggregation transformations.

Given that V_{ir} is the server i visit ratio, S_{ir} is the service time per visit, and X_r is the throughput for class r, the aggregate class service time per visit is

$$S_i = \frac{\text{Total service rendered by } i}{\text{Total number of completions at } i},$$

$$= \frac{\sum_{r=1}^{R} V_{ir} S_{ir} X_r}{\sum_{r=1}^{R} V_{ir} X_r},$$

the visit ratio is

$$V_i = \frac{\text{Total number of completions at } i}{\text{Total number of system completions}},$$

$$= \frac{\sum\limits_{r=1}^{R} V_{ir} X_r}{\sum\limits_{r=1}^{R} X_r},$$

and total customer population is

$$N = \sum_{r=1}^{R} N_r,$$

where N_r is the class r population. Due to the loss of information, an exact reverse mapping does not exist. Particular mapping depends on the application. We illustrate the concepts below.

Example 1: Data Collection and Reduction

When the analyst is interested in an overall system performance measures without concern to specific job types, a single class model is usually sufficient. The data measurement and reporting procedure performs this aggregation automatically. Since the analyst is not interested in performance measures by classes, the reverse mapping is an identity.

Example 2: Sauer and Chandy Model for Priorities

Consider a system in which there are R priority classes at CPU and other devices use First-Come-First-Served scheduling. To analyze this system, Sauer and Chandy construct models $M_1, \ldots, M_R$, one for each priority class [SAUE75b]. M_r is a three class model: classes H_r, r and L_r. Class H_r is the aggregate class for all classes with priority higher than that of class r. Class L_r is the aggregate class for classes with priority less than that of r. M_r is solved to determine the class r throughput, X_r; the solution procedure replaces all devices except CPU by a flow-equivalent server (decomposition) and then solves global balance equations.[2] Since throughputs are needed to

_____
2. See Example 1 for Server Aggregation Transformation (Section 4.5.3).

perform class aggregation and are initially unknown, the M_r's are iteratively solved to obtain final solution.

Example 3: Class Aggregation for Complexity Reduction

The cost of solving a multiclass model rises as $RK \prod (N_r + 1)$ with number of classes. To reduce the complexity, Zahorjan aggregates "similar" classes [ZAHO80]. The forward mapping is same as the one considered in the beginning. However, since we are now interested in performance measures by class, we have to use heuristic reverse mappings. Zahorjan has proposed that

$$\bar{n}_{ir} = \frac{X_r V_{ir} S_{ir}}{\sum\limits_{j=1}^{R} X_j V_{ij} S_{ij}} \ \bar{n}_{ir} .$$

Because of the heuristic and incorrect estimates of X_r, $\sum_{i=1}^{K} \bar{n}_{ir}$ need not equal N_r, the X_r are heuristically corrected

$$\hat{X}_r = (\alpha + \frac{N_r}{\sum\limits_{i=1}^{K} \bar{n}_{ir}}) \ \frac{X_r}{\alpha + 1} .$$

α is a positive constant; typically $\alpha = 1$. The model is solved iteratively with new estimate for $\hat{X}_r$. For details, see [ZAHO80].

4.5.7 Load Scaling Transformation

Product form solution algorithms consume too much space and time for systems with a large load N_0. One approach to reduce the complexity is by scaling down loads: let the number of customers in M be $N = N_0/k$, where N_0 is the population in M_0 and k is some constant. The intuition is that a customer in M corresponds to a batch of k customers in M_0.

Because of this intuition, a possible scaling for service times is:

$$S_i' = kS_i.$$

The corresponding reverse mapping is:

$$X_i(N_0) = X_i'(N_0/k).$$

The resulting solution is in error because in M_0 jobs do not travel in batches of k.

Zahorjan has suggested another mapping [ZAHO80]. The device factor for fixed-rate server i in M_0 is

$$F_i(n) = (V_iS_i)^n.$$

Let

$$V_i'S_i' = (V_iS_i)^k,$$

so that in M

$$F_i'(n/k) = F_i(n),$$

where F_i' is the device factor in M. The reverse mapping is:

$$X_i(N_0) = (X_i'(N_0/k))^{1/k}.$$

This mapping is also approximate because jobs in M_0 are not actually batched.

4.5.8 Response Time Modeling Transformation

Response time modeling is a basic transformation underlying several exact and approximate models. This transformation provides a separate model for response time for each device of the system, together with a method of integrating the separate response times into overall system metrics. This section will illustrate this transformation with: the single class MVA algorithm [REIS80], the multiclass MVA algorithm [REIS80], Bard's approximation for FCFS servers with different service time per visit for each class [BARD79], two approximations for preemptive priority scheduling [BRYA83, CHAN83], and a variant of the Extended Product Form (EPF) model [SHUM76, SHUM77].

The basis for response time modeling is the equations of Mean Value Analysis (MVA), which have the form

$$R_i = f_i(P_i, \bar{n}_i) \qquad i = 1, \ldots, K,$$

$$X_0 = N / \sum_{i=1}^{K} V_i R_i, \tag{4.24}$$

$$\bar{n}_i = X_0 V_i R_i \qquad i = 1, \ldots, K.$$

The first equation gives the response time of device i in terms of the parameters P_i of that device and the queue length $\bar{n}_i$ there. The second and third equations integrate the set of response times $\{R_i\}$ to produce the system throughput X_0 and the queue lengths $\{\bar{n}_i\}$. Note that the queue lengths satisfy the consistency requirement $\bar{n}_1 + \cdots + \bar{n}_K = N$. The second and third equations hold for any flow-balanced system.

For any server in flow-balance, the response satisfies the relation

$$R_i = \sum_{n \geq 1} n S_i(n) \, p_{Ai}(n - 1),$$

where $p_{Ai}(n)$ is the fraction of arrivals who see $n_i(t) = n$ [BUZE80a]. For a fixed-rate server, this reduces to

$$R_i = S_i(1 + \bar{n}_{Ai}).$$

In a product form queueing network, the arrival theorem [BUZE80a, BUZE80b, REIS80, SEVC79] guarantees $\bar{n}_{Ai}(N) = \bar{n}_i(N - 1)$, whereupon

$$R_i(N) = S_i(1 + \bar{n}_i(N - 1)). \tag{4.25}$$

In other words, Eqn. (4.25) is the response time model which, when

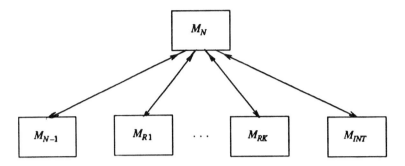

Legend:

M_n — Original model with n customers

M_{Ri} — Response time model for queue i

M_{INT} — Performance Measure INTegrator to compute X, n_i

Figure 4.4: Model hierarchy for MVA response time
modeling transformation.

substituted into the schema (4.24), yields the equations for a product form
network.

Equations yielding approximate solutions for non-product form networks
can be constructed from an approximate model for the response time of nonautonomous or unfair devices. Figure 4.4 illustrates the modeling pattern
being used here. The models M_{Ri} provide the response times $\{R_i\}$. The model
M_{INT} combines the $\{R_i\}$ to calculate the other metrics of the system.

Multi-class Product Form Networks

Consider an R class product form network with N_r customers in class r,
$r = 1, \ldots, R$. As a condition for product form solution, the service time per
visit S_{ir} is equal for each class at FCFS server i. The arrival theorem
[SEVC79] gives for the the class r response time

$$R_{ir}(\underline{N}) = \sum_{j=1}^{R} \bar{n}_{Aijr}(\underline{N})S_{ij} + S_{ir}$$

$$= \sum_{j=1}^{R} \bar{n}_{ij}(\underline{N} - \underline{1}_r)S_{ij} + S_{ir}$$

$$= S_{ir}(1 + \sum_{j=1}^{R} \bar{n}_{ij}(\underline{N} - \underline{1}_r)), \qquad (4.26)$$

where $\bar{n}_{Aijr}(\underline{N})$ is the mean number of class j jobs seen by a class r job upon arrival at server i and $\underline{1}_r$ is a population vector with 1 class r job and 0 jobs for other classes.

Multi-class FCFS Servers

The arrival theorem does not hold for a network containing a FCFS device with different mean service times in each class. For an approximation, Bard [BARD79] assumed that the arrival theorem holds nonetheless -- i.e., the mean number of class j customers seen at server i by an arriving class r customer:

$$\bar{n}_{Aijr}(\underline{N}) = \bar{n}_{ij}(\underline{N} - \underline{1}_r).$$

With this assumption, class r response time

$$R_{ir}(\underline{N}) = S_{ir} + \sum_{j=1}^{R} \bar{n}_{Aijr}(\underline{N})S_{ij}$$

$$= S_{ir} + \sum_{j=1}^{R} \bar{n}_{ij}(\underline{N} - \underline{1}_r)S_{ij}. \qquad (4.27)$$

Priority Servers

Consider a preemptive priority-scheduled server. A response time model can be constructed from these observations with respect to class r:

1. The customers with lower priority (class j, $j > r$) do not delay class r customers.

2. Assumption that the arrival theorem still holds, i.e.,

$$\bar{n}_{Aijr}(\underline{N}) = \bar{n}_{ij}(\underline{N} - \underline{1}_r).$$

3. The number of high priority customers (class j, $j < r$) that arrive during the time the tagged class r customer is at server i is

$$R_{ir}(\underline{N})\lambda_{ijr}(\underline{N}),$$

where $\lambda_{ijr}(\underline{N})$ is the arrival rate of class j customers at server i during the residence of the tagged class r customer at i.

Therefore,

$$R_{ir}(\underline{N}) = S_{ir} + \sum_{j=1}^{r} \bar{n}_{ij}(\underline{N} - \underline{1}_r)S_{ij} + \sum_{j=1}^{r-1} R_{ir}(\underline{N})\lambda_{ijr}(\underline{N})S_{ij},$$

or,

$$R_{ir}(\underline{N}) = \frac{S_{ir} + \sum_{j=1}^{r} \bar{n}_{ij}(\underline{N} - \underline{1}_r)S_{ij}}{1 - \sum_{j=1}^{r-1} \lambda_{ijr}(\underline{N})S_{ij}}. \tag{4.28}$$

Chandy and Laksmi [CHAN83] estimate $\lambda_{ijr}(\underline{N})$ as

$$\lambda_{ijr}(\underline{N}) = V_{ij}X_j(\underline{N} - \bar{n}_{ij}(\underline{N}) \cdot \underline{1}_j), \tag{4.29}$$

where $X_j(\underline{N})$ is the system throughput for class j when $\underline{N}$ jobs are present in the network. This approximation is based on the following argument. Because on the average $\bar{n}_{ij}(\underline{N})$ class j customers are present at server i, $\lambda_{ijr}(\underline{N})/V_{ij}$ should equal the class j system throughput with $\bar{n}_{ij}(\underline{N})$ fewer class j customers in the network. This argument is inexact because the $\bar{n}_{ij}(\underline{N})$ customers seen upon arrival by a class r job must leave server i before the tagged class r customer can be processed at server i -- hence, these $\bar{n}_{ij}(\underline{N})$ class j jobs may be among the arrivals while the tagged customer is at server i. The approximation is likely to be poor when the time spent by class j jobs in the rest of the network is no longer than the time spent at the server i or when the priority of class j is much higher than the priority of class r. In both cases, a class j customer is likely to cycle back to server i before the tagged customer leaves. Chandy and Laksmi's experiments confirm this intuition. The data in Appendix A show that the approximation may perform poorly even when class j transit time in the rest of the network is large compared to the response time at server i.

Bryant and Krzesinski [BRYA83] use a simpler estimate for $\lambda_{ijr}(\underline{N})$:

$$\lambda_{ijr}(\underline{N}) = V_{ij}X_j(\underline{N}).\tag{4.30}$$

This approximation is at the other extreme from the Chandy and Laksmi approximation. It says that the arrival rate of the class j jobs during the residence time of the class r job is unaffected by the number of class j jobs seen by the class r job at the time of arrival. It is valid only if class j jobs do not loop back to i or if they have preemptive priority over all other jobs at all other devices. The approximation is likely to overestimate λ_{ijr}. The overestimate of λ_{ijr} will lead to an overestimate in R_{ir} and an underestimate of class r throughput. The data presented in Appendix A corroborate these intuitions.

EPF Extension for General Service Times

The Extended Product Form approximation attempts to account for the coefficient of variation (CV) of service time at a device [SHUM76, SHUM77]. The original idea was that in the product form solution,

$$p(\underline{n}) = \frac{F_1(n_1) \cdots F_K(n_K)}{G},$$

the device factors $F_i(n_i)$ are unnormalized solutions to the $M/M/1/N$ queueing system. Shum and Buzen proposed to replace each device factor with the unnormalized solutions of the $M/G/1/N$ queueing system. The method is among the most accurate known for networks whose servers have

CV much different from 1, but it is difficult to program and does not always find a solution consistent with the throughput equations of the system [BALB79].

The method can be approached using the schema of Figure 4.4. The Pollaczek-Khinchin formula for an $M/G/1$ queue says that the response time is

$$R_i = S_i \left(1 + \frac{U_i(CV_i^2 + 1)}{2(1 - U_i)} \right). \tag{4.31}$$

When combined with the equations

$$X_0 = N / \sum_{i=1}^{K} V_i R_i, \text{and}$$
$$U_i = X_0 V_i S_i,$$

a system of equations results in which given parameters $\{S_i\}$, $\{CV_i\}$ and $\{V_i\}$, an iterative solution will yield the quantities $\{U_i\}$ and $\{R_i\}$. A better solution will be obtained by using the response time formula for an $M/G/1/N$ queue.

A summary of these response time models appears in Box 4.2.

4.5.9 Delay Server Introduction Transformation

This transformation introduces a delay server in the transformed model to stand as a surrogate for some delay in the system. The amount of delay is usually determined by iteration.

Examples of this useful transformation were encountered in the Jacobson-Lazowska method for simultaneous resource possession [JACO82] and in the Heidelberger-Trivedi model of complementary delays for analyzing internal program concurrency [HEID83].

Product Form Response Time Model (MVA) at a FCFS Server (Single Class):

$$R_i(N) = S_i(1 + \bar{n}_i(N - 1))$$

Product Form Response Time Model (MVA) at a FCFS Server (Multi-class):

$$R_{ir}(\underline{N}) = S_{ir}(1 + \sum_{j=1}^{R} \bar{n}_{ij}(\underline{N} - \underline{1}_r))$$

Bard's Response Time Model for FCFS with Different Service Times:

$$R_{ir}(\underline{N}) = S_{ir}(1 + \sum_{j=1}^{R} \bar{n}_{ij}(\underline{N} - \underline{1}_r))$$

Bryant-Krzesinski's Response Time Model for Preemptive Priority:

$$R_{ir}(\underline{N}) = \frac{S_{ir} + \sum_{j=1}^{r} \bar{n}_{ij}(\underline{N} - \underline{1}_r)S_{ij}}{1 - \sum_{j=1}^{r-1} S_{ij} V_{ij} X_j(\underline{N})}$$

Chandy-Laksmi's Response Time Model for Preemptive Priority:

$$R_{ir}(\underline{N}) = \frac{S_{ir} + \sum_{j=1}^{r} \bar{n}_{ij}(\underline{N} - \underline{1}_r)S_{ij}}{1 - \sum_{j=1}^{r-1} S_{ij} V_{ij} X_j(\underline{N} - \bar{n}_{ij}(\underline{N})\underline{1}_j)}$$

$M/G/1$ Extension (EPF) for General Service Time at FCFS Server:

$$R_i = S_i\left(1 + \frac{U_i(CV_i^2 + 1)}{2(1 - U_i)}\right).$$

Box 4.2: Summary of response time models.

CHAPTER 5

CONSISTENT SOLUTION,

ITERATION AND CONVERGENCE

Iteration is often used to obtain a consistent and correct solution of a model. This chapter examines the consistency requirements for a correct solution and the convergence proofs for iterative algorithms. Two easy techniques that exploit the monotonic behavior of queueing networks are developed to prove convergence. These techniques are illustrated by proving convergence of

1) the Bard-Schweitzer MVA-based approximation [SCHW79],

2) the Jacobson-Lazowska method discussed in Chapter 3 [JACO82], and

3) shadow CPU preemptive priority algorithm [SEVC77].

We show that iterative algorithms may have multiple convergence points and exemplify it by presenting a network for which the shadow CPU algorithm has two stable fixed points. We show that these fixed points indicate the bistable behavior of the system.

5.1 Consistent Solution

A minimal requirement for the correctness of a solution generated by a model's SOLVE procedure is consistency, which has two aspects:

A. *A consistent solution must be consistent with parameters.* For example:

1) The device queue lengths must sum to the number of customers in the network -- i.e., the Load Conservation Law must holds;

2) The Utilization Law, $S = U/X$, must be satisfied.

B. *A consistent solution must not contradict known information about the solution of the system.* For example:

1) The throughput equations must be satisfied -- i.e., the Forced Flow Law must hold;

2) Little's law must be satisfied at each device;

3) The estimates for throughputs of two classes must be equal if they are equal in the real system (e.g., in the FORK-JOIN models discussed in Chapter 4),

4) If two estimates are obtained for the same measure from two different methods (models), they should be equal or reasonably close. (E.g., as discussed in Section 3.3, in the Jacobson-Lazowska model for simultaneous resource possession, both M_1 and M_2 can provide estimates for network throughput); and

5) If a performance measure of submodel M_1 is used as a parameter for another submodel M_2, the value of the measure in the solution must equal the value of the parameter used to solve M_2 (e.g., q_{PP} in the Jacobson-Lazowska model of Section 3.3).

When a proposed model generates inconsistent solutions, corrective action is needed. Four different cases of inconsistency arise and are discussed

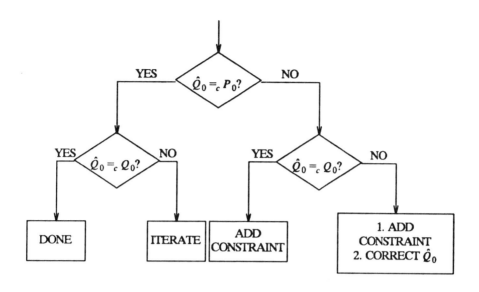

Figure 5.1: Decision tree for inconsistent solutions.

below. The corrective actions are summarized in the decision tree in Figure 5.1. The following notation is used:

$\hat{Q}_0 =_c P_0$: the solution is consistent with the parameters. This is type **A** consistency.

$\hat{Q}_0 =_c Q_0$: the solution is consistent with known information about itself. If the solution procedure is iterative, the solution must be consistent with its previous estimate. This is type **B** consistency.

Case I: $\hat{Q}_0 =_c P_0$ & $\hat{Q}_0 =_c Q_0$

This is the desired outcome: A consistent solution to the problem has been obtained.

Case II: $\hat{Q}_0 =_c P_0$ & $\hat{Q}_0 \neq_c Q_0$

The consistency violation that $\hat{Q}_0$ is inconsistent with itself but is consistent with the parameters occurs commonly. To remove this inconsistency, the normal practice is iteration. Examples include iterations in the Sevcik's shadow CPU model, in the Jacobson-Lazowska model for simultaneous resource possession [JACO82] and in the Heidelberger-Trivedi model for FORK and JOIN [HEID82, HEID83]. The iteration may be speeded up by using techniques such as Aitken's Δ^2 method [STOE80] or other heuristics.

Case III: $\hat{Q}_0 \neq_c P_0$ & $\hat{Q}_0 =_c Q_0$

The solution is consistent with itself but is inconsistent with parameters. The recourse is to add new equations to the model that express the missing consistency constraints.

We will illustrate with the shadow CPU model for preemptive priority scheduling at CPU. (See Section 4.3.) For brevity, we will focus the discussion on class L and CPU.

Assume that Eqns. (4.7), (4.9), (4.11) and (4.13) are used as forward mappings rather than Eqns. (4.8), (4.10), (4.12) and (4.14). In other words, assume that the forward mapping specifies

$$S'_{CPU-L,L} = \frac{p_0(n_{CPU,L} \geq 1)}{X_{CPU,L}}. \tag{4.13}$$

The reverse mapping (Eqn. (4.15)) is now expanded to compute device throughputs as $\hat{X}_{ir} = X'_{ir}$. In particular,

$$\hat{X}_{CPU,L} = X'_{CPU-L,L}. \tag{5.1}$$

Now consider the solution of the model. With initial solution $p_0^{(0)}(n_{CPU,L} > 0)$ and $X_{CPU,L}^{(0)}$,

$$S_{CPU-L,L}^{'(0)} = \frac{p_0^{(0)}(n_{CPU,L} \geq 1)}{X_{CPU,L}^{(0)}}.$$

We solve M to compute $p^{(1)}(n_{CPU-L,L} \geq 1)$ and $X_{CPU-L,L}^{'(1)}$. This solution satisfies the Utilization Law in M, therefore,

$$S_{CPU-L,L}^{'(0)} = \frac{p^{(1)}(n_{CPU-L,L} \geq 1)}{X_{CPU,L}^{'(1)}}.$$

From Eqns. (4.15) and (5.1), the next estimate of stretched out CPU-L service time is

$$S_{CPU-L,L}^{'(1)} = \frac{p_0^{(1)}(n_{CPU,L} \geq 1)}{X_{CPU,L}^{(1)}}$$

$$= \frac{p^{(1)}(n_{CPU-L,L} \geq 1)}{X_{CPU,L}^{'(1)}}$$

$$= S_{CPU-L,L}^{'(0)}.$$

The same result holds for other devices. Thus, the algorithm converges in one iteration to the initial *assumed, arbitrary* solution; this solution, therefore, may not bear any relationship to the correct solution. This solution may also be inconsistent with parameters: the Utilization Law (Eqns. (4.2), (4.3), (4.4) and (4.5)) may not be satisfied. E.g., if $S_{CPU-L,L}^{(0)} = S_{CPU,L}$,

$$p_0^{(1)}(n_{CPU,L} > 0, n_{CPU,H} = 0) < p_0^{(1)}(n_{CPU,L} > 0),$$

and therefore, Eqn. (4.5) is not satisfied.

The problem is remedied by incorporating the parameter constraints (Eqns. (4.2), (4.3), (4.4) and (4.5)) into the reverse mapping, e.g.,

$$\hat{X}_{CPU,L} = \frac{p(n_{CPU-H,H} = 0, n_{CPU-L,L} \geq 1)}{S_{CPU,L}}.$$

With this reverse mapping, we get the transformation used in Chapter 4 (Eqns. (4.8), (4.10), (4.12) and (4.14)).

As a result of this transformation, $\hat{X}_{ir}$ may not satisfy the throughput laws. I.e., the solution may become inconsistent with itself ($\hat{Q}_0 \neq_c Q_0$). As mentioned in the Case II, iteration can be used to remedy the problem. Each iteration reduces the deviation from flow balance. It can be shown that the convergence criterion $|S_{CPU-L,L}^{'(i)} - S_{CPU-L,L}^{'(i-1)}| < \epsilon_1$ is equivalent to testing if $|X_{CPU,L}^{(i)} - V_{CPU,L}X_L^{(i)}| < \epsilon_2$, where both ϵ_1 and ϵ_2 are arbitrarily small constants. This implies that the converged solution is flow-balanced.

Case IV: $\hat{Q}_0 \neq_c P_0$ & $\hat{Q}_0 \neq_c Q_0$

This solution is neither consistent with itself nor with the parameters. There are two corrective actions. One is to add constraints to remove the Type A inconsistency, thereby reducing this to Case III. The other is to correct $\hat{Q}_0$ in a way that tends to reduce the Type B inconsistency, and iterate. The second approach is illustrated by the Chandy-Herzog-Woo method for modeling high coefficient of variation at FCFS servers [CHAN75a], Zahorjan's class aggregation method [ZAHO80], and the EPF method [SHUM76, SHUM77].

When the remedial procedures mentioned in the Cases II - IV fail, the alternatives are:

1) Relax some consistency constraints. The model may have been overspecified and no completely consistent solution may exist.

2) Modify (redesign) the transformations.

3) Accept the inconsistent solution but seek to minimize the inconsistency according to some measure. The EPF method illustrates: it minimizes the weighted deviation of device throughputs from bottleneck device

throughput, or equivalently, it minimizes the weighted deviation of device arrival and output rates from each other [SHUM76, SHUM77, BALB79].

The main point is that **Type A** inconsistencies are removed by redesigning the model; **Type B** inconsistencies are removed by iterating on the proposed solution. Whether Type B inconsistencies are removable depends on the model's constituent transformations.

5.2 Convergence Theorems for Iterative Algorithms

In its most general form, the iteration problem can be expressed as finding a fixed point ξ of an iteration function Φ, i.e., find a ξ such that

$$\xi = \Phi(\xi).$$

An iterative algorithm for solving this problem is:

> Initially assume $\hat{x} = x_0$.
> **repeat**
> $x = \hat{x}$
> $\hat{x} = \Phi(x)$
> **until** $|\hat{x} - x| < \epsilon$.

This iterative algorithm will converge iff Φ has a stable fixed point. The following basic theorem from numerical analysis determines when Φ has a stable fixed point [ORTE70, STOE80].

Theorem 5.1 (Basic Numerical Analysis Theorem): The iterative algorithm for finding a fixed point of Φ converges to $\xi \in S$ if

1) for all $x \in S$, $\Phi(x) \in S$, and

2) for all $x, y \in S$, $|\Phi(x) - \Phi(y)| \leq K |x - y|, 0 \leq K < 1$,

i.e., the algorithm converges, or equivalently, Φ has a stable fixed point in S if Φ is a contraction mapping on S.

Proof: Let $x_i \in S$. Then, by (1) $x_{i+1} = \Phi(x_i) \in S$, and $x_{i+2} = \Phi(x_{i+1}) \in S$. By (2)

$$|x_{i+2} - x_{i+1}| = |\Phi(x_{i+1}) - \Phi(x_i)| \leq K |x_{i+1} - x_i| < |x_{i+1} - x_i|.$$

Thus, assuming $x_k \in S$, successive differences $|x_{i+1} - x_i|$ get smaller for $i > k$. Therefore, the iteration converges. $\square$

If Φ is a differentiable function of one variable x, Theorem 5.1 requires that $|d\Phi/dx| < 1$ at $x = \xi$. If Φ is a differentiable function of many variables, then the Theorem needs that at $x = \xi$, $|D\Phi| < 1$, where $D\Phi$ is the Jacobian of Φ. For details, the reader is referred to [ORTE70, STOE80], or any good text on numerical analysis.

Let us apply these general results in the metamodeling framework. The iteration function Φ is a composition of F, SOLVE, and R:

$$\hat{Q}_0 = \Phi(Q_0) = R(SOLVE(M, F(P_0, Q_0))).$$

Its derivative (Jacobian) can be computed by an application of the chain rule. Williams and Bhandiwad [WILL76], and Gordon and Dowdy [GORD80] worked out the derivatives when SOLVE is the Convolution algorithm. They are presented in Section 5.2.2.

Unfortunately, the general theory of convergence is often not very helpful in proving the convergence of the iterative algorithms that arise in the modeling process. The reason is that we often want to prove the convergence for a class of networks and not for a particular network with given parameters. In such general cases, it is notoriously difficult to get bounds on the derivatives. In fact, such bounds may not exist because the function can be contractive in some regions and expansive in others; see Figure 5.2.

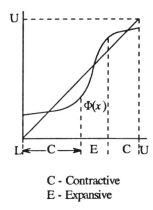

C - Contractive
E - Expansive

Figure 5.2: An iteration function with contractive and expansive intervals.

Queueing networks exhibit certain monotone behaviors [GORD80, WILL76, SURI83]. These behaviors can be exploited to argue that the iteration function has properties sufficient to force any sequence of estimates resulting from an allowable initial condition to converge on a fixed point. The following two theorems give sufficient conditions for convergence.

Theorem 5.2 (Monotone Bounded Sequence Theorem): Suppose the algorithm generates estimates $x_0, x_1, \ldots,$ such that $x_i \leq U$ and for $i > k$, $x_{i+1} \geq x_i$. Then the algorithm converges.

Sketch of Proof: If $x_{i+1} = x_i$ for $i > k$, the algorithm obviously converges. Assume $x_{i+1} > x_i$, let $d_i > 0$ and $d_i > d_{i+1}$. Then

$$\lim_{j \to \infty} \frac{d_j}{d_i} = \lim_{j \to \infty} \frac{d_{i+1}}{d_i} \frac{d_{i+2}}{d_{i+1}} \cdots \frac{d_j}{d_{j-1}} = 0,$$

which implies that the algorithm converges. $\qquad \square$

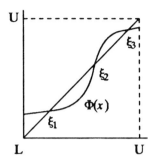

Figure 5.3: Alternating stable and unstable fixed points.

Corollary: If $x_i \geq L$ and $x_{i+1} \leq x_i$ for all $i > k$, the iteration converges.

Theorem 5.3 (Monotone Bounded Iteration Function Theorem): Suppose that $\Phi(x)$ is monotone increasing, bounded, and continuous on the interval $[L, U]$. Suppose $\Phi(L) = LB > L$ and $\Phi(U) = UB < U$. Then:

1. There is at least one stable fixed point in $[L, U]$.
2. Stable and unstable fixed points alternate.

Sketch of Proof: Figure 5.3 illustrates that a continuous bounded curve that lies above 45-degree ($y = x$) line for $x = L$ and below that line for $x = U$ must cross that line an odd number of times. A crossing may be called a down (up) crossing if $\Phi(x)$ passes from above the line to below (or below to above) as x increases. Down- and up- crossings must alternate. In Figure 5.3, ξ_1 and ξ_3 are down-crossings while ξ_2 is an up-crossing.

The slope of the monotone increasing function $\Phi(x)$ is at least 0 everywhere. Near a down-crossing, the slope of $\Phi(x)$ must be less than 1. Near an up-crossing, the slope of $\Phi(x)$ must be greater than 1. Therefore, by Theorem 5.1, down-crossings are stable fixed points and the up-crossings are unstable fixed points.   □

Corollary: Theorem 5.3 also holds when $\Phi(L) = L$ or $\Phi(U) = U$.

Sketch of Proof: If $\Phi(L) = L$, then $\xi_1 = L$. If ξ_1 is a down-crossing, Theorem 5.3 obviously holds; if ξ_1 is an up-crossing, there must be a down-crossing $\xi_2 \leq U$ on the path from $\Phi(\xi_1^+)$ to $\Phi(U)$. Similarly, if $\Phi(U) = U$, then $\xi_k = U$. If ξ_k is a down-crossing, Theorem 5.3 obviously holds; if ξ_k is an up-crossing, there must be a down-crossing $\xi_{k-1} \geq L$ on the path from $\Phi(L)$ to $\Phi(\xi_k^-)$.   □

NOTE: If $\Phi(x)$ is tangent to the line $y = x$ at a fixed point ξ, then the above theorem holds with the interpretation that multiple fixed points exist at ξ. If

$$\frac{d^i \Phi(x)}{dx^i}\bigg]_\xi = \begin{cases} 1 & i = 1 \\ 0 & i = 2, \dots, n \\ \neq 0 & i > n, \end{cases}$$

is equal n. Figure 5.4 illustrates a double fixed point; $\xi = \xi_1 = \xi_2$.

5.3 Monotonicity Results for Queueing Networks

In this section, we present some results concerning monotonic behavior of product form queueing networks. We first review Suri's results [SURI83] on monotonicity of throughput and queue length distribution as network population is changed. Then we consider the change in network throughput and device utilization as a function of parameter variation.

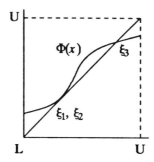

Figure 5.4: A multiple fixed point.

5.3.1 Monotonicity in Customer Population

Suri [SURI83] presents following definitions to define monotonicity in single class networks.

- A network is *N-monotonic* if $X(n) \geq X(n-1)$ for $n \leq N$.

- Server i is *N-monotonic* if $p(n_i \geq k \mid n) \geq p(n_i \geq k \mid n-1)$ for all k and for $n \leq N$. (Note that if a server is N-monotonic, $\bar{n}_i(N) \geq \bar{n}_i(N-1)$.)

- A network (server) is ∞ *-monotonic* if it is N-monotonic for all N.

Suri shows that

1. A network with fixed-rate servers only is ∞ -monotonic.

2. Each fixed-rate server in an N-monotonic network is N-monotonic.

3. If $S_i(n) \leq S_i(n-1)$ (or $Rate_i(n) \geq Rate_i(n-1)$) for all i and n, the network and every server in it are ∞ -monotonic.

4. If $S_i(n) \leq S_i(n-1)$ (or $Rate_i(n) \geq Rate_i(n-1)$) for all i and $n = 1, \ldots, N$, the network and every server in it are N-monotonic.

5. Let $\overline{M}_i$ be the complementary network for i, i.e., the original network with server i removed. If $\overline{M}_i$ is N-monotonic, server i is N-monotonic.

Suri does not treat multi-class networks in [SURI83]. However, it is easy to show that if all the devices are independent:

$$X_r(\underline{n} - \underline{1}_s) - X_r(\underline{n}) = \begin{cases} > 0 & \text{if } r \neq s \\ < 0 & \text{if } r = s \end{cases} \tag{5.2}$$

and

$$\bar{n}_{ir}(\underline{n} - \underline{1}_s) - \bar{n}_{ir}(\underline{n}) = \begin{cases} > 0 & \text{if } r \neq s \\ < 0 & \text{if } r = s, \end{cases} \tag{5.3}$$

where $\underline{1}_s$ denotes a population vector with 1 class s customer and 0 customers for all other classes.

5.3.2 Monotonicity in Parameters

Williams and Bhandiwad [WILL76], and Gordon and Dowdy [GORD80] have computed derivatives for the normalization constant G and performance metrics as a function of service demands. From these derivatives, certain inferences can be made about the monotonic behavior of the metrics as parameters are varied. We discuss these results below. In this discussion, $G_K(\cdot)$ is the normalization constant vector after the last server (server K) has been dealt with.

Single Class Networks with Fixed-Rate Servers

The derivatives are:

$$\frac{\partial G_K(n)}{\partial D_i} = \frac{G_K(n)}{D_i} \, \bar{n}_i(n) \tag{5.4}$$

$$\frac{\partial X(n)}{\partial D_i} = \frac{X(n)}{D_i} [\bar{n}_i(n-1) - \bar{n}_i(n)]. \tag{5.5}$$

By the ∞ -monotonicity of these networks, we see that

$$\frac{\partial X(n)}{\partial D_i} < 0.$$

Since $U_i(n) = X(n)D_i$, it can be shown that

$$\frac{\partial U_k(n)}{\partial D_i} \leq 0 \quad \text{for } k \neq i, \text{ and}$$

$$\frac{\partial U_i(n)}{\partial D_i} \geq 0.$$

Single Class Networks with Variable-Rate Servers

The derivatives are same as in (5.1) and (5.5) with the assumption that $D_i = V_i S_i(1)$.

If $S_i(n) \leq S_i(n-1)$ for all i, and n, by the ∞ -monotonicity of such networks,

$$\frac{\partial X(n)}{\partial D_i} < 0.$$

Multi-Class Networks with Fixed-Rate Servers

The derivatives are

$$\frac{\partial G_K(\underline{n})}{\partial D_{ir}} = \frac{G_K(\underline{n})}{D_{ir}} \, \bar{n}_{ir}(\underline{n}) \tag{5.6}$$

$$\frac{\partial X_s(\underline{n})}{\partial D_{ir}} = \frac{X_s(\underline{n})}{D_{ir}} \, [\bar{n}_{ir}(\underline{n}-\underline{1}_s) - \bar{n}_{ir}(\underline{n})]. \tag{5.7}$$

Eqn. (5.4) again guarantees the monotonicity.

5.4 Convergence Proof for Bard-Schweitzer Algorithm

The Bard-Schweitzer equations are an approximation to the equations of mean value analysis for solving product form queueing networks [SCHW79]. These equations can be solved iteratively using the algorithm presented in Section 1.2.8. Until recently, no proof of convergence of this algorithm had been known. Then Eager and Sevcik, and us proved the convergence independently for the single class networks. Eager and Sevcik showed that a unique solution is guaranteed when initially all N jobs are enqueued at the bottleneck device [EAGE83b]. Their proof exploits the fact that the sequence of queue length estimates is monotonic, but does not handle the initial condition stated in the algorithm. Below we present a convergence proof of the algorithm as stated. This proof is based on Theorem 5.2 (the Monotone Bounded Sequence Theorem).

The iteration function can be written as

$$\hat{\bar{n}}_i = \Phi_i(\bar{n}_1, \ldots, \bar{n}_K)$$

$$= \frac{ND_i(1 + \dfrac{N-1}{N}\,\bar{n}_i)}{\displaystyle\sum_{l=1}^{K} D_l(1 + \dfrac{N-1}{N}\,\bar{n}_l)} \qquad i = 1, \ldots, K,$$

where $D_i = V_i S_i$ is the total service demand at server i.

Claim: Without loss of generality, assume $D_1 < D_2 < \cdots < D_K$. Let $\bar{n}_i^{(0)} = N/K$, $i = 1, \ldots, K$. Let $\bar{n}_i^{(1)}, \bar{n}_i^{(2)}, \ldots$, be the sequence of mean queue length estimates produced by the algorithm. Then for each i there exists an iteration index I_i (possibly 0 or ∞) such that the sequence $\bar{n}_i^{(0)}, \ldots, \bar{n}_i^{(I_i)}$ is monotonically increasing and the sequence $\bar{n}_i^{(I_i)}$, $\bar{n}_i^{(I_i+1)}, \ldots$ is monotonically decreasing; see Figure 5.5.

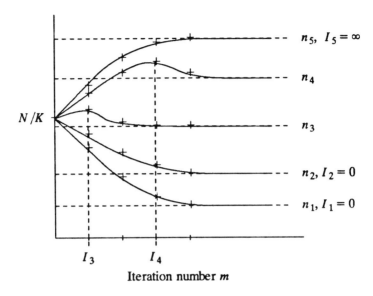

Caution: Picture NOT drawn to scale.

Figure 5.5: Mean queue length estimate sequences for
the Bard-Schweitzer Approximation.

Proof: The proof consists of three parts. In the first we show that if on
some iteration $\bar{n}_i$ increases, then $\bar{n}_{i+1}$ also increases. In the second we
show that given that $\bar{n}_i$, $i = 1, \ldots, k_m$ decreased and $\bar{n}_i$,
$i = k_m + 1, \ldots, K$ increased on iteration m, $\bar{n}_i$, $i = 1, \ldots, k_m$, will
decrease on the next iteration. In the third we show by induction that
the claim is valid.

Part I: Given that $\bar{n}_i^{(0)}$, $\bar{n}_i^{(1)}$, $\ldots$, $\bar{n}_i^{(m)}$, is a monotonically increasing
sequence, the sequence $\bar{n}_{i+1}^{(0)}$, $\bar{n}_{i+1}^{(1)}$, $\ldots$, $\bar{n}_{i+1}^{(m)}$, is also increasing.
Proof: Because $D_{i+1} > D_i$, $\bar{n}_{i+1}$ has to attain a higher value than $\bar{n}_i$.
Since $\bar{n}_i^{(0)} = \bar{n}_{i+1}^{(0)}$, $\bar{n}_{i+1}$ cannot start decreasing before $\bar{n}_i$ does. $\square$

Part II: For some integer k_m, If $\bar{n}_i^{(m)} < \bar{n}_i^{(m-1)}$ for $i = 1, \ldots, k_m$, and $\bar{n}_i^{(m)} > \bar{n}_i^{(m-1)}$ for $i = k_m+1, \ldots, K$, then $\bar{n}_i^{(m+1)} < \bar{n}_i^{(m)}$ for $i = 1, \cdots, k_m$. I.e., the $\bar{n}_i$ can be partitioned into contiguous increasing and decreasing sets.

Proof: For $i = 1, \ldots, k_m$,

$$\bar{n}_i^{(m+1)} = \frac{ND_i(1 + \frac{N-1}{N} \bar{n}_i^{(m)})}{\sum_{l=1}^{K} D_l(1 + \frac{N-1}{N} \bar{n}_l^{(m)})}$$

$$< \frac{ND_i(1 + \frac{N-1}{N} \bar{n}_i^{(m-1)})}{\sum_{l=1}^{K} D_l(1 + \frac{N-1}{N} \bar{n}_l^{(m)})}$$

$$< \frac{ND_i(1 + \frac{N-1}{N} \bar{n}_i^{(m-1)})}{\sum_{l=1}^{K} D_l(1 + \frac{N-1}{N} \bar{n}_l^{(m-1)})}$$

$$= \bar{n}_i^{(m)}$$

because

$$\sum_{l=1}^{K} D_l(1 + \frac{N-1}{N} \bar{n}_l^{(m)}) > \sum_{l=1}^{K} D_l(1 + \frac{N-1}{N} \bar{n}_l^{(m-1)}). \qquad \square$$

Part III: Proof by Induction.

Basis: The claim is valid for $m = 1$ because

$$\bar{n}_1^{(1)} < \bar{n}_2^{(1)} < \cdots < \bar{n}_K^{(1)},$$

and therefore, there is some k_1 such that

$$\bar{n}_i^{(1)} < \bar{n}_i^{(0)} = N/K, \text{ for } i = 1, \ldots, k_1, \text{ and}$$
$$\bar{n}_i^{(1)} > \bar{n}_i^{(0)} = N/K, \text{ for } i = k_1+1, \ldots, K.$$

Hypothesis: The claim is valid for some iteration m. Therefore, by Part I and II, there is some k_m such that

(1) for $i = 1, \ldots, k_m$, there exist I_i such that $\bar{n}_i^{(0)}, \ldots, \bar{n}_i^{(I_i)}$ is monotonically increasing, and $\bar{n}_i^{(I_i)}, \bar{n}_i^{(I_{i+1})}, \ldots,$ is monotonically decreasing; and

(2) for $i = k_m + 1, \ldots, K$, $\bar{n}_i^{(0)}, \ldots, \bar{n}_i^{(m)}$ is monotonically increasing (i.e., $I_i \geq m$).

Induction: We now show that the claim is valid for the next iteration -- the $m + 1$st iteration. By Part II,

$$\bar{n}_i^{(m+1)} < \bar{n}_i^{(m)}, \quad i = 1, \ldots, k_m.$$

Let $k_{m+1} \geq k_m$ be the smallest integer such that

$$\bar{n}_{k_{m+1}+1}^{(m+1)} > \bar{n}_{k_{m+1}+1}^{(m)}.$$

Then, by Part I,

$$\bar{n}_i^{(m+1)} > \bar{n}_i^{(m)}, \quad i = k_{m+1} + 1, \ldots, K.$$

Also $\bar{n}_i^{(m+1)} < \bar{n}_i^{(m)}$ for $i = k_m + 1, \ldots, k_{m+1}$, i.e.,

$$I_i = m + 1, \quad i = k_m + 1, \ldots, k_{m+1}.$$

Hence, by induction, the claim is valid for all m. $\qquad\qquad\square$

Since $\bar{n}_i$ sequence is bounded above by N and bounded below by 0, by Theorem 5.2, the iteration converges.

5.5   Convergence Proof for the Jacobson-Lazowska Method

The Jacobson-Lazowska method was studied in Chapter 3. To recapitulate, it involves iteration between two models M_1 and M_2. M_1 is the primary resource congestion model. It consists of the rest of the system R, delay server QD, and the primary resource shadow server PS. It computes q_{PP}

$(= q_1)$, the delay due to primary resource congestion. M_2 is the secondary subsystem congestion model. It consists of the rest of the system R, delay server PD, and the secondary resource shadow server QS. It computes $q_Q + q_{PQ}$ $(= q_2)$, the delay due to secondary subsystem congestion.

The mappings can be written as:

$$M_1: \qquad q_{PP} = \Psi_1(q_{PQ} + q_Q) \qquad \text{or} \quad q_1 = \Psi_1(q_2),$$

$$M_2: \qquad q_{PQ} + q_Q = \Psi_2(q_{PP}) \qquad \text{or} \quad q_2 = \Psi_2(q_1).$$

Now we consider $d\Psi_1/dq_2$. Since all primary and secondary resources are fixed rate servers, the service rate of the shadow server PS is non-decreasing. Then assuming that the service rate of R is non-decreasing (i.e., the service rate of its equivalent server is non-decreasing), increasing q_2 decreases network throughput and response time at server PS.[1] Thus, increasing q_2 decreases

$$q_1 = q_{PP} = R_{PS} - (S_P + S_Q),$$

where $S_P + S_Q$ is the total service demand in the primary-secondary subsystem. Thus, $d\Psi_1/dq_2 = dq_1/dq_2 < 0$. Similarly, $d\Psi_2/dq_1 = dq_2/dq_1 < 0$.

To prove the convergence, Jacobson and Lazowska argue that because $dq_1/dq_2 < 0$, and $dq_2/dq_1 < 0$, starting with $q_2^{(0)} = 0$, $q_1^{(1)}$ is at its maximum value. Therefore, $q_2^{(1)} = \Psi_2(q_1^{(1)}) > 0$. This produces $q_1^{(2)} < q_1^{(1)}$, and so on. Hence, $q_1^{(i)}$'s form a monotonically decreasing sequence, and $q_2^{(i)}$'s form a monotonically increasing sequence; see Figure 5.6. Since the following upper and lower bounds for q_1 and q_2 exist:

---

1. If the service rates of R may decrease with queue length (e.g., due to overhead or thrashing), then increasing q_1 (q_2) decreases queue length at R which means jobs will be processed faster. This increase in throughput will increase the queue length and response time at shadow server QS (PS). Hence, q_2 (q_1) will increase.

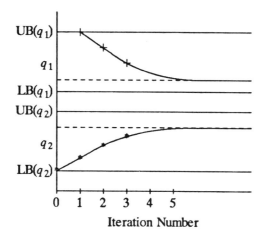

$$q_1 = q_{PP}, \quad q_2 = q_{PQ} + q_Q$$

Figure 5.6: Convergence in the Jacobson-Lazowska method.

$$UB(q_1) = \Psi_1(0), \qquad LB(q_1) = 0,$$

$$UB(q_2) = \Psi_2(0), \qquad LB(q_2) = 0,$$

by the Monotonic Bounded Sequence Theorem (Thm. 5.2), the algorithm is guaranteed to converge.

A simpler proof is obtained by observing that the iteration function Φ can be written as

$$\hat{q}_1 = \Phi_1(q_1) = \Psi_1(\Psi_2(q_1)).$$

Therefore,

$$d\Phi_1/dq_1 = d\Psi_1/dq_2 \cdot d\Psi_2/dq_1 > 0.$$

Because the bounds exist, by Theorem 5.3, the iteration function has at least one stable fixed point and the convergence is guaranteed.

Observe that the second proof indicates that there may be multiple stable fixed points. Also, both proofs require that R's service rate be non-decreasing. Otherwise convergence is not guaranteed. Jacobson and Lazowska have not stated this assumption.

5.6 Convergence Proof for Sevcik's Shadow CPU Algorithm

We now consider the convergence of Sevcik's shadow CPU algorithm for preemptive priority at CPU. The proof employs the Monotone Bounded Iteration Function Theorem (Thm. 5.3). The following discussion is equally applicable (with minor modifications) to the improved fixed-rate shadow CPU algorithm developed in Chapter 3.

Sevcik's basic model was discussed in Section 2.4. To recapitulate, M_0 is a system with preemptive priority service at CPU, M_1 is the system with one additional shadow server CPU-L, and the forward mapping is

$$F(U_H) = S_L' = \frac{S_L}{(1 - U_H)},$$

where S_L and S_L' are actual and elongated CPU service times for class L and $U_H = X_H S_H$ is class H CPU utilization. M_1 is assumed to have a product form solution and is solvable by the Convolution or the MVA algorithm. The reverse mapping is an identity.

The iteration function is computed by composing F, SOLVE and R and is given by:

$$\hat{U}_H = \Phi(U_H) = \text{SOLVE}(S_L') = \text{SOLVE}(F(U_H)).$$

(Other parameters do not change during the iteration.) The iteration function derivative is:

$$\frac{d\hat{U}_H}{dU_H} = \frac{d\hat{U}_H}{dS_L'} \cdot \frac{dS_L'}{dU_H}$$

$$= \frac{\hat{U}_H}{1 - U_H} \left[\bar{n}_L(N_L, N_H - 1) - \bar{n}_L(N_L, N_H) \right] \tag{5.8}$$

because

$$\frac{dS_L'}{dU_H} = \frac{S_L'}{1 - U_H},$$

and

$$\frac{d\hat{U}_H}{dS_L'} = S_H \frac{d\hat{X}_H}{dS_L'}$$

$$= S_H \frac{\hat{X}_H}{S_L'} \left[\bar{n}_L(N_L, N_H - 1) - \bar{n}_L(N_L, N_H) \right]$$

$$= \frac{\hat{U}_H}{S_L'} \left[\bar{n}_L(N_L, N_H - 1) - \bar{n}_L(N_L, N_H) \right].$$

The derivative in Eqn. (5.8) is not, in general, less than 1 in magnitude everywhere. This is because both factors $U_H/(1 - U_H)$ and $\bar{n}_L(N_L, N_H - 1) - \bar{n}_L(N_L, N_H)$ may be greater than 1. The latter factor can be greater than 1 because by adding a class H job can increase congestion elsewhere in the system and reduce the number of class L jobs at the CPU. Moreover, the derivative can be negative because the second factor can be negative. These two possibilities preclude a straight forward proof of convergence for all values of model parameters.

Because the the iteration parameter U_H is bounded between 0 and 1, the iteration is guaranteed to converge whenever the derivative is non-negative for all values of U_H. This requires that the second factor in Eqn. (5.8) be non-negative. A sufficient condition for this is that the rest of the network include only those servers whose service-rate functions do not rise "superlinearly," i.e., whose service-rate functions obey the constraint

$$Rate(n) \leq \frac{n}{n-1} Rate(n-1).$$

If a superlinear server is in the network, removal of a class H job may lead to much reduced service rate at that server; this will produce an increase in the class L transit time through the rest of the network and reduce the class L queue length at the CPU.

A superlinear server is, in effect, a "standby capacity" server that suddenly provides a sharp increase in resources when the queue length becomes sufficiently long. Such servers are not encountered in real systems.

Non-superlinear servers are common. They include fixed rate servers, multiservers, delay servers (infinite servers), processor sharing servers, servers whose service rates increase less than linearly with queue length, and servers whose rates decrease with queue length. The generality of this class explains why the iteration function for Sevcik's algorithm is monotone and why no one has found a practical system for which the algorithm diverges.

Figure 5.7 shows the parameters of a simple, two-station cyclic network with fixed rate servers. The Sevcik iteration function for this network has only one fixed point. This fixed point is stable. Recall, however, that the Theorem 5.3 does not guarantee a unique fixed point. Figure 5.8 shows another network whose iteration function has three fixed points; by Theorem 5.3, only two of these are stable. The iterative algorithm will converge on a solution that depends on the initial guess $U_H^{(0)}$. For example, $U_H^{(0)} = 0$ will cause convergence to the smaller solution $U_H = 0.34$. $U_H^{(0)} = 1$ will cause convergence to the larger solution, $U_H = 0.95$. Neither of these solutions is close to the value of $U_H = 0.66$ obtained by solving the exact model, the global balance equations of the network. These two solutions, however, have

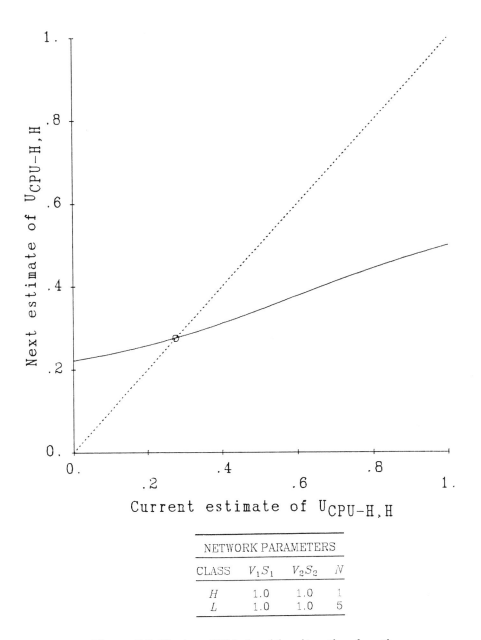

Figure 5.7: Shadow CPU algorithm iteration function - one stable fixed point.

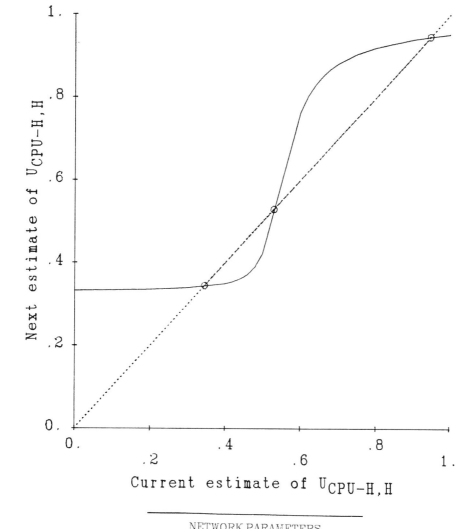

NETWORK PARAMETERS					
CLASS	V_1	S_1	V_2	S_2	N
H	1	0.1	1	0.005	1
L	1	0.05	21	0.005	40

Figure 5.8: Shadow CPU algorithm iteration function -
multiple fixed points.

a physical interpretation; we will report below on the simulation and global balance analysis results that indicate that the system is bistable with two possible operating points.

5.7 Anomalies

Two types of anomalous behavior can be encountered with iterative algorithms: divergence and multiple stable fixed points. These behaviors will be explained below and illustrated with examples in the shadow CPU model.

5.7.1 Divergence

If the derivative of the iteration function is negative in some range, the function is not monotone increasing and Theorem 5.3 may not apply. An iterative algorithm may fail to find any solution for such a network. As note above, in the shadow CPU model such a network must contain a superlinear sever.

Figure 5.9 shows the parameters of a two-station cyclic network including a superlinear server with rate function

$$\{Rate\,(n\,),\ n\ =\ 1,\ \ldots,6\} = \{1,\ 1,\ 1,\ 1,\ 1,\ 1000\}.$$

The iteration function has a negative slope everywhere. The function has one unstable fixed point. The iteration suffers oscillatory divergence.

5.7.2 Multiple Stable Fixed Points

Figure 5.8 showed an instance of a network having two stable solutions; the iterative algorithm can find either one depending on the initial guess of U_H. A question arises: Do these fixed points represent physically observable phenomena, or are they a defect of the modeling technique?

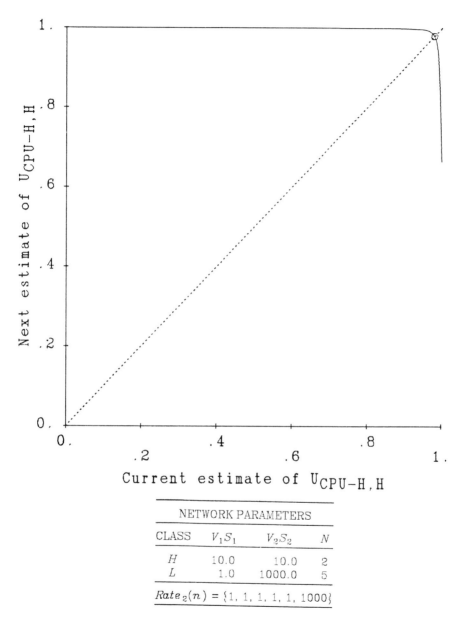

NETWORK PARAMETERS			
CLASS	$V_1 S_1$	$V_2 S_2$	N
H	10.0	10.0	2
L	1.0	1000.0	5
$Rate_2(n) = \{1, 1, 1, 1, 1, 1000\}$			

Figure 5.9: Shadow CPU algorithm iteration function -
no stable fixed point.

To answer this question, we simulated the network of Figure 5.8 for 40,000 seconds. A trace of the class H CPU utilization (U_H) over each 5 seconds window is displayed in Figure 5.10. (Class H CPU service time per visit is 0.1 seconds; class L CPU service time per visit is 0.05 seconds.) While U_H is normally around 95%, the system occasionally enters the state in which U_H is low (about 35%) for a significant period. We conclude that both high and low values of U_H observed in the simulation are both stable operating points in the corresponding real system. The two levels correspond to the two stable fixed points of the iteration function. Thus, we see that the model correctly predicted the bistable behavior of the system and the multiple stable fixed points are not a defect of the modeling technique.

The solution of the global balance equations also shows the bistable behavior. The steady state probability distribution is given in Table 5.1 and plotted in Figure 5.11. Curve C is the marginal CPU queue length distribution for class L. It has two well defined peaks. The right peak occurs when almost all class L jobs are queued at the CPU; in these states the class H job experiences relatively little contention at server 2; consequently, both X_H and U_H are high. This fact is demonstrated by the dominance of the conditional probability curve B ($\Pr(n_{1L} \mid n_{1H} = 1)$) over the conditional probability distribution curve A ($\Pr(n_{1L} \mid n_{1H} = 0)$). Just the opposite happens at the left peak which occurs when almost all class L jobs are queued at server 2. In this case the class H job experiences substantial delay at the server, and thus, U_H and X_H are low. The dominance of the right peak over the left peak corresponds to the observation from the simulation that the system spends most of its time in high U_H state.

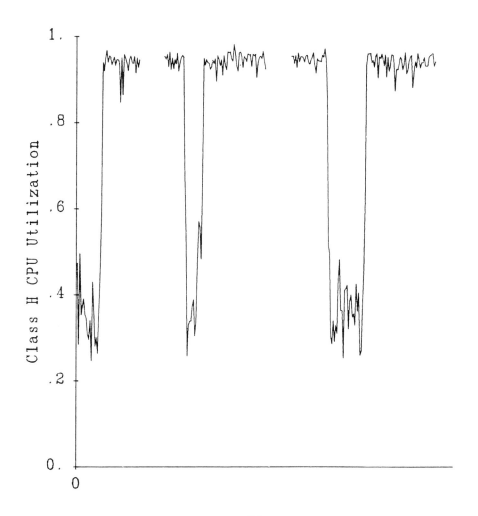

Time

Each sample indicates CPU utilization in the preceding
5 second interval. CPU utilization during the intervals
250 - 28500 and 28930 - 38925 seconds was about 95%.

Figure 5.10: Class *H* CPU utilization trace for bistable system.

These observations about the bistable behavior of the preemptive priority systems are reminiscent of the behavior of a multiprogrammed virtual memory system susceptible to thrashing [COUR75, COUR77]. When the multiprogramming level is low, jobs spend little time waiting at paging devices and the system throughput is high. When multiprogramming level becomes very high, the system begins thrashing, paging increases, jobs spend a large amount of time waiting for pages, and consequently, the throughput drops.

The impact of the potential bistable behavior on the design and simulation of preemptive priority systems is outlined in Appendix D.

Table 5.1: State probability distribution for the example in Figure 5.8.

(a) Model parameters.

CLASS	S_1	V_1	D_1	S_2	V_2	D_2	N
H	0.10	1	0.10	0.005	1	0.005	1
L	0.05	1	0.05	0.005	21	0.105	40

Server 1 is the preemptive priority scheduled CPU.

(b) Probabilities.

j	$p(0,j)$	$p(1,j)$	$p(*,j)$	CDF: $p(n_{1L} \leq j)$
0	.863e-01	.216e-01	.108e+00	.108e+00
1	.504e-01	.234e-01	.738e-01	.182e+00
2	.345e-01	.205e-01	.550e-01	.237e+00
3	.257e-01	.169e-01	.426e-01	.279e+00
4	.199e-01	.138e-01	.337e-01	.313e+00
5	.157e-01	.112e-01	.269e-01	.340e+00
6	.125e-01	.914e-02	.217e-01	.362e+00
7	.101e-01	.750e-02	.176e-01	.379e+00
8	.815e-02	.619e-02	.143e-01	.394e+00
9	.663e-02	.514e-02	.118e-01	.405e+00
10	.542e-02	.430e-02	.972e-02	.415e+00
11	.446e-02	.362e-02	.808e-02	.423e+00
12	.369e-02	.307e-02	.676e-02	.430e+00
13	.307e-02	.262e-02	.569e-02	.436e+00
14	.256e-02	.225e-02	.482e-02	.440e+00
15	.216e-02	.195e-02	.410e-02	.444e+00
16	.182e-02	.170e-02	.352e-02	.448e+00
17	.155e-02	.149e-02	.304e-02	.451e+00
18	.132e-02	.132e-02	.264e-02	.454e+00
19	.113e-02	.117e-02	.230e-02	.456e+00
20	.977e-03	.105e-02	.202e-02	.458e+00
21	.846e-03	.944e-03	.179e-02	.460e+00
22	.737e-03	.858e-03	.159e-02	.461e+00
23	.645e-03	.786e-03	.143e-02	.463e+00
24	.568e-03	.725e-03	.129e-02	.464e+00
25	.503e-03	.676e-03	.118e-02	.465e+00
26	.450e-03	.637e-03	.109e-02	.466e+00
27	.406e-03	.608e-03	.101e-02	.467e+00
28	.372e-03	.590e-03	.962e-03	.468e+00
29	.347e-03	.584e-03	.931e-03	.469e+00
30	.332e-03	.594e-03	.927e-03	.470e+00
31	.329e-03	.628e-03	.957e-03	.471e+00
32	.343e-03	.696e-03	.104e-02	.472e+00
33	.379e-03	.825e-03	.120e-02	.473e+00
34	.453e-03	.107e-02	.152e-02	.475e+00
35	.595e-03	.154e-02	.213e-02	.477e+00
36	.870e-03	.253e-02	.340e-02	.480e+00
37	.144e-02	.492e-02	.636e-02	.487e+00
38	.276e-02	.118e-01	.146e-01	.501e+00
39	.642e-02	.387e-01	.451e-01	.546e+00
40	.199e-01	.434e+00	.454e+00	.100e+01

The state $p(i,j) = \Pr[n_{1L} = i, n_{1L} = j]$. Global Performance
Measures: $U_{1H} = 0.66324$, $X_H = 6.6324$; $U_{1L} = 0.25043$, $X_{L1} = 5.0086$.

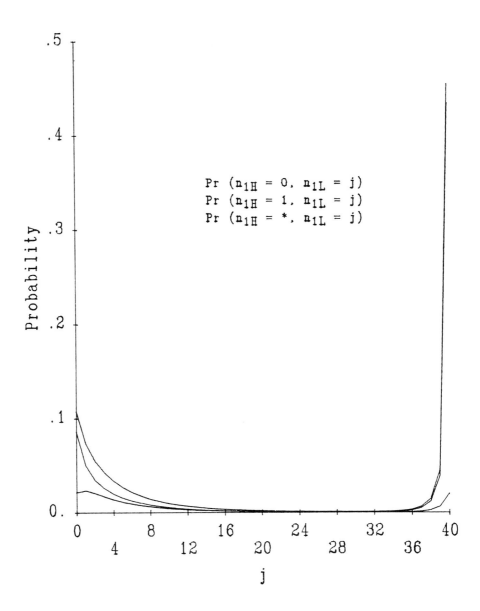

Figure 5.11: Probability distribution for bistable system.

CHAPTER 6

CONCLUSION

The main goals of this research were a critical examination of the modeling process and a characterization of the method by which approximate models are developed. From this research emerged metamodeling, a methodology for modeling.

Metamodeling provides a keen insight in the model development process and a methodology or template for approximate solution procedure development. In this methodology, solution procedures for complex models are constructed by recursively transforming a complex model into a set of simpler models. These transformations change the state space of the model. The relationships between the original and transformed state spaces can be used to determine the parameters of the transformed models. Once a consistent set of models is obtained, they can be solved by iteration.

Metamodeling is to modeling as structured programming, hierarchical design, and program proof rules are to software development. Just as one is likely to construct reliable software more efficiently using the software development methodology, an analyst is likely to construct accurate models more efficiently using the techniques of metamodeling.

REFERENCES

AFSH82   P.V. Afshari, S.C. Bruell and R.Y. Kain, "Modeling a New Technique for Accessing Shared Busses," *Proc. Computer Network Performance Symposium* printed as *Performance Evaluation Review 11*, 1 (Spring 1982) pp.3-13.

AGRA83   S.C. Agrawal and J.P. Buzen, "The Aggregate Server Method for Analyzing Serialization Delays in Computer Systems," *ACM TOCS 1*, 2 (May 1983) pp. 116-143.

AGRA84   S.C. Agrawal, J.P. Buzen and A.W. Shum, "Response Time Preservation: A General Technique for Developing Approximate Algorithms for Queueing Networks," to be presented at ACM/SIGMETRICS Conf. on Measurement and Modeling of Computer Systems, Cambridge, MA. 1984.

AGRE82   J.R. Agre and S.K. Tripathi, "Modeling Reentrant and Non-Reentrant Software," *Proc. 1982 ACM SIGMETRICS Conf. on Measurement and Modeling of Computer Systems, Seattle, Aug. 30 - Sept. 1, 1982* printed as *Performance Evaluation Review 11*, 4 (Winter 1982-83) pp. 163-178.

ALME79   G.T. Almes and E.D. Lazowska, "The Behavior of Ethernet-like Computer Communications Networks," *Proc. 7th Symposium on Operating Systems Principles, 10-12 Dec. 1979*, pp. 66-81.

BADE76   M. Badel and A.V.Y. Shum, "Accuracy of An Approximate Computer System Model," in *Proc. Modelling and Performance Evaluation of Computer Systems, Stresa, Italy*, (1976) pp. 11-34.

BALB79   G. Balbo, "Approximate Solutions of Queueing Network Models of Computer Systems," Ph.D. Thesis, Purdue University, W. Lafayette, IN. (1979)

BARD79   Y. Bard, "Some Extensions to Multiclass Queueing Network Analysis," in *Performance of Computer Systems*, Arato *et al*. Eds., North-Holland, New York, NY. (1979) pp. 51-62.

BARD80   Y. Bard, "A Model of Shared DASD and Multipathing," *Comm. ACM 23*, 10 (Oct. 1980) pp. 564-583.

BASK75   F. Baskett, K.M. Chandy, R.R. Muntz and F.G. Palacios, "Open, Closed, and Mixed Networks of Queues with Different Classes of Customers," *J. ACM 22*, 2 (1975) pp. 248-260.

BGS80   *BEST/1 User's Guide*, BGS Systems, Inc., Waltham, MA. (1980).

BRAN74   A.E. Brandwajn, "A Model of a Time-Sharing Virtual Memory System Solved Using Equivalence and Decomposition Methods," *Acta Informatica 4*, 1 (1974) pp. 11-47.

BRAN82   A.E. Brandwajn, "Fast Approximate Solution of Multiprogramming Models," *Proc. 1982 ACM SIGMETRICS Conf. on Measurement and Modeling of Computer Systems, Seattle, Aug 30-Sept 1, 1982* printed as *Performance Evaluation Review 11*, 4 (Winter 1982-83) pp. 141-149.

BROW75   J.C. Browne, K.M. Chandy, R.M. Brown, T.W. Keller, D.F. Towsley and C.W. Dizzly, "Hierarchical Techniques for the Developemnt of Realistic Models of Complex Computer Systems," *Proc. IEEE 63*, 6 (June 1975) pp. 966-975.

BRUE80   S.C. Bruell, G. Balbo, *Computational Algorithms for Single and Multiple Class Closed Queueing Network Models*, Series on Programming and Operating Systems, Elsevier/North-Holland Publishing Co., New York (1980).

BRUM82   J.A. Brumfield, "Operational Analysis of Queueing Phenomenon," Ph.D. Thesis, Dept. of Computer Sciences, Purdue University, West Lafayette, IN. 47906 (1982).

BRYA83   R.M. Bryant and A.E. Krzesinski, "The MVA Pre-empt Resume Priority Approximation," *pre-RC*, IBM T.J. Watson Research Center, Yorktown Heights, N.Y. (1983).

BUZE71   J.P. Buzen, "Queueing Network Models of Multiprogramming," Ph.D. Thesis, Harvard University, Cambridge, MA. (1971).

BUZE73   J.P. Buzen, "Computational Algorithms for Closed Queueing Networks with Exponential Servers," *Comm. ACM 16*, 9 (Sept. 1973) pp. 527-531.

BUZE76a   J.P. Buzen, "Fundamental Operational Laws of Computer System Performance," *Acta Informatica 7, 2* (1976) pp. 167-182.

BUZE76b   J.P. Buzen, "Operational Analysis : the Key to the New Generation of Performnace Prediction Models," *Proc. IEEE COMPCON 76*, Washington, DC, (1976) pp. 166-171.

BUZE78a   J.P. Buzen *et al.*, "BEST/1 - Design of a Tool for Computer System Capacity Planning," *Proc. 1978 AFIPS National Computer Conference 47*, AFIPS Press, Montvale, N.J. (1978) pp. 447-455.

BUZE78b   J.P. Buzen, "Operational Analysis: An Alternative to Stochastic Modeling," *Performance of Computer Installations*, D. Ferrari (Ed.), North-Holland Publishing Co. (1978) pp. 175-194.

BUZE80a   J.P. Buzen and P.J. Denning, "Measuring and Calculating Queue Length Distributions," *Computer 13*, 4 (April 1980) pp.33-44.

BUZE80b   J.P. Buzen and P.J. Denning, "Operational Treatment of Queue Distributions and Mean-Value Analysis," *Computer Performance 1*, 1 (June, 1980) pp. 6-15.

BUZE83   J.P. Buzen and S.C. Agrawal, "Metamodeling and Its Application to Queueing Networks," Tech. Report CSD-TR-385, Dept. of Computer Science, Purdue University, West Lafayette, IN. (1983)

CHAN75a   K.M. Chandy, U. Herzog and L. Woo, "Approximate Analysis of General Queuing Networks," *IBM J. of Research and Development 19*, 1 (Jan. 1975) pp. 43-49.

CHAN75b   K.M. Chandy, U. Herzog and L. Woo, "Parametric Analysis of Queuing Networks," *IBM J. of Research and Development 19*, 1 (Jan. 1975) pp. 36-42.

CHAN77   K.M. Chandy, J.H. Howard and D.F. Towsley, "Product Form and Local Balance in Queuing Networks," *J. ACM 24*, 2 (1977) pp. 250-263.

CHAN78   K.M. Chandy and C.H. Sauer, "Approximate Methods for Analyzing Queueing Network Models of Computer Systems," *Computing Surveys 10*, 3 (Sept. 1978) pp. 281-317.

CHAN80   K.M. Chandy and C.H. Sauer, "Computational Algorithms for Product Form Queueing Networks," *Comm. ACM 23*, 10 (Oct. 1980) pp. 573-593.

CHAN82   K.M. Chandy and D. Neuse, "Linearizer: A Heuristic Algorithm for Queueuing Network Models of Computing Systems," *Comm. ACM 25*, 2 (Feb. 1982) pp. 126-134.

CHAN83   K.M. Chandy and M.S. Laksmi, "An Approximation Technique for Queueing Networks with Preemptive Priority Queues," Tech. Report, Dept. of Comp. Sc., Univ. of Texas at Austin, Austin, TX. (1983).

COFF73   E.G. Coffman, Jr. and P.J. Denning, *Operating System Theory*, Prentice Hall, New York (1973).

COUR75   P.J. Courtois, "Decomposability, Instabilities, and Saturation in Multiprogramming Systems," *Comm. ACM 18*, 7 (July 1975) pp. 371-376.

COUR77   P.J. Courtois, *Decomposability: Queueing and Computer System Applications*, Academic Press, New York (1977).

COX65   D.R. Cox and H.D. Miller, *The Theory of Stochastic Processes*, John Wiley & Sons, Inc., New York (1965).

DENN78   P.J. Denning and J.P. Buzen, "The Operational Analysis of Queueing Network Models," *Computing Surveys 10*, 3 (Sept. 1978) pp. 225-261.

DENN82   P.J. Denning and W. Kowalk, "Error Analysis of the Mean Busy Period of a Queue," CSD-TR-DRAFT, Dept. of Comp. Sc., Purdue University, W. Lafayette, IN. (March 1982).

EAGE83a D.L. Eager and K.C. Sevcik, "Performance Bound Hierarchies for Queueing Networks," *ACM TOCS 1*, 2 (May, 1983) pp. 99-115.

EAGE83b D.L. Eager and K.C. Sevcik, "An Analysis of an Approximation Algorithm for Queueing Networks," Tech. Report, Department of Computer Science, Univ. of Toronto, Toronto (1983).

GAVE68 D.P. Gaver, "Diffusion Approximations and Models for Certain Congestion Problems," *J. Appl. Probab. 5*, (1968) pp. 607-623.

GELE75 E. Gelenbe, "On Approximate Computer Models," *J. ACM 22*, 2 (April 1975) pp. 261-269.

GELE82 E. Gelenbe and I. Mitrani, "Control Policies in CSMA Local Area Networks: Ethernet Controls," *Proc. 1982 ACM SIGMETRICS Conf. on Measurement and Modeling of Computer Systems, Seattle, Aug 30-Sept 1, 1982* printed as *Performance Evaluation Review 11*, 4 (Winter 1982-83) pp. 233-240.

GORD67 W.J. Gordon and G.F. Newell, "Closed Queueing Systems with Exponential Servers," *Ops. Res. 15*, (1967) pp. 245-255.

GORD80 K.D. Gordon and L.W. Dowdy, "The Impact of Certain Parameter Estimation Errors in Queueing Network Models," *Proc. Performance '80, Toronto, Canada* printed as *Performance Evaluation Review 9*, 2 (Summer 1980) pp. 3-9.

HEID82 P. Heidelberger and K.S. Trivedi, "Queueing Network Models for Parallel Processing with Asynchronous Tasks," *IEEE Trans. Computers C-31*, 11 (Nov. 1982) pp. 73-82.

HERZ75 U. Herzog, L. Woo and K.M. Chandy, "Solution of queueing problems by a recursive technique," *IBM J. Research and Development 19*, 5 (May 1975) pp. 295-300.

HEID83 P. Heidelberger and K.S. Trivedi, "Analytical Queueing Models for Programs with Internal Concurrency," *IEEE Trans. Computers C-32*, 1 (Jan. 1983) pp. 73-82.

HOYM82 K.P. Hoyme, S.C. Bruell, P.V. Afshari, and R.Y. Kain, "A Tree-structured MVA Algorithm," Tech. Report 82-17, Computer Science Department, University of Minnesota, Minneapolis, MN. (Dec. 1982).

IRA77   *Users's Manual for the CADS (Computer Analysis and Design System)*, Information Research Associates, Austin, TX. (1977)

JACK57 J.R. Jackson, "Networks of Waiting Lines," *Oper. Res. 5*, (1957) pp. 518-521.

JACK63 J.R. Jackson, "Jobshop-like Queueing Systems," *Manage. Sci. 10*, 1 (1963) pp. 131-142.

JACO82 P.A. Jacobson and E.D. Lazowska, "Analyzing Queueing Networks with Simultaneous Resource Possession," *Comm. ACM 25*, 2 (Feb. 1982) pp. 142-151.

JACO83 P.A. Jacobson and E.D. Lazowska, "A Reduction Technique for Evaluating Queueing Networks with Serialization Delays," *Proc. Performance'83*, University of Maryland, College Park. North-Holland (1983) pp. 45-59.

KELL76 T.W. Keller, "COmputer Systems Models with Passive Resources," Ph.D. Thesis, Dept. of Computer Science, Univ. of Texas at Austin, Austin, TX. (1976).

KLEI75 L. Kleinrock, *Queueing Systems Volume I: Theory*, Wiley, New York, NY (1975).

KLEI76 L. Kleinrock, *Queueing Systems Volume II: Computer Applications*, Wiley, New York, NY (1976).

KOWA81 W. Kowalk, "Extensions of Operational Analysis," in *Messung, Modellierung und Bewertung von Rechensystemen*, Informatik-Fachberichte No. 41, Springer. (February 1981).

KUEH79 P.J. Kuehn, "Multiqueue Systems with Nonexhaustive Cyclic Service," *BSTJ 58*, 3 (March 1979) pp. 671-698.

KUMA80   B. Kumar and E.S. Davidson, "Computer System Design Using a Hierarchical Approach to Performance Evaluation," *Comm. ACM 23*, 9 (Sept. 1980) pp. 511-521.

LABE80   J. Labetoulle and G. Pujolle, "Isolation Method in a Network of Queues," *IEEE Trans. Software Engineering SE-6*, 4 (July 1980) pp. 373-381.

LAM83   S.S. Lam and Y.L. Lien, "A Tree Convoluted Algorithm for the Solution of Queueing Networks," *Comm. ACM 26*, 3 (March 1983) 203-215.

LAZO82   E.D. Lazowska and J. Zahorjan, "Multiple Class Memory Constrained Queueing Networks," *Proc. 1982 ACM SIGMETRICS Conf. on Measurement and Modeling of Computer Systems, Seattle, Aug 30-Sept 1, 1982* printed as *Performance Evaluation Review 11*, 4 (Winter 1982-83) pp. 130-140.

MARI78   R. Marie, "Modelisation par Reseaux de Files d'Attente," Ph.D. Thesis, Universite' de Rennes, France, (Dec. 1978).

MOOR71   C.G. Moore III, "Network Models for Large-Scale Time Sharing Systems," Ph.D. Thesis, Tech. Rep. 71-1, Dept. of Industrial Eng., Univ. of Michigan, Ann Arbor, MI. (1971).

ORTE70   J.M. Ortega and W.C. Rheinboldt, *Iterative Solution of Nonlinear Equations in Several Variables,* Academic Press, New York, NY (1970).

REIS80   M. Reiser and S.S. Lavenberg, "Mean Value Analysis of Closed Multichain Queueing Networks," *J. ACM 27*, 2 (April 1980) pp. 313-322.

SAUE75a   C.H. Sauer, "Configuration of Computing Systems: An Approach Using Queueing Network Models," Ph.D. Thesis, Dept. of Computer Science, Univ. of Texas at Austin, Austin, TX. (1975).

SAUE75b   C.H. Sauer and K.M. Chandy, "Approximate Analysis of Central Server Models," *IBM J. Research and Development 19*, 3 (May 1975) pp. 301-313.

SAUE81a C.H. Sauer, "Approximate Solution of Queueing Networks with Simultaneous Resource Possession," *IBM J. of Research and Development 25*, 6 (Nov. 1981) pp. 894-903.

SAUE81b C.H. Sauer and K.M. Chandy, *Computer System Performance Evaluation*, Prentice-Hall, Englewood Cliffs, N.J. (1981).

SAUE82a C.H. Sauer, E.A. MacNair and J.F. Kurose, "The Research Queueing Package Version 2: Introduction and Examples," IBM Research Report RA-138, IBM T. J. Watson Research Center, Yorktown Heights, NY (April 1982).

SAUE82b C.H. Sauer, E.A. MacNair and J.F. Kurose, "The Research Queueing Package: Past, Present and Future," *Proc. of NCC* (June 1982) pp. 273-280.

SAUE83 C.H. Sauer, "Computational Algorithms for State-Dependent Queueing Networks," *ACM TOCS 1*, 1 (Feb. 1983) pp. 67-92.

SCHE67 A. Scherr, *An Analysis of Time-Shared Computer Systems*, MIT Press, Cambridge, MA. (1967).

SCHW78 H.D. Schwetman, "Hybrid Simulation Models of Computer Systems," *Comm. ACM 21*, 9 (Sept. 1978) pp. 718-723.

SCHW79 P. Schweitzer, "Approximate Analysis of Multiclass Closed Networks of Queues," *Presented at the Int. Conf. Stochastic Control and Optimization*, Amsterdam, Netherlands (1979).

SCHW80 H.D. Schwetman, "Implementing the Mean Value Algorithm for the Solution of Queueing Network Models," Tech. Report CSD-TR-355, Dept. Computer Sciences, Purdue University, West. Lafayette, IN. (Dec. 1980).

SELB73 S.M. Selby, *Standard Mathematical Tables*, The Chemical Rubber Co., Cleveland, Ohio (1973).

SEVC77 K.C. Sevcik, "Priority Scheduling Disciplines in Queueing Network Models of Computer Systems," *Proc. IFIP Congress 77*, North-Holland Publishing Co., Amsterdam (1977) pp. 565-570.

SEVC79   K.C. Sevcik and I. Mitrani, "The Distribution of Queueing Network
          States at Input and Output Instants," in *Performance of Computer
          Systems*, Arato *et al.* Eds., North-Holland, New York, NY. (1979)
          pp. 319-335.

SHUM76   A.W. Shum, "Queueing Models for Computer Systems with
          General Service Time Distributions," Ph.D. Thesis, Harvard
          University, Cambridge, MA. (1976).

SHUM77   A.W. Shum and J.P. Buzen, "The EPF Technique: A Method for
          Obtaining Approximate Solutions to Closed Queueing Networks
          with General Service Times," *Proc. Third Symposium on Measuring,
          Modeling, and Evaluating Computer Systems*, Bonn-Bad Godesborg,
          B.R.D., North Holland (1977) pp. 201-220.

SIMO61   H.A. Simon and A. Ando, "Aggregation of Variables in Dynamic
          Systems," *Econometrica 29*, (1961) pp. 111-138.

SMIT80a   C.U. Smith, "The Prediction and Evaluation of the Performance of
          Software from Extended Design Specifications," Ph.D. Thesis,
          Department of Computer Science, University of Texas at Austin,
          Austin, TX. (Aug. 1980).

SMIT80b   C.U. Smith and J.C. Browne, "Aspects of Software Design Analysis:
          Concurrency and Blocking," *Proc. Performance'80, Toronto, Canada,
          printed as Performance Evaluation Review 9*, 2 (Summer 1980) pp.
          245-253.

SPIR79   J.R. Spirn, "Queueing Networks with Random Selection for
          Service," *IEEE Transactions on Software Engineering 5*, 3 (May 1979)
          pp. 287-289.

STEW78   W.J. Stewart, "A Comparison of Numerical Techniques in Markov
          Modeling," *Comm. ACM 21*, 2 (Feb. 1978) pp. 144-152.

STOE80   J. Stoer and R. Bulirsch, *Introduction to Numerical Analysis*,
          Springer-Verlag, New York, N.Y. (1980).

SURI83a   R. Suri, "Characterization of Monotonicity in Closed Queueing
          Networks," TR-06-83, Center of Research in Computing
          Technology, Harvard University, Cambridge, MA. (Feb. 1983)

SURI83b   R. Suri, "Robustness of Queueing Networks," *J. ACM* (July 1983).

THOM83   A. Thomasian, "Queueing Network Models to Estimate Serializaiton Delays in Multiprogrammed Computer Systems," *Proc. Performance'83*, University of Maryland, College Park. North-Holland (1983) pp. 61-81.

TOLO79   S.J. Tolopka, "Solution of General Queueing Networks Using Norton's Theorem," Tech. Report TR-314, Department of Computer Sciences, Purdue University, West Lafayette, IN. (Sept. 1979).

TOWS78   D.F. Towsley, K.M. Chandy and J.C. Browne, "Models for Parallel Processingg Within Programs: Application to CPU:I/O and I/O:I/O Overlap," *Comm. ACM 21*, 10 (Oct. 1978) pp. 821-831.

TOWS80   D.F. Towsley, "Queueing Network Models with State-Dependent Routing," *J. ACM 27*, 2 (April 1980) pp. 323-337.

VANT80   H.T. Vantilborgh, R.L. Garner and E.D. Lazowska, "Near-Complete Decomposabilitiy of Queueing Networks With Clusters of Strongly Interacting Servers," *Proc. Performance'80* printed as *Performance Evaluation Review 9*, 2 (Summer 1980) pp. 81-92.

WILH77   N.C. Wilhelm, "A General Model for the Performance of Disk Systems," *J. ACM 24*, 1 (Jan. 1977) pp. 14-31.

WILL76   A.C. Williams and R.A. Bhandiwad, "A Generating Function Approach to Queueing Network Models of Multiprogrammed Computer Systems," *Network 6,* (1976) pp. 1-22.

ZAHO80   J. Zahorjan, "The Approximate Solution of Large Queueing Network Models," Ph.D. Thesis, Dept. of Computer Science, University of Toronto, Toronto, Canada (1980).

ZAHO81   J. Zahorjan and E. Wong, "A Solution of Separable Queueing Network Models Using Mean Value Analysis," *ACM/SIGMETRICS Conf. on Measurement and Modeling of Computer Systems, Las Vegas, Nevada, Sept. 14-16, 1981* printed as *Performance Evaluation Review 10, 3* (Fall 1981) pp. 80-85.

ZAHO82   J. Zahorjan, K.C. Sevcik, D.L. Eager and B. Galler, "Balanced Job
Bound Analysis of Queueing Networks," *Comm. ACM 25*, 2 (Feb.
1982) pp. 134-141.

Appendix A

Comparison of Models of Preemptive Priority Systems

In this appendix, we present some numerical results about the accuracy of approximate models for preemptive priority systems. The models considered are:

- *Sevcik's OLD shadow CPU model*, which has fixed-rate shadow server CPU-L to represent class L CPU processing;

$$
\begin{aligned}
S_{L,CPU-L} &= \frac{1}{p(n_{H,CPU} = 0)} S_{L,CPU} \\
&= \frac{1}{1 - p(n_{H,CPU} > 0)} S_{L,CPU}.
\end{aligned}
$$

- *NEW shadow CPU model*, which has fixed-rate shadow server CPU-L to represent class L CPU processing;

$$
\begin{aligned}
S_{L,CPU-L} &= \frac{p(n_{L,CPU} \geq 1)}{p(n_{H,CPU} = 0, n_{L,CPU} \geq 1)} S_{L,CPU} \\
&= \frac{1}{p(n_{H,CPU} = 0 \mid n_{L,CPU} \geq 1)} S_{L,CPU} \\
&= \frac{1}{1 - p(n_{H,CPU} > 0 \mid n_{L,CPU} \geq 1)} S_{L,CPU}.
\end{aligned}
$$

If we assume that

$$
p(n_{H,CPU} > 0 \mid n_{L,CPU} \geq 1) = p(n_{H,CPU} > 0),
$$

the NEW model and Sevcik's OLD model are equivalent.

- *LD shadow CPU model*, which has variable-rate shadow server CPU-L to represent class L CPU processing;

$$
S_{L,CPU-L}(n) = \frac{p(n_{L,CPU} = n)}{p(n_{H,CPU} = 0, n_{L,CPU} = n)} \, S_{L,CPU}
$$

$$
= \frac{1}{p(n_{H,CPU} = 0 \mid n_{L,CPU} = n)} \, S_{L,CPU}
$$

$$
= \frac{1}{1 - p(n_{H,CPU} > 0 \mid n_{L,CPU} = n)} \, S_{L,CPU}.
$$

- *Bryant-Krzesinski Response Time Model*, is an MVA based approximation [BRYA83];

$$
R_{ir}(\underline{N}) = \frac{S_{ir} + \sum_{j=1}^{r} \bar{n}_{ij}(\underline{N} - \underline{1}_r)}{1 - \sum_{j=1}^{r-1} X_j(\underline{N}) S_{ij}}.
$$ [See Chapter 4.]

- *Chandy-Laksmi Response Time Model*, is another MVA based approximation [CHAN83];

$$
R_{ir}(\underline{N}) = \frac{S_{ir} + \sum_{j=1}^{r} \bar{n}_{ij}(\underline{N} - \underline{1}_r)}{1 - \sum_{j=1}^{r-1} X_j(\underline{N} - \bar{n}_{ij}(\underline{N})\underline{1}_j) S_{ij}}.
$$ [See Chapter 4.]

In Table A.1, we present data for a test network. The data includes class H and L throughputs and errors in their estimates. The errors are computed by using exact solution for the network obtained by global balance analysis. We now summarize the results of the investigation.

The model NEW is consistently more accurate than the model OLD; the difference is maximum when class L population, N_L, is 1. Figure A.1 displays the elongated service time, after the iteration has converged, for CPU-L for

Table A.1: Comparison of different models for preemptive priority systems.

(a) Class H throughput comparison.

N_L	THROUGHPUT						% ERROR				
	GB	OLD	NEW	LD	BK	CL	OLD	NEW	LD	BK	CL
1	0.2511	0.2473	0.2500	0.250	0.2549	0.2508	-1.5	-0.4	-0.4	1.5	-0.1
2	0.2378	0.2314	0.2354	0.237	0.2421	0.2346	-2.7	-1.0	-0.3	1.8	-1.3
3	0.2261	0.2181	0.2227	0.225	0.2289	0.2189	-3.5	-1.5	-0.5	1.2	-3.2
4	0.2156	0.2066	0.2115	0.215	0.2161	0.2043	-4.2	-1.9	-0.3	0.2	-5.2
5	0.2062	0.1966	0.2015	0.207	0.2038	0.1911	-4.7	-2.3	-0.4	-1.2	-7.3
6	0.1977	0.1877	0.1926	0.199	0.1922	0.1792	-5.1	-2.6	0.7	-2.8	-9.4
7	0.1900	0.1798	0.1845	0.192	0.1815	0.1685	-5.4	-2.9	1.1	-4.5	-11.3

(b) Class L throughput comparison.

N_L	THROUGHPUT						% ERROR				
	GB	OLD	NEW	LD	BK	CL	OLD	NEW	LD	BK	CL
1	0.0266	0.0485	0.0417	0.0417	0.0212	0.0309	82.3	56.8	56.8	-20.3	16.2
2	0.0479	0.0760	0.0681	0.0645	0.0406	0.0572	58.7	42.2	34.7	-15.2	19.4
3	0.0656	0.0959	0.0882	0.0811	0.0588	0.0794	46.2	34.5	23.6	-10.4	21.0
4	0.0807	0.1117	0.1044	0.0943	0.0758	0.0984	38.4	29.4	16.9	-6.1	21.9
5	0.0938	0.1248	0.1179	0.105	0.0916	0.1148	33.0	25.6	11.9	-2.3	22.4
6	0.1053	0.1359	0.1294	0.115	0.1061	0.1295	29.1	22.9	9.2	0.8	23.0
7	0.1156	0.1455	0.1395	0.124	0.1194	0.1424	25.9	20.7	7.3	3.3	23.2

M_0 is a 2-class closed network with two fixed-rate servers.
Demands: $D_{H1} = D_{H2} = D_{L1} = D_{L2} = 3$. $N_H = 4$.

GB: Global Balance Solution (Exact Solution).
OLD: Sevcik's Basic Model [SEVC77] [Chapter 2].
NEW: Modified Sevcik's Model [Chapter 3].
    (It does not use the additional independence assumption.)
LD: Load Dependent shadow CPU Model [Chapter 4].
BK: Bryant and Krzesinski's Model [BRYA83] [Chapter 4].
CL: Chandy and Laksmi's Model [CHAN83] [Chapter 4].

different class L populations. The higher value of stretched out service time for NEW leads to its better accuracy.

Comparison of columns OLD, NEW and LD reveals that LD is significantly more accurate than both Sevcik's OLD model and the NEW model. The data plotted in Figure A.2 shows that CPU-L service function is, indeed, load-dependent.

Now examine the accuracy of Bryant-Krzesinski model. As predicted in Chapter 4, the class L throughput, X_L, is underestimated (at low N_L).

Chandy-Laksmi method overestimates X_L and thus corroborates our error analysis in Chapter 4.

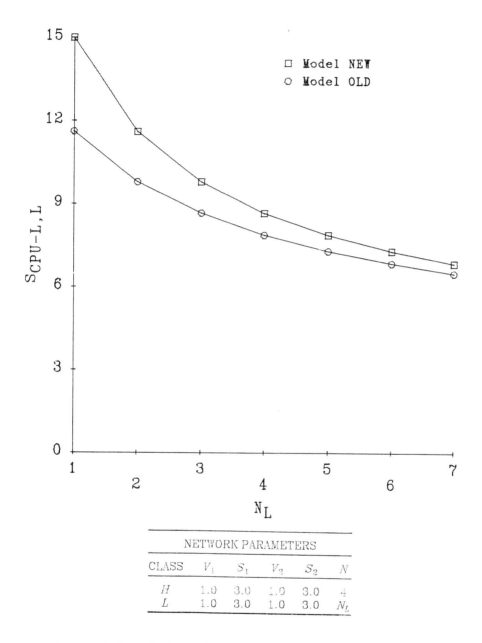

Figure A.1: Stretched out CPU-L service time vs. class *L* population.

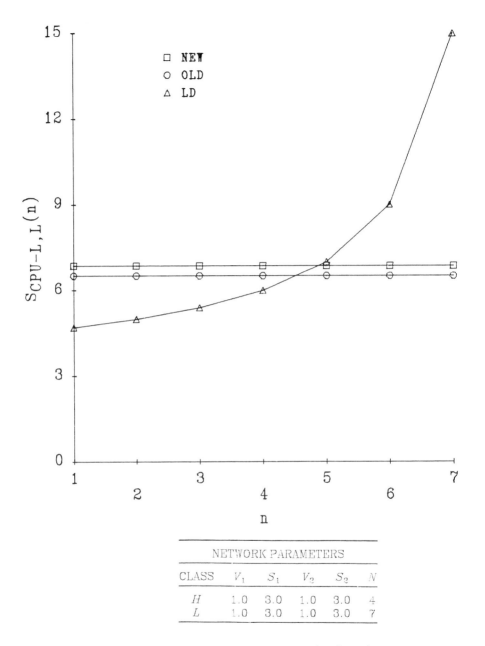

Figure A.2: Stretched out CPU-L service function.

Appendix B

The Aggregate Server Method

for Multi-Class Networks

In this appendix, we present extensions to the aggregate server method for modeling serialization delays in multi-class mixed networks. The extensions are intended for networks in which critical sections are not shared between customers of different classes.

In Chapter 3, we developed the aggregate server model for analyzing serialization delays in single class closed networks. We obtained this model by applying two transformation to the original model. The first transformation was a *load concealment transformation* that created a shadow server for each physical server and each processing phase. The second transformation was a *server aggregation transformation* that aggregated shadow servers for each serialized phase into a single server. This same basic scheme is now used to develop extensions for multi-class mixed networks.

The plan for the the appendix is as follows. We first present an extension for single class, open networks with one critical section. This extension is obtained via an "exact" load concealment transformation. We then examine a heuristic extension for open and mixed-networks with multiple critical sections. Preliminary experimental evidence suggests that the heuristic works better than the "exact" load concealment transformation.

B.1 Open Network Model with Exact Load Concealment Transformation

In this section, we develop a model for a single class open network with one critical section. In this analysis, we use an "exact" load concealment transformation; this transformations is a straightforward extension of the transformation used in Chapter 3 and 4.

Original Model M_0

The original model is a single class open network with one critical section and PS servers. This model satisfies all assumptions for a product form solution except for serialization.

The TOTAL service time requirements for each phase can be expressed as derived variables. With arrival rate λ, they are:

$$S_{0i} = \frac{\sum_{r \geq 1} \sum_{k=0}^{1} \frac{r}{r+k} \, p(n_{0i} = r, n_{1i} = k)}{\lambda}, \tag{B.1}$$

$$S_{1i} = \frac{\sum_{r \geq 0} \frac{1}{r+1} \, p(n_{0i} = r, n_{1i} = 1)}{\lambda}. \tag{B.2}$$

Load Concealment Transformation - Model M_1

By applying the load concealment transformation on each server in M_0, we obtain a shadow server for each phase and each server. The elongated service times for these shadow servers are:

$$S_{0i}^{'} = \frac{p(n_{0i} \geq 1)}{\lambda}$$

$$= \frac{p(n_{0i} \geq 1)}{\displaystyle\sum_{r \geq 1} \sum_{k=0}^{1} \frac{r}{r+k} p(n_{0i} = r, n_{1i} = k)} S_{0i}, \qquad \text{[by using (B.1)]} \quad (B.3)$$

$$S_{1i}^{'} = \frac{p(n_{1i} = 1)}{\lambda}$$

$$= \frac{p(n_{1i} = 1)}{\displaystyle\sum_{r \geq 0} \frac{1}{r+1} p(n_{0i} = r, n_{1i} = 1)} S_{1i}. \qquad \text{[by using (B.2)]} \quad (B.4)$$

Server Aggregation Transformation - Model M_2

We now aggregate all shadow servers for the critical section phase into a single server CS (server $K+1$). The service time of this server is:

$$S_{CS} = S_{K+1} = \sum_{i=1}^{K} S_{1i}^{'}. \qquad (B.5)$$

By reindexing the other servers, we obtain

$$S_i = S_{0i}^{'}, \quad i = 1, \cdots, K. \qquad (B.6)$$

As seen in Chapter 3, this model has only fair, autonomous servers. Therefore, we solve it by *assuming* that the service times are homogeneous. Each queue is solved independently; the solution is:

$$p(n_i = r) = (1 - \lambda S_i)(\lambda S_i)^r. \qquad (B.7)$$

Consequently,

$$p(n_i \geq 1) = \sum_{r \geq 1} p(n_i = r) = \sum_{r \geq 1} (1 - \lambda S_i)(\lambda S_i)^r = \lambda S_i. \qquad (B.8)$$

This solution is easily mapped back into the solution for M_1 as follows:

$$p(n_{1i} = 1) = p(n_{1i} = 1 \mid n_{CS} \geq 1) \cdot p(n_{CS} \geq 1)$$

$$= \frac{S'_{1i}}{S_{CS}} \lambda S_{CS} = \lambda \cdot S'_{1i}, \qquad (B.9)$$

$$p(n_{0i} = r, n_{1i} = k) = p(n_{0i} = r) \cdot p(n_{1i} = k). \qquad (B.10)$$

By an identity reverse mapping for M_1, this is the solution for M_0 as well.

Iteration: Simplification of Parameter Expressions

Since the state probabilities are initially unknown, we are forced to solve the model iteratively. During an iteration, the new estimates of the stretched out service times is computed from Eqns. (B.3) and (B.4)). By substituting the probabilities obtained from the previous iteration, we get

$$\hat{S}'_{0i} = \frac{p(n_{0i} \geq 1)}{\displaystyle\sum_{r \geq 1} \sum_{k=0}^{1} \frac{r}{r+k} \, p(n_{0i} = r, n_{1i} = k)} \, S_{0i}$$

$$= \frac{p(n_{0i} \geq 1)}{\displaystyle\sum_{r \geq 1} [p(n_{0i} = r) - \frac{1}{r+1} \, p(n_{0i} = r, n_{1i} = 1)]} \, S_{0i}$$

$$= \frac{p(n_{0i} \geq 1)}{\displaystyle\sum_{r \geq 1} [p(n_{0i} = r) - \frac{1}{r+1} \, p(n_{0i} = r) \, p(n_{1i} = 1)]} \, S_{0i} \quad [\text{by (B.10)}]$$

$$= \frac{p(n_{0i} \geq 1)}{p(n_{0i} \geq 1) - p(n_{1i} = 1) \displaystyle\sum_{r \geq 1} \frac{1}{r+1} \, p(n_{0i} = r)} \, S_{0i}$$

$$= \frac{\lambda S'_{0i}}{\lambda S'_{0i} - \lambda S'_{1i} (1 - \lambda S'_{0i}) \displaystyle\sum_{r \geq 1} \frac{1}{r+1} \, (\lambda S'_{0i})^r} \, S_{0i} \quad [\text{by (B.5) - (B.9)}]$$

By computing the sum given in the denominator,[1] we get

$$\hat{S}'_{0i} = \cfrac{\lambda S'_{0i}}{\lambda S'_{0i} - \lambda S'_{1i}(1 - \lambda S'_{0i})\cfrac{-\lambda S'_{0i} - \ln(1 - \lambda S'_{0i})}{\lambda S'_{0i}}} S_{0i}. \tag{B.11}$$

Similarly it can be shown that

$$\hat{S}'_{1i} = -\cfrac{\lambda S'_{0i}}{(1 - \lambda S'_{0i})\ln(1 - \lambda S'_{0i})} S_{1i}. \tag{B.12}$$

At the fixed point of the iteration, $\hat{S}'_{0i} = S'_{0i}$, and $\hat{S}'_{1i} = S'_{1i}$. Therefore, by eqns. (B.11) and (B.12):

$$S'_{0i} = \cfrac{\lambda S'_{0i}}{\lambda S'_{0i} + \lambda S'_{1i}(1 - \lambda S'_{0i}) + \cfrac{\lambda S'_{1i}(1 - \lambda S'_{0i})\ln(1 - \lambda S'_{0i})}{\lambda S'_{0i}}} S_{0i}$$

$$= \cfrac{\lambda S'_{0i}}{\lambda S'_{0i} - \cfrac{\lambda S_{1i}\lambda S'_{0i}}{\ln(1 - \lambda S'_{0i})} - \lambda S_{1i}} S_{0i}. \qquad \text{[by (B.12)]}$$

Thus,

$$\lambda S'_{0i} - \frac{\lambda S_{1i}\lambda S'_{0i}}{\ln(1 - \lambda S'_{0i})} - \lambda S_{1i} = \lambda S_{0i},$$

and hence, $S'_{0i}\ (\geq S_{0i})$ is a zero of

$$S'_{0i}\ln(1 - \lambda S'_{0i}) - S_{1i}\lambda S'_{0i} - (S_{0i} + S_{1i})\ln(1 - \lambda S'_{0i}) = 0. \tag{B.13}$$

---

1. For computing the sums in these equations, consider the series $S = \sum_{r \geq 1} 1/(r+1)x^{r+1}$. Then $dS/dx = \sum_{r \geq 1} x^r = x/(1-x)$. Thus, $S = \int x/(1-x)dx = 1 - x - \ln(1-x)$. On the other hand, however, consider $S' = \sum_{r \geq 0} 1/(r+1)x^{r+1}$. $dS'/dx = \sum_{r \geq 0} x^r = 1/(1-x)$. Thus, $S' = \int 1/(1-x)dx = -\ln(1-x)$. Note that, though, initially, $S' = S + x$, their sums as obtained from the integration differ by an additional constant 1 (a paradox). We take the sum $S' = -\ln(1-x)$ as the correct one and then compute $S = S' - x$. Experiments have shown that this is better than the other expression for S which leads to an extremely high overestimate of response time, and causes some difficulties in evaluation. Moreover, [SELB73, pg. 413] lists $-x - \ln(1-x)$ as an alternate expression for S.

This zero can be computed by using a numerical technique such as Newton's Method [STOE80]. Using this value of $S_{0i}^{'}$, we have,

$$S_{1i}^{'} = -\frac{\lambda S_{0i}^{'}}{(1 - \lambda S_{0i}^{'}) \ln(1 - \lambda S_{0i}^{'})} S_{1i}. \qquad (B.14)$$

Note that by this analysis, we have eliminated the iteration between models M_0, M_1 and M_2. Instead, the iteration is now required to find the roots of the equation in (B.13).

This extension is summarized in Box B.1 and will be referred to as algorithm A1. Preliminary validation results are presented after discussing a heuristic load concealment transformation.

B.2 Open Network Model with Heuristic Load Concealment Transformation

In the preceding section we used an "exact" load concealment transformation to analyze a single critical section network. (This transformation is exact in the sense that if the correct values of the probabilities are known, the elongated service times will be correct.) The same transformation can be used for multiple critical sections. However, the resulting equations for elongated service times cannot be easily simplified and expanded. Therefore, we seek a simple heuristic for computing elongated service times. One such heuristic is based on the observation that if U_0 is the server utilization due to non-phase z customers, only $1 - U_0$ fraction of the server capacity is available to class z customers. Therefore, it can be proposed that the service time should be stretched out by a factor of $1/(1 - U_0)$,[2] i.e.,

---

2. This heuristic is not exact because it does not take into account joint probabilities. The exact expressions for the stretchout factor are given by (B.3) and (B.4).

Example: The aggregate server method for open networks (Algorithm A1) (*one critical section only*).

M_0: Single class open network of K PS/FCFS devices, 1 critical section.
P_0: $\{S_{zi}, \lambda\}$; S are TOTAL service requirements.
Q_0: { state probabilities, e.g., $p(n_{0i} = r, n_{zi} = 1)$}.

M_1: 2 isomorphic networks with a critical section queue.
P_1: $\{S_{zi}', \lambda\}$.
Q_1: {state probabilities, e.g., $p(n_{0i} = r, n_{1i} = 1)$}.

$\mathbf{F_1}$: Load Concealment Transformation (from exact analysis):
  $S_{0i}'(\geq S_{0i})$ is a zero of

  $$S_{0i}\ln(1 - \lambda\, S_{0i}') - S_{1i}\,\lambda\, S_{0i}' - (S_{0i} + S_{1i})\ln(1 - \lambda\, S_{0i}') = 0.$$

  $$S_{1i}' = -\frac{S_{1i}\,\lambda\, S_{0i}'}{(1 - \lambda\, S_{0i}')\ln(1 - \lambda\, S_{0i}')}.$$

$\mathbf{R_1}$: Identity.

SOLVE(M_1, P_1):**SOLVE**(M_2, P_2).

Iteration: Not Required.
    (Though, the S_{0i}' is to evaluated using an iterative method.)

M_2: Model with critical section network aggregated into a single server
    total $K + 1$ servers: shadow physical servers $1, \cdots, K$;
    shadow critical section server $K + 1$.
P_2: $\{S_i, \lambda\}$.
Q_2: {state probabilities, e.g., $p(n_i = r, n_{K+1} \geq 1)$}.

$\mathbf{F_2}$: Server Aggregation Transformation.

  $$S_i = S^{'0i}, \quad i = 1, \cdots, K, \ S_{K+1} = \sum_{i=1}^{K} S^{'1i}.$$

$\mathbf{R_2}$: Identity:

  $$p(n_{1i} = 1) = \frac{S_{1i}'}{S_{K+1}}\, p(n_{K+1} \geq 1),$$

  $$p(n_{0i} = r, n_{1i} = 1) = \frac{S^{'1i}}{S_{K+1}}\, p(n_i = r, n_{K+1} \geq 1),$$

  etc.

SOLVE(M_2, P_2):$p(n_i = r) = (1 - \lambda S_i)(\lambda S_i)^r$,
    $$p(n_i = r, n_j = l) = p(n_i = r)\, p(n_j = l).$$

Iteration: Not Required.

Box B.1: The aggregate server method for
single class open networks with one critical section.

$$S' = \frac{1}{1 - U_O} \, S.$$

U_O can be directly calculated from arrival rate and the total service requirement for each phase. Therefore, the resulting algorithm, A2, is non-iterative. The transformations employing this heuristic are summarized in Box B.2.

B.3 Preliminary Validation for Single Class Open Networks

To establish the feasibility of these algorithms, we summarize the preliminary validation results. An extensive validation is a part of future investigation.

Table B.1 compares the algorithms A1 (Box B.1) and A2 (Box B.2) with the simulation results. For this network, the system response time predicted by A1 is about 25% less than the simulated value. The response time estimated by A2 is within 3% of the simulated value. The estimated waiting time for entry into the critical section is about 47% less for A1 and 13% less for A2 from the simulated value. This indicates that the "heuristic" algorithm A2 is likely to perform much better than the "exact" algorithm A1. This result is somewhat surprising and counter intuitive. A possible explanation is that by overestimating stretchout factors, A2 corrects for the errors due to the homogeneity assumptions used in Eqns. (B.3) - (B.10).

Table B.2 further validates the heuristic algorithm A2 against the simulation results for a two critical section open network. Once again, the results are fairly satisfactory: system response time is estimated within 8% and and wait time for heavily used critical section CS1 is within 10%.

(As an aside, experiments have indicated that the heuristic does not work well for single class closed networks. While it is satisfactory for low

Example: The aggregate server method heuristic for open networks (Algorithm A2).

M_0: Single class network of K PS/FCFS devices, Z critical sections.
P_0: $\{S_{zi}, \lambda\}$; S's are TOTAL service requirements.
Q_0: {state probabilities, e.g., $p(n_{0i} = r, n_{zi} = 1)$}.

M_1: network with $Z+1$ isomorphic networks.
P_1: $\{S_{zi}^{\cdot}, \lambda\}$.
Q_1: {state probabilities $p(n_{0i} = r, n_{zi} = 1)$}.

$\mathbf{F_1}$: Load Concealment Transformation (a heuristic)
$$S_{zi}^{\cdot} = \frac{S_{zi}}{1 - U_0} = \frac{S_{zi}}{1 - \sum_{\substack{q=0 \\ q \neq z}}^{Z} \lambda S_{qi}}.$$

$\mathbf{R_1}$: Identity.

SOLVE(M_1, P_1):**SOLVE**(M_2, P_2).

Iteration: Not Required.

M_2: Model with critical section network aggregated into a single server;
    total $K+Z$ servers: shadow physical servers $1, \cdots, K$,
    shadow critical section servers $K+1, \cdots, K+Z$.
P_2: $\{S_i, \lambda\}$.
Q_2: { state probabilities $p(n_i = r, n_{K+z} \geq 1)$}.

$\mathbf{F_2}$: Server Aggregation Transformation:
$$S_i = S_{0i}^{\cdot}, \ i = 1, \cdots, K,$$
$$S_{K+z} = \sum_{i=1}^{K} S_{zi}^{\cdot}, \quad z = 1, \cdots, Z.$$

$\mathbf{R_2}$: Identity:
$$p(n_{zi} = 1) = \frac{S_{zi}^{\cdot}}{S_{K+z}} p(n_{K+z} \geq 1), \ z = 1, \cdots, Z,$$
$$p(n_{0i} = r, n_{zi} = 1) = \frac{S_{zi}^{\cdot}}{S_{K+z}} p(n_i = r, n_{K+z} \geq 1), \ z = 1, \cdots, Z.$$

SOLVE(M_2, P_2):$p(n_i = r) = (1 - \lambda S_i)(\lambda S_i)^r$,
$$p(n_i = r, n_j = l) = p(n_i = r) \cdot p(n_j = l).$$

Iteration: Not Required.

Box B.2: The aggregate server method heuristic for single class open networks.

Table B.1: Preliminary validation of the aggregate server method for a single class open network with one critical section.

(a) Model Parameters (for M_0 and M_1).

Arrival Rate $\lambda = 0.67625$.

Server	Simulation $(M_0)^1$		A1 (M_1)		A2 (M_1)	
	S_0	S_1	S_0'	S_1'	S_0'	S_1'
1	0.5052	0.2385	0.553	0.304	0.602	0.362
2	0.3345	0.2377	0.365	0.275	0.399	0.307
3	0.3388	0.2408	0.370	0.279	0.405	0.312

[1] Measured in Simulation.
A1 and A2 are algorithms in Box B.1 and Box B.2 respectively.
S_0 is total non-serialized requirement.
S_1 is total serialized requirement.
Superscript ' denotes elongated service times.

(b) Parameters for M_2 and performance measures.

Server	A1 (M_2)		A2 (M_2)		Simulation
	S	R	S	R	
1	0.553	0.883	0.602	1.015	
2	0.365	0.485	0.399	0.546	
3	0.370	0.493	0.405	0.558	
4 (CS)	0.858	2.044	0.981	2.914	
R_0	3.91		5.03		5.187
W_{CS}	1.186		1.933		2.23

R_0 is system response time.
W_{CS} is the queueing time for CS entry.

Table B.2: Preliminary validation of the aggregate server method for a single class open network with two critical sections.

(a) Model parameters.

Arrival Rate $\lambda = 0.19225$.

Server	Service Time (M_0)[1]			Elongated Service Time (M_1)		
	NCS	CS1	CS2	NCS	CS1	CS2
1	1.000	1.01	0.537	1.423	1.434	0.875
2	0.598	2.01	0.427	1.125	2.503	1.302
3	0.605	0.00	0.649	0.691	0.000	0.734

[1] M_0 quantities are those measured in simulation.

(b) Performance Measure Comparison.

Measure	A2 (Box B.2)	Simulation
System Response Time R_0	27.00	25.04
Wait for CS1 entry W_{CS1}	12.26	13.57
Wait for CS2 entry W_{CS2}	3.70	1.61

customer population, its accuracy deteriorates rapidly as the number of customers increase.)

B.4 Heuristic Extension for Multiclass Mixed Networks

The basic idea of a Load Concealment Transformation followed by Server Aggregation is also applicable to mixed networks. An analysis using the "exact" load concealment transformation is theoretically possible but poses practical difficulties in evaluation and simplification. On the other hand, the heuristic discussed in Section B.2 can be easily extended as follows:

1. Start with an R class mixed network M_0 in which a critical section is not visited by customers of two classes, i.e., critical sections are not shared between classes.

2. Transform this network into R isomorphic networks $M_{01}, \cdots, M_{0R}$ such that only one class r is visible in M_{0r} and other classes $1, \cdots, r-1, r+1, \cdots, R$ are invisible. As a heuristic, stretchout factor can be taken as $1/(1-U_O)$ where U_O is the TOTAL server utilization due to invisible classes.

3. Solve each M_r by applying the aggregate server method.

The necessary transformations are summarized in Box B.3. The hierarchy for this set of transformations is shown in Figure B.1.

Table B.3 validates the heuristic against simulation for a two-class closed network with two critical sections. The results are encouraging and further evaluation is warranted.

B.5   Conclusion

In this appendix we have presented heuristic extensions of the aggregate server method for mixed networks. In this exercise, the metamodeling framework allowed us to abstract away the details of solving the equations and rise to a conceptual level. At this level, we were able to think about the model development as a series of transformations. Once the nature of these transformations was identified, it was easy to see the extensions of the basic model.

Example: The aggregate server method for multi-class mixed networks

M_0: R class mixed network of K PS/FCFS devices, Z critical section.
    Critical sections are not shared between classes.
P_0: $\{S_{rzi}, \lambda_r, N_r\}$; S are TOTAL service requirements.
Q_0: $\{X_r, R_r\}$.

For $r = 1, \cdots, R$,
M_{0r}:   Single class isomorphic network for class r.
P_{0r}: $\{S_{zi}^{\cdot}, \lambda\}$ if class r is an open class;
        $\{S_{zi}, N\}$ if class r is a closed class.
Q_{0r}: $\{R,$ state probabilities$\}$ if r is open;
        $\{X, R,$ state probabilities$\}$ if r is closed.

$\mathbf{F_{0r}}$: Load concealment transformation (classes concealed).

$$S_{zi}^{\cdot} = \frac{S_{rzi}}{1 - \displaystyle\sum_{\substack{l=0 \\ l \neq r}}^{R} \sum_{q=0}^{q=Z} U_{lzi}},$$

    where $U_{lzi} = \lambda_l S_{lzi}$ if l is open; $U_{lzi} = X_l S_{lzi}$ otherwise.

$\mathbf{R_{0r}}$:   Identity.

SOLVE(M_{0r}, P_{0r}):Aggregate server method.

Iteration: Required between closed models only.
          (Compute initial throughputs by assuming
          that M_0 is product form).
          Open models should be solved last.

Box B.3: The aggregate server method heuristic for mixed networks.

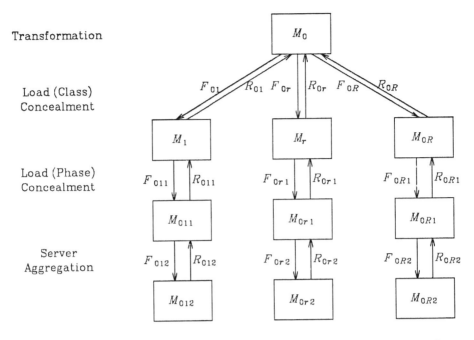

Transformation

Load (Class)
Concealment

Load (Phase)
Concealment

Server
Aggregation

Figure B.1: Hierarchy for the aggregate server model for mixed networks.

Table B.3: Preliminary validation of the heuristic aggregate server method for a two class closed network with two critical sections.

(a) Specified Service Times.

Server	Class 1		Class 2	
	S_0	S_1	S_0	S_2
1	1.00	0.833	1.00	0.556
2	0.70	1.667	0.80	0.444
3	0.70	0.000	0.70	0.667

(b) Throughput Comparison.

Population		Number of Iterations	Heuristic		Simulation	
Class 1	Class 2		Class 1	Class 2	Class 1	Class 2
4	2	5	0.229	0.203	0.213	0.218
3	3	5	0.197	0.257	0.197	0.261

Appendix C

Response Time Preservation Transformation

The response time preservation (RTP) transformation entails replacing a subsystem by a set of equivalent servers where the response time under an assumed arrival process equals that at the replaced subsystem. This tranformation leads to a powerful and general approximate solution procedure development technique. The technique was first presented at the ACM SIGMETRICS Conference on Measurement and Modeling of Computer Systems, 1984.

The RTP based approximation development technique was conceptualized and formalized in the metamodeling framework presented in the main body of the monograph. The power and the generality of this technique illustrate the usefulness of the metamodel. Therefore, with the permission of the ACM, we reprint the paper below. Sections and other referenceable items have been renumbered according to the convention adopted in this monograph.

RESPONSE TIME PRESERVATION:

A General Technique for Developing
Approximate Algorithms for Queueing Networks

Subhash C. Agrawal
Jeffrey P. Buzen
Annie W. Shum

BGS Systems, Inc.

One University Office Park
Waltham, MA. 02254

ABSTRACT

Response Time Preservation (RTP) is introduced as a general technique for developing approximate analysis procedures for queueing networks. The underlying idea is to replace a subsystem by an equivalent server whose response time in isolation equals that of the entire subsystem in isolation. The RTP based approximations, which belong to the class of decomposition approximations, can be viewed as a dual of the Norton's Theorem approach for solving queueing networks since it matches response times rather than throughputs. The generality of the RTP technique is illustrated by developing solution procedures for several important queueing systems which violate product form assumptions. Examples include FCFS servers with general service times, FCFS servers with different service times for multiple classes, priority scheduling, and distributed systems.

C.1 Introduction

Queueing network models have been found to be extremely useful and cost-effective in analyzing the performance of complex computer systems. The wide applicability of these models is due primarily to the discovery of efficient computational algorithms [Buzen 73, Bruell and Balbo 80, Reiser and Lavenberg 80] for product-form queueing networks [Baskett et. al. 75]. Many real systems, however, exhibit characteristics that violate the product form

Published in the *Proceedings of the 1984 ACM Sigmetrics Conference on Measurement and Modeling of Computer Systems* (August 1984). Copyright 1984, Association for Computing Machinery, Inc., reprinted by permission.

assumptions. Typical examples include priority scheduling at a server, queueing for passive resources such as critical sections and memory, I/O path contention, database concurrency algorithms, and blocking.

Various approximations have been developed to handle networks with such properties [Agrawal 83a, Bard 79, Bard 80, Brandwajn 74, Brandwajn 82, Courtois 75, Potier and Leblanc 80, Graham 78]. While each approximation may appear to involve an entirely different technique, Agrawal and Buzen have unified their characterization through a general framework termed metamodeling [Agrawal 83b, Buzen and Agrawal 83]. As explained by them, the principal idea in developing an approximation is to the original network into one or more simpler networks, solve these simpler networks, and then integrate their solutions to obtain an approximate solution of the original system. Each one of the approximations mentioned above can be viewed as an application of a transformation or a series of such transformations. Transformations for a number of approximation techniques are discussed in [Agrawal 83b].

In this paper we present a general approximation development technique which entails isolating the subsystem from the original model, analyzing the isolated subsystem under an assumed arrival process and replacing the subsystem by an equivalent server whose response time under the assumed arrival process equals that of the isolated subsystem. Since the underlying transformation preserves the isolated system response time, it is called a Response Time Preservation transformation. The resulting approximation procedure is called a Response Time Preservation (RTP) based approximation.

We first motivate the RTP technique by developing an approximation for modeling FCFS servers with general service times in a queueing network. Then we specify the general technique in Section C.3 and present some specific mappings in Section C.4. These mappings are followed by additional examples in Section C.5. Some considerations in developing an effective RTP approximation are discussed in Section C.6. Section C.7 compares the RTP approach and the Norton's Theorem approach [Chandy et. al. 75] as two decomposition based solution approximation development procedures.

One of the most important aspects of the RTP approximation is that it is a general technique for developing approximate solution procedures for a wide class of non-product form queueing systems. It is not our intent here to evaluate extensively the accuracy of any individual RTP based approximation. Rather, we wish to emphasize the underlying concept and the essential steps of the RTP procedure so that the reader can develop specific RTP based approximations for individual problems. Detailed analyses of the accuracy of specific RTP based approximations is a subject for future research.

C.2   Example: FCFS Servers with General Service Times

Consider a single class closed queueing network containing a FCFS server as shown in Figure C.1a. If the service time at this server is not exponentially distributed, the queueing network does not possess an efficiently computable product form solution. A number of approximation procedures have been proposed for solving such networks [Shum and Buzen 77, Marie 78, Balbo 79].

As an alternative to these previously published approaches, consider the following intuitive technique for solving such networks: Replace the general FCFS server by an equivalent server with exponentially distributed service times. The resulting network, as depicted in Figure C.1b, possesses a product form solution and thus is easily solvable.

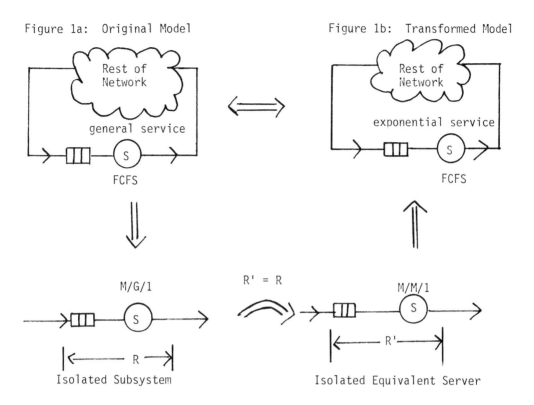

Figure C.1: RTPA for an FCFS server with general service time.

The primary issue now is to obtain the service times at the equivalent server. For a good approximation, one important condition is that the response time of a job at the general FCFS server should be the same as its response time at the equivalent server. As an approximation to this condition, we equate the response time of a job at the two servers when they are taken out of the system and analyzed by assuming that the arrivals are generated by a Poisson or homogeneous arrival process. See Figure C.1c.

The next step is to compute the two response times. If the general FCFS server has throughput equal to X and service time equal to S with a coefficient of variation CV, then by the Pollaczek-Khinchin formula for an $M/G/1$ queue with FCFS scheduling [Kleinrock 75], the open system response time is given by:

$$R = S + \frac{(1 + CV^2)S\ U}{2\ (1 - U)} \qquad \text{(C.1)}$$

where $U = XS$ is the server utilization.

Let the service time at the exponential equivalent server be S'. Then, the response time at this server is given by the standard $M/M/1$ formula:

$$R' = \frac{S'}{1 - XS'}$$

Our response time preservation technique requires that

$$R' = R.$$

Solving for S' and substituting R' by R, the effective service time at the equivalent server is:

$$S' = \frac{R}{1 + XR} \qquad \text{(C.2)}$$

The complete solution procedure for the closed queueing network is iterative and outlined below:

1. Assume initial throughput X'.
2. Repeat
   $X = X'$
   For general server i
       Compute R_i using eqn. (C.1).
       Compute S_i' using eqn. (C.2).
   Obtain new throughput X' of the product form network containing the equivalent server by using MVA or Convolution.
   Until $| X' - X | < \epsilon$.

Note that, in this procedure, we create a product form network of servers whose response times and throughput rates approximate those of the original non-product form network. To calculate server utilizations in the original network, we simply multiply the approximate server throughputs by the original service times.

The data presented in Table C.1 shows that the method yields reasonably accurate throughputs for moderate CVs (up to 5). Device utilizations and system response time have comparable accuracy. Errors are larger for higher CVs. When service times are exponential, the method is exact. See Appendix C.A for a more systematic examination of this particular approximation.

C.3   Response Time Preservation Approximation

The Response Time Preservation approximation used implicitly in the previous section can be generalized to provide a powerful approximation development technique. To this end, let us abstract the technique from the preceding example.

Start with an original model (M_0) whose parameters (P_0) include device service times and whose performance metrics (Q_0) include system throughput. M_0 is not easily solvable because it contains a non-product form subsystem, namely the FCFS server with general service times. Construct a product-form

Table C.1: Accuracy of RTPA for networks with general service times
at an FCFS server.

Network Description

DEVICE i	V_i	S_i	$V_i S_i$
CPU	10	28 ms	280 ms
DISK 1	7	40 ms	280 ms
DISK 2	2	280 ms	560 ms

NETWORK POPULATION $N = 6$

MODEL	CV			NO. OF	CPU THROUGHPUT		% ERROR
#	CPU	DISK 1	DISK 2	ITER.	EXACT	APPROX.	
1	0.6	1.0	1.0	1	0.01744	0.01743	-0.1
2	2.0	1.0	1.0	1	0.01703	0.01695	-0.5
3	5.0	1.0	1.0	4	0.01588	0.01517	-4.5
4	10.0	1.0	1.0	8	0.01487	0.01310	-11.9
5	1.0	0.6	1.0	1	0.01745	0.01743	-0.1
6	1.0	2.0	1.0	1	0.01703	0.01695	-0.5
7	1.0	10.0	1.0	8	0.01483	0.01310	-11.7
8	1.0	1.0	0.6	3	0.01765	0.01750	-0.8
9	1.0	1.0	2.0	4	0.01662	0.01687	1.5
10	1.0	1.0	5.0	17	0.01567	0.01531	-2.3
11	1.0	1.0	10.0	34	0.01541	0.01368	-11.2
12	0.6	2.0	10.0	31	0.01500	0.01278	-14.8
13	10.0	2.0	0.6	8	0.01489	0.01328	-10.8
14	5.0	2.0	10.0	21	0.01363	0.00942	-30.9
15	10.0	2.0	0.6	33	0.01353	0.00886	-34.5

NOTES: These are some of the models evaluated in [Balbo 79]. The exact solutions were obtained by Balbo using global balance techniques.

If the CV's are ignored, CPU throughput for all models = 0.01735.

We are unable to explain the error for model 9.

queueing network (M) by replacing the non-product form subsystem (general server) with an equivalent product form subsystem (an "equivalent" server). The forward mapping F from M_0 to M determines the parameters of the equivalent subsystem, e.g., the service time of the equivalent server. F is such that the response time of the non-product form subsystem under an assumed arrival process (in this case Markovian) is equal to the response time of the equivalent product form subsystem under the same arrival process. The reverse mapping R from M to M_0 equates X_0, the throughput of M_0, to X which is the throughput of M.

To be able to parameterize the equivalent subsystem, we need to compute the response time of the non-product form subsystem under the assumed arrival process. To accomplish this, construct an auxiliary model M_1 representing only the subsystem with the assumed arrival process. The forward mapping F_1, from M_0 to M_1, computes the parameters of the subsystem including the parameters of the arrival process. In the special case of Markovian arrivals, only the mean arrival rate is required. In general, the arrival rate equals the network throughput times the appropriate visit ratio. However, the throughput is not known a priori and is, therefore, iteratively computed.

The structure of an RTP based approximation procedure immediately follows: Let M_0 be a model of a system with N subsystems each of which can be analyzed in isolation (say, as an open system). Then the RTP approximation procedure is:

0. Assume initial system throughput X_0.

1. Isolate and solve each subsystem M_i, $i = 1, \cdots, N$
    a. Using forward mapping F_i, compute arrival process parameters,
       e.g. arrival rate at M_i.
    b. Solve M_i in isolation and calculate the
       subsystem's response time R_i.

2. Construct and solve transformed system model M.

    a. F: Using forward mapping F, compute effective service time at the
       equivalent server representing subsystem i.
    b. Solve M (with product form algorithms)
       and compute new throughput X_n.

3. If $|X_n - X_0| < \epsilon$ STOP
   else $X_0 = X_n$
        go to 1

An RTP based approximation can be developed whenever solutions can be obtained for the subsystems in isolation. It is based on the assumption that if the response time of a subsystem in isolation equals the response time of the equivalent server in isolation, then it is likely that the response time at the equivalent server in the transformed model M will equal the response time at the subsystem in the original model M_0. This assumption is reminiscent of the On-line = Off-line behavior implicit in traditional Norton's Theorem based decomposition approximations [Brandwajn 74, Chandy et.al. 75, Courtois 75, Denning and Buzen 78]. We discuss this analogy and compare the two approaches in Section C.7. We now present some forward mappings for computing the effective service times at the equivalent server(s) in specific cases.

C.4 Forward Mappings for Equivalent Servers

One of the crucial steps in developing an RTP based approximation is to characterize the equivalent server representation for a subsystem and to compute a customer's effective service time. The choice of equivalent server(s) is affected by a number of considerations that are detailed in Section C.6. One consideration is the nature of the arrival process used in the analysis of the isolated subsystem. If the arrival process is assumed to be Poisson or homogeneous, some of the forward mappings for computing effective service times at the equivalent server(s) are relatively simple. If the arrival process assumed for the isolated subsystem analysis is similar to the one observed at the subsystem in the network, the forward mapping may be trivial. Some of these mappings are presented in terms of the following theorems. The mappings are differentiated by the number of classes and the number of equivalent servers.

Theorem C.4.1 - Single Class Equivalent Server: Assume that the forward mapping F_i used to isolate a single class subsystem yields an open network having Poisson arrivals with rate X. Let the response time of the isolated subsystem under this mapping be R. Then, the effective service time at the response time preserving equivalent server is:

$$S' = \frac{R}{1 + XR} \qquad (C.3)$$

Proof: From equations (C.1) and (C.2) of the general FCFS server example. $\qquad \square$

Corollary C.1: Assume that the forward mapping F_i used to isolate a multi-class subsystem yields an open network in which customer class r has Poisson arrivals with rate X_r for $r = 1, \ldots, c$. Let R_r be the response time of customer class r under this mapping. Assume that in the equivalent product form network each customer class is processed by a dedicated equivalent server. Then the effective service time of class r at its equivalent server is given by

$$S_r{}' = \frac{R_r}{1 + X_r R_r}, \quad r = 1, \cdots, c. \tag{C.4}$$

An alternative approach for constructing equivalent servers for a multiclass subsystem is given by the following theorem.

Theorem C.4.2 - Multiple Class Equivalent Server: Assume that the forward mapping F_i used to isolate a multi-class subsystem yields an open network in which customer class r has Poisson arrivals with rate X_r for $r = 1, \ldots, c$. Let R_r be the response time of customer class r under this mapping. Assume that, in the equivalent product form network, all customer classes are processed by a single equivalent server using a processor sharing discipline. The effective service time for class r, $S_r{}'$, $1 \le r \le c$, is given by:

$$S_r{}' = \frac{R_r}{1 + \sum_{i=1}^{c} X_i R_i}, \tag{C.5}$$

Proof: Class r response time at the equivalent server is

$$R_r{}' = \frac{S_r}{1 - \sum_{i=1}^{c} X_i S_i}, \tag{C.6}$$

It is easy to verify that the solution given by equation (C.5) satisfies the above equation. And since eqn. (C.6) represents a system of c equations in c unknowns, the solution is unique. □

When the interarrival times at subsystem M_i are not exponentially distributed, the calculations of effective service times are not necessarily as simple. In general, for a given arrival process at M_i, if the response time function of the equivalent server is

$$R_i{}' = f_i(S_i{}'), \qquad (C.7)$$

then by the RTP approximation $R_i{}' = R_i$, and therefore the effective service time is given by

$$S_i{}' = f_i{}^{-1}(R_i). \qquad (C.8)$$

If the equivalent server is just a delay server (i.e., an infinite or no-queueing server) then $S_i{}'$ simply equals the response time R_i. It is sometimes desirable to use delay servers when developing RTP approximations. For example, assume that the isolated subsystem can be analyzed under an arrival process that approximates closely the arrival process observed at the subsystem in the original network. Let the isolated subsystem's response time be R. Then, one appropriate forward mapping F is to replace the subsystem by a delay server with delay R.

C.5   Additional Applications of the RTP Technique

In this section we show how RTP based approximations can be developed for a number of networks that violate product form conditions. Complete equations are presented for RTP approximations of multi-class FCFS servers and priority servers. This is followed by a discussion of distributed systems and a brief outline of how RTP could be used to integrate isolated models of nodes, communication networks and synchronization delays. These examples provide an indication of the broad applicability of the RTP approach.

C.5.1 Different Service Times at an FCFS Server

Consider a c-class closed queueing network M_0 with an FCFS server, i. In general, the mean and variance of the service time at server i for each customer class is different. In this case, the network does not have a product form solution. An RTP based approximation that is a multi-class generalization of the case treated in Section C.2 can be obtained by applying Theorem C.4.2. The approximation entails replacing server by a processor sharing equivalent server i' (Model M). To accomplish this, we first need to find the response time for each class at the isolated server (Model M_i).

Model M_i

This model consists of an isolated FCFS server visited by c classes, each with Poisson arrivals and general service times. The arrival rate of class r is $V_{ir}X_r$, where V_{ir} is the number of class r visits to server i in M_0 and X_r is class r throughput in M_0. The mean and coefficient of variation of the service time are S_{ir} and CV_{ir}, respectively. The response time of class r, R_{ir}, is computed as follows.

Total arrival rate at the isolated server

$$X_i = \sum_{r=1}^{c} V_{ir}X_r.$$

Mean effective service time at the server is given by

$$S_i = \frac{\sum_{r=1}^{c} S_{ir}V_{ir}X_r}{X_i}.$$

Coefficient of variation square for the effective service time is given by

$$CV_i^2 = \frac{\sum\limits_{r=1}^{c} (1 + CV_{ir}^2) S_{ir}^2 V_{ir} X_r}{S_i^2} - 1.$$

Then from the Pollaczek-Khinchin formula, the wait time for all jobs is

$$W_i = \frac{(1 + CV_i^2) S_i^2 X_i}{2(1 - X_i S_i)}.$$

The isolated system response time of class r is

$$R_{ir} = S_{ir} + W_i.$$

Transformed Model M

Because all jobs receive "non-discriminatory" service at server i in M_0, an appropriate equivalent server is a single server visited by all classes. The effective service time is computed by the forward mapping specified in Theorem C.4.2.

Note that the preceding analysis assumes generally distributed service times at server i. In the special case where these service times are exponentially distributed, the model still violates product form assumptions unless all classes have the same mean service time. For exponentially distributed cases where the mean service times may differ, Bard has proposed an MVA based approximate solution [Bard 79]. Table C.2 shows the accuracy of the RTP approximation for the limited set of examples considered in [Bard 79]. We also note that the RTP method provides exact results for product form queueing networks with load independent FCFS servers.

Table C.2: Accuracy of RTPA for multi-class networks with FCFS servers.

DEVICE	CLASS 1			CLASS 2		
i	V_{i1}	S_{i1}	$V_{i1}S_{i1}$	V_{i2}	S_{i2}	$V_{i2}S_{i2}$
1	18	7	126	8	11	88
2	5	20	100	13	8	104
3	10	2	20	15	3	45

POPULATION		# RTPA	RESPONSE TIME					
CLASS 1	CLASS 2		CLASS 1			CLASS 2		
		ITER.	SIM.	RTPA	BARD	SIM.	RTPA	BARD
5	5	8	1140	1115	1154	1156	1120	1208
50	50	14	12267	12952	12022	9070	8566	9316

NOTE: The example and simulation results are taken from [Bard 79].

C.5.2 Priority Scheduling in Computer Systems

Consider a computer system in which a device, say the CPU, gives preemptive priority to class 1 customers over class 2. The assumptions for product form solution are violated at the CPU, and thus an efficient approximation procedure is necessary. Some approximations have been discussed in [Sevcik 77, Agrawal 83b, Chandy and Laksmi 83, Bryant et. al. 83]. We now present another approximation based on the general RTP approximation technique.

The idea is to replace the CPU by equivalent CPUs, CPU1 and CPU2. The service times at these devices are computed such that the class 1 and class 2 response times at CPU1 and CPU2 in isolation are the same as the class 1 and class 2 response times at original CPU in isolation. The response times at the original CPU are obtained via auxiliary model M_1.

Model M $_1$

This model is constructed by taking the CPU out of the system and examining it in isolation. The interarrival times at the isolated CPU are assumed to be distributed exponentially. The response times can be directly calculated using well-known formulae [Kleinrock 76]:

$$R_1 = S_1 + \frac{(1 + CV_1^2)S_1 U_1}{2(1 - U_1)}$$

$$R_2 = \frac{S_2 (1 - U_1) + ((1 + CV_1^2)S_1 U_1 + (1 + CV_2^2)S_2 U_2)/2}{(1 - U_1)(1 - U_1 - U_2)},$$

where S_r is per visit CPU service time, U_r is CPU utilization and CV_r is coefficient of variation for service time for class r.

Transformed Model M

In this model, the CPU is replaced by CPU1 and CPU2. The effective service times of these "shadow" CPUs are computed by using Theorem C.4.1, Corollary C.1.

Since the throughputs are not known initially, they are computed iteratively.

We present some numerical results in Table C.3. The network under consideration is a two-station cyclic network. Two station cyclic networks are perhaps the worst-case for this algorithm because the principal source of the error in the approximation is the mismatch between the arrival process assumed for the isolated CPU analysis and the arrival process encountered at the CPU in the network.

To obtain an idea of the relative accuracy of some of the approximation methods cited earlier, we compare the errors for model 1 in note 5 of Table C.3. Note that the RTP approximation, which is based on general principles

Table C.3: Accuracy of RTPA for network with preemptive priority scheduling.

MODEL	S			THROUGHPUT		%
#	CLASS	CPU	DISK	EXACT	RTPA	ERROR
1	1	3	3	0.2156	0.2066	1.9
	2	3	3	0.0807	0.1117	13.3
2	1	3	1	0.3302	0.3305	0.1
	2	3	1	0.0031	0.0031	0
3	1	1	3	0.2566	0.2583	0.7
	2	3	1	0.2261	0.2227	-1.5
4	1	3	1	0.3282	0.3303	0.6
	2	1	3	0.0103	0.0100	-2.9
5	1	1	1	0.6446	0.6472	0.4
	3	3	3	0.0885	0.0977	10.4

NOTES:

1. System is a 2-queue cyclic network.
2. Customer population of each class = 4.
3. Exact throughputs were calculated using global-balance solution technique.
4. With given approximate solution for models 2 and 4, CPU utilization exceeds 1. When this happens, reduce class 1 throughput to make utilization 1. Therefore:

MODEL	ADJUSTED X_1	% ERROR
2	0.3302	0
4	0.3300	0.5

5. Comparison of different methods:

MODEL	% ERROR IN THROUGHPUT				
#	CLASS	RTPA	SEVCIK	BRYANT ET. AL.	CHANDY LAKSMI
1	1	1.9	-4.2	0.2	-5.2
	2	13.3	38.4	-6.1	21.9

that are completely independent of this particular application, compares favorably with other approximations that were specifically motivated by and tailored for the analysis of networks with preemptive priority servers. Of course, only a few cases are presented in our table, so no general conclusion can be drawn. Nevertheless, the combination of generality, simplicity, and relative accuracy exhibited by the RTP approach in this example is noteworthy.

The approximation procedure for modeling non-preemptive priority scheduling is similar to the procedure outlined above for preemptive priority. Instead of the preemptive priority equations, use non-preemptive priority equations for analysis of the open system (model M_1) (e.g., equation 3.30 in [Kleinrock 76]). The accuracy of the non-preemptive priority approximation is expected to be comparable to that for the preemptive priority approximation.

C.5.3 Distributed Systems

A model of a distributed processing system must represent both nodes and a communication network. The protocols used to manage the network make it difficult to treat them adequately as product form servers. However, many networks have been analyzed in isolation under Poisson arrival assumption.

The RTP approach is well suited for integrating these open-model solutions into a comprehensive product form model that represents both nodes and networks To apply the RTP approach in such cases, represent the network as a product form server. The service time for this server is obtained from existing analyses of the network operating in isolation under Poisson or homogeneous arrivals [Berry and Chandy 83, Gelenbe and Mitrani 82, Kuehn 79, Marathe and Kumar 81].

The solution procedure follows the same steps as the FCFS example given at the start of this paper, except that the Pollaczek-Khinchin formula is replaced by the appropriate equation for the network response time.

Another issue that arises when modeling distributed processing systems is the synchronization delays that occur when computations proceeding in parallel on several nodes need to coordinate their operations. In such cases, it is sometimes possible to compute the expected synchronization delays by modeling each node and network as an open system, and then adding up individual response times to determine the length of each parallel path. Once the expected delay due to path synchronization is determined, an additional server can be added to the model to represent this delay. RTP techniques can be used to determine the service time of this server.

C.6 Some Considerations in Developing an RTP Approximation

In this section we discuss three important considerations in developing an effective RTP based approximation. These are: the number of equivalent servers, the type of equivalent servers, and the nature of the arrival process used in the analysis of the isolated subsystems.

C.6.1 Number of Equivalent Servers

This issue arises when considering a multi-class subsystem. Corollary C.1 provides a forward mapping that creates several FCFS (PS) servers, each dedicated to a single class, while Theorem C.4.2 can be used to create a single FCFS (PS) server capable of serving all classes. The problem is deciding which type of mapping to use when solving a specific problem.

ITER.	ARRIVAL RATE		REST. TIME		EFFECTIVE SERVICE TIME		THROUGHPUT	
	1	2	1	2	1	2	1	2
1	.2156	.0807	8.5	95	.8093	9.05	.2424	.0823
2	.2424	.0823	11.0	528	.2335	11.21	.2550	.0782
3	.2550	.0782	12.8	34329	.0048	12.77	.2597	.0739
4	.2597	.0737	13.6	1.7e12	1.e-11	13.57	seenote2	

NOTES:
1. Initial guess is exact solution from global balance solution.
2. The iteration seems to be stabilizing around $X_1 = 0.26.$ and $X_2 = 0.07$. Iteration was discontinued at this point because of too small a value for class 1 effective service time. Nonetheless, these results show that the answers are rather inaccurate.

MODEL: 2 queue cyclic network with priority queueing at server 1.
$D_{ir} = 3$, $N_r = 4$, $i = 1,2$, $r = 1,2$.

Table C.4: One equivalent server RTP model for priority server.

To illustrate the issue, recall the preemptive priority scheduling system discussed in Section C.5. Class 1 customers have priority over class 2 customers at the CPU and therefore they do not have to wait for class 2 customers. In this case, since class 1 customers do not suffer any contention at all from class 2 customers, we chose to use one equivalent server for each class. However, if we use only one equivalent processor sharing server for both classes, the number of low priority class 2 customers at that server would influence the completion rate of class 1 customers. As shown by the data in Table C.4, the performance measures are quite inaccurate in this case. Results of intermediate calculations are also presented in Table C.4. They show that some serious numerical difficulties may arise as well.

On the other hand, consider a 2-class network with different per visit service times for the two classes at an FCFS server. In this case, the two classes freely contend with each other so one multiclass equivalent server is the appropriate choice. This reasoning was used implicitly in Section C.5.1.

If we use separate servers for each class, the network would be partitioned into two subnetworks, one for each class. This partitioning eliminates the dynamic interaction between the two classes that occurs in the original multiclass system. As a result both the accuracy and the numerical properties of the method suffer. This point is illustrated in Appendix C.B.

While the choice between a single server with multiple workloads or multiple servers with dedicated workloads is clear for these two examples, in general the decision may not be as straightforward. Fortunately the problem is not as severe as it may seem at first because an improper choice of the structure often leads to easily identifiable problems such as numerical instability. These problems serve as the indicators of inappropriate structural decisions. The analyst should be aware of these problems and experiment with different alternatives to reach a judicious conclusion.

C.6.2 Equivalent Server Type

Possible types of equivalent servers are numerous and include the FCFS/PS server, the delay server, the mult-server and the load-dependent server. One aspect affecting the choice of server type is the level of concurrency in the subsystem. If the level of concurrency is low, (e.g., as in the general FCFS server examples discussed in Sections C.2 and C.5), an FCFS/PS server is an appropriate choice. On the other hand, if the level of concurrency in the subsystem is high, then a mult-server, a load dependent server, or even a delay server may be more appropriate. Examples of highly concurrent subsystems include mult-CPUs with priority scheduling, or a computer network with alternate paths.

A second consideration that affects the choice of server type is the complexity of the forward mapping F for calculating necessary parameters of the equivalent servers (equation (C.8)). When the equivalent server is a single server or a delay server, the parameter calculation is simple and the required formulae were given in Section C.4. On the other hand, if the equivalent server is a mult-server with M individual processors, the forward mapping involves finding the root of an M-degree polynomial.

The third major consideration in selecting an appropriate server type is the arrival process assumed at the isolated subsystem. We discuss this issue in detail next.

C.6.3 Arrival Process at the Isolated Subsystem

The arrival process assumed at the isolated subsystem not only affects the solvability of the isolated subsystem and the equivalent server, but also guides the selection of the appropriate equivalent server. The principal factor is the similarity between the arrival process observed at the subsystem when it is embedded in the original model and the one assumed at the isolated subsystem. If the two are similar, even a delay server may be adequate to represent the subsystem in the transformed approximate model. An example of such a method is Zahorjan and Lazowska's approximate MVA algorithm for networks incorporating load-dependent servers [Zahorjan and Lazowska 84]. In this algorithm, a load dependent server is replaced by a delay server. The delay is computed by analyzing the load dependent server under a load dependent arrival process generated by an equivalent server for the rest of the network. The service rates of the equivalent server for the rest of the network are computed approximately. An FCFS server can also be used, but determining its service time is more involved.

If the arrival processes in the isolated subsystem and the original model are quite different, the server type should be chosen such that the effect of the discrepancy can be mitigated. The general FCFS server example illustrates. In the original network, the interarrival times at the general server are a function of the number of customers at that server. For the isolated subsystem analysis, however, we assume that the inter-arrival times are exponentially distributed with fixed mean $1/X$. As a result, the queue length at the isolated general server can exceed the number of customers in the network and the response time R can be much larger than what will be observed in the original network.

Let us now determine the type of the replacement server. The response time at a delay server is not affected by the arrival process, and therefore if a delay server is used as a replacement for the general server, the network throughput will be underestimated. The response time at an exponential FCFS server, on the other hand, depends on the arrival process in a way similar to the response time at a general FCFS server. Therefore, using an exponential FCFS server as a replacement for the general server mitigates the error due to the arrival process discrepancy.

The interaction between the arrival process and type of equivalent server also provides a clue to the accuracy of the EPF method [Shum and Buzen 77] and Marie's method [Marie 78] for solving networks containing general servers. Both of these methods accurately represent the load dependent nature of the arrival process for the general server analysis. Due to the interaction between the arrival process and service process, the response time and queue length distribution at the general server are similar to the ones that may be observed at a load dependent server. Both methods incorporate this effect. Because both methods introduce very small in each step of the approximation, their accuracy is very good.

C.7 RTP and Decomposition

As mentioned earlier, an RTP based approximation is essentially a decomposition approximation [Courtois 77]: we isolate a subsystem, analyze it under an "arbitrarily" assumed arrival process and use the isolated system's response time to parameterize its equivalent server(s). This technique of equating a subsystem's On-line behavior with its Off-line behavior can be regarded as a dual of Norton's Theorem approach [Chandy et. al. 75]. In the latter approach, we isolate a subsystem, analyze it as a closed system (i.e., under constant load or finite population), and use its throughput to parameterize an equivalent server. To see the duality, note that in the analysis of an open system, the throughput is usually known and the response time (mean queue length) is calculated. On the other hand, in the analysis of a closed system, the customer population (system queue length) is known and the throughput is normally calculated.

Both RTP and the Norton's Theorem approach lead to a state space transformation. The Norton's Theorem usually aggregates a set of states into a composite state and reduces the size of state space. Besides reducing the state space size by aggregation, RTP can also change the inherent state space structure and introduce new servers. This transformation is evident in the priority server analysis.

It is important to point out that these two techniques are complimentary and are not substitutes for one another. They can be effectively combined to develop solutions for complex systems. Consider, for example, a multiclass interactive system with a given maximum level of multiprogramming and priority scheduling at the CPU. To analyze such a system, we first apply the RTP approximation to obtain the central system throughputs under constant loads. Then as a second step, using the Norton's Theorem approach, we use these throughputs to characterize the equivalent server for the central system and solve the terminal-central system model. Another example of a technique that combines both approaches is the one outlined earlier for distributed systems.

Another point to be considered is when to use either RTP or the Norton's Theorem approach. The choice is usually fairly clear as their application domains are different. The Norton's Theorem approach is usually applied when the isolated subsystem's throughput can be easily computed under constant population. In its typical application, the subsystem consists of multiple devices and has a product form solution, but there is a delay in a passive resource queue before entering the subsystem.

The RTP approach, on the other hand, is applicable whenever the isolated system's response time can be easily computed under a chosen arrival process. In a typical application, the isolated subsystem violates product form assumptions, but it not preceded by a passive resource queue. Examples of such systems include FCFS general servers, priority queues, computer networks, etc.

C.8 Conclusion

The Response Time Preservation (RTP) is a general technique for developing approximate analysis procedures for queueing networks that contain subsystems which can be analyzed in isolation. The technique involves replacing the subsystem by equivalent servers. These servers are parameterized by using performance metrics obtained from isolated subsystems. Typically, the isolated system is analyzed as an open system, though other kinds of arrival processes, in principle, can also be used.

The RTP methodology provides an elegant, effective and efficient procedure for developing approximations. It is basically a decomposition approximation and can be regarded as a dual of the Norton's Theorem approach. The key elements of the approach entail selection of the number and type of equivalent servers as well as the arrival process used for isolated subsystem analysis. We provide practical guidelines on these matters. All these issues and the generality of the method are illustrated by presenting approximations for analyzing FCFS servers with general service times, FCFS servers in multi-class networks with different per visit service times for different classes, and priority queueing.

ACKNOWLEDGEMENTS

We are grateful to Ethan Bolker for pointing out the simple solution given by equation (C.5) for the linear system described by equation (C.6).

REFERENCES

[Agrawal 83a]
S.C. Agrawal and J.P. Buzen, "The aggregate server method for analyzing serialization delays in computer systems," *ACM TOCS*, Vol. 1, No. 2 (May 1983), pp. 116-143.

[Agrawal 83b]
S.C. Agrawal, "Metamodeling: A study of approximations in queueing networks," *Ph.D. Dissertation*, Dept. of Computer Science, Purdue University, West Lafayette, IN. (August 1983).

[Balbo 79]

G. Balbo, "Approximate solutions of queueing network models of computer systems," *PhD. Dissertation,* Dept. of Computer Science, Purdue University, West Lafayette, IN. (December 1979).

[Bard 79]

Y. Bard, "Some extensions to multiclass queueing network analysis," in *Performance of Computer Systems,* Arato et. al. Eds., North-Holland, New York, NY, (1979) pp. 51-62.

[Bard 80]

Y. Bard, "A model of shared DASD and multipathing," *Comm. ACM* 23, 10 (October 1980) pp. 564-583.

[Baskett et. al. 75]

F. Baskett, K.M. Chandy, R.R. Muntz and F.G. Palacios, "Open, closed, and mixed networks of queues with different classes of customers," *J. ACM* 22,2 (1975) pp. 248-260.

[Berry and Chandy 83]

R. Berry and K.M. Chandy, "Performance models of token ring local area networks," *Proc. 1983 ACM SIGMETRICS Conf. on Measurement and Modeling of Computer Systems, Minneapolis, August 29-31, 1983* printed as *Performance Evaluation Review* Special Issue August 1983, pp. 266-274.

[Brandwajn 74]

A.E. Brandwajn, "A model of a time-sharing virtual memory system solved using equivalence and decomposition methods," *Acta Informatica* 4,1 (1974) pp. 11-47.

[Brandwajn 82]

A.E. Brandwajn, "Fast approximate solution of multiprogramming models," *Proc. 1982 ACM SIGMETRICS Conf. on Measurement and Modeling of Computer Systems,* Seattle, Aug 30-Sept 1, 1982 printed as *Performance Evaluation Review* 11,4 (Winter 1982-83) pp. 141-149.

[Bruell and Balbo 80]

S.C. Bruell and G. Balbo, "Computational algorithms for single and multiple class closed queueing network models," *Series on Programming and Operating Systems,* Elsevier/North Holland Publishing Co., New York (1980).

[Bryant et. al. 83]

R.M. Bryant, A.E. Krzesinski and P. Teunissen, "The MVA pre-empt resume priority approximation," *Proc. 1983 ACM SIGMETRICS Conf. on Measurement and Modeling of Computer Systems,* Minneapolis, August 29-31, 1983 printed as *Performance Evaluation Review* Special Issue August 1983, pp. 12-27.

[Buzen 73]

J.P. Buzen, "Computational algorithms for closed queueing networks with exponential servers," *Comm. ACM* 16,9 (Sept. 1973) pp. 527-531.

[Buzen and Agrawal 83]

J.P. Buzen and S.C. Agrawal, "State space transformations in queueing network models," *Proc. 1983 ACM SIGMETRICS Conf. on Measurement and Modeling of Computer Systems,* Minneapolis, August 29-31, 1983 printed as *Performance Evaluation Review* Special Issue August 1983, pp. 55-69.

[Chandy et.al. 75]

K.M. Chandy, U. Herzog and L. Woo, "Parametric analysis of queueing networks," *IBM Journal of Research and Development* Vol. 19, No. 1 (January 1975) pp. 36-42.

[Chandy and Sauer 78]

K.M. Chandy and C.H. Sauer, "Approximate methods for analyzing queueing networks," *Computing Surveys,* Vol. 10, No. 3 (September 1978) pp. 281-317.

[Chandy and Laksmi 83]

K.M. Chandy and M.S. Laksmi, "An approximation technique for queueing networks with preemptive priority queues," Technical Report Dept. of Comp. Sc., Univ. of Texas at Austin, Austin, TX (1983).

[Courtois 75]

P.J. Courtois, "Decomposability, instabilities, and saturation in multiprogramming systems," *Comm. ACM* 18,7 (July 1975) pp. 371-376.

[Courtois 77]

P.J. Courtois, *Decomposability: Queueing and Computer System Applications,* Academic Press, New York (1977).

[Denning and Buzen 78]
P.J. Denning and J.P. Buzen, "The operational analysis of queueing network models," *Computing Surveys,* 10,3 (September 1978) pp. 225-261.

[Gelenbe and Mitrani 82]
E. Gelenbe and I. Mitrani, "Control policies in CSMA local area networks: Ethernet controls," *Proc. 1982 ACM SIGMETRICS Conf. on Measurement and Modeling of Computer Systems,* Seattle, Aug 30-Sept 1, 1982 printed as *Performance Evaluation Review* 11,4 (Winter 1982-83) pp. 233-240.

[Graham 78]
G.S. Graham, Editor, "Special Issue on Queueing Network Models," *Computing Surveys,* 10,3 (Sept. 1978).

[Kleinrock 75]
L. Kleinrock, *Queueing Systems Volume I: Theory,* Wiley, New York, NY (1975).

[Kleinrock 76]
L. Kleinrock, *Queueing Systems Volume II: Computer Applications,* Wiley, New York, NY (1976).

[Kobayashi 78]
H. Kobayashi, *Modeling and Analysis: An Introduction to System Performance Evaluation Methodology,* Addison-Wesley Publishing Co., Reading, Mass. (1978).

[Kuehn 79]
P.J. Kuehn, "Multiqueue systems with nonexhaustive cyclic service," *BSTJ,* Vol. 58(3) pp. 671-698 (1979).

[Lazowska and Zahorjan 82]
E.D. Lazowska and J. Zahorjan, "Multiple class memory constrained queueing networks," *Proc. 1982 ACM SIGMETRICS Conf. on Measurement and Modeling of Computer Systems,* Seattle, Aug 30-Sept 1, 1982 printed as *Performance Evaluation Review* 11,4 (Winter 1982-83) pp. 130-140.

[Marathe and Kumar 81]

     M. Marathe and S. Kumar, "Analytical models for an Ethernet-like local area network," *Proc. 1981 ACM SIGMETRICS Conf. on Measurement and Modeling of Computer Systems,* Las Vegas, September 14-16, 1981 printed as *Performance Evaluation Review* 10,3 (Fall 1981-82) pp. 205-215.

[Marie 78]

     R. Marie, "Modelisation par resseaux de files d'attente," *Ph.D. Thesis,* Universite' de Rennes, France, (December 1978).

[Potier and LeBlanc 80]

     D. Potier and Ph. LeBlanc, "Analysis of locking policies in database management systems," *Comm. ACM* 23,10 (October 1980) pp. 584-593.

[Reiser and Lavenberg 80]

     M. Reiser and S.S. Lavenberg, "Mean value analysis of closed multichain queueing networks," *J. ACM* 27,2 (April 1980) pp./ 3113-322.

[Sevcik 77]

     K.C. Sevcik, "Priority scheduling disciplines in queueing network models of computer systems" *Proc. IFIP Congress 77,* North-Holland Publishing Co., Amsterdam (1977) pp. 565-570.

[Shum and Buzen 77]

     A.W. Shum and J.P. Buzen, "The EPF technique: A method for obtaining approximate solutions to closed queueing networks with general service times," *Proc. Third Symposium on Measuring Modeling, and Evaluating Computer Systems,* Bonn-Bad Godesborg, B.R.D., North Holland (1977) pp. 201-220.

[Zahorjan and Lazowska 84]

     J. Zahorjan and E. Lazowska, "Incorporating load dependent servers in approximate mean value analysis", University of Washington Tech. Rpt. 84-02-01, (February 1984).

Appendix C.A: Accuracy of RTP Approximation for FCFS Servers

We now consider the results of a systematic study of a machine repairman model and a two FCFS queue cyclic network. These two systems represent two extreme cases. In the machine repairman model the general server is subjected to a load dependent arrival process, with arrival rate

$$
A_m(n) = \begin{cases} \dfrac{N-n}{\text{think time}} = (N-n)A & n = 0, \ldots, N-1 \\ 0 & n > N. \end{cases}
$$

In the two queue models, the general server is subjected to a fixed rate arrival process:

$$
A_t(n) = \begin{cases} M_1 & n = 0, \ldots, N-1 \\ 0 & n > N, \end{cases}
$$

where $M_1 = 1/S_1$ is the service rate of the server 1. In a real system, the arrival process at the general server will have some intermediate arrival rates

$$
A_r < A_r(n) < (N-n)A_r
$$

(and possibly $A_r(n-1) < A_r(n)$). Therefore, the evaluation of the accuracy of the RTP approximation for these two models can provide a good indication of the method's accuracy.

The machine repairman model is solved exactly as an $M/G/1//N$ system [Buzen and Goldberg 74]. Table C.5 presents the results of the study. In the experiment, the mean and the coefficient variation of the service time were 1.0 and CV, respectively. $THINK$ is the think time, N is the number of customers in the network; R_N is the response time of the general server and X_N is the network throughput. (X_N also equals the general server utilization). ERA and EXA are the relative percent errors in the RTP estimates of general server response time and system throughput, respectively. ERP and EXP are

Table C.5: Accuracy of RTPA for machine repairman models.

CV	THINK	N	R_N	ERA	ERP	X_N	EXA	EXP
0.0	0.400	2	1.633	1.8	5.0	0.984	-1.4	-3.9
0.0	1.000	5	4.000	0.2	0.4	1.000	-0.2	-0.3
0.0	2.000	10	8.000	0.0	0.0	1.000	-0.0	-0.0
0.0	1.000	2	1.368	-2.6	9.7	0.845	1.5	-5.3
0.0	2.500	5	2.641	2.9	8.8	0.973	-1.5	-4.3
0.0	5.000	10	5.024	1.5	3.3	0.998	-0.8	-1.6
0.0	2.000	2	1.213	-8.4	9.9	0.622	3.3	-3.6
0.0	5.000	5	1.663	-2.8	19.8	0.750	0.7	-4.7
0.0	10.000	10	2.180	0.2	25.3	0.821	-0.0	-4.3
0.0	5.000	2	1.094	-7.2	6.7	0.328	1.3	-1.2
0.0	12.500	5	1.199	-3.9	13.9	0.365	0.3	-1.2
0.0	25.000	10	1.254	-2.3	18.0	0.381	0.1	-0.9
0.0	10.000	2	1.048	-4.4	4.1	0.181	0.4	-0.4
0.0	25.000	5	1.089	-2.1	7.6	0.192	0.1	-0.3
0.0	50.000	10	1.106	-1.1	9.2	0.196	0.0	-0.2
2.000	0.400	2	1.751	5.1	-2.1	0.930	-4.0	1.7
2.000	1.000	5	4.047	-0.2	-0.8	0.991	0.2	0.6
2.000	2.000	10	8.005	-0.1	-0.1	1.000	0.0	0.0
2.000	1.000	2	1.588	13.9	-5.6	0.773	-7.9	3.5
2.000	2.500	5	3.121	2.6	-7.9	0.890	-1.4	4.6
2.000	5.000	10	5.501	-1.8	-5.7	0.952	0.9	3.1
2.000	2.000	2	1.455	20.3	-8.3	0.579	-7.9	3.6
2.000	5.000	5	2.406	10.4	-17.2	0.675	-3.3	5.9
2.000	10.000	10	3.514	4.5	-22.2	0.740	-1.2	6.1
2.000	5.000	2	1.286	19.8	-9.3	0.318	-3.9	1.9
2.000	12.500	5	1.699	12.3	-19.7	0.352	-1.5	2.4
2.000	25.000	10	1.994	8.1	-25.8	0.370	-0.6	1.9
2.000	10.000	2	1.180	13.4	-7.6	0.179	-1.4	0.8
2.000	25.000	5	1.377	7.3	-14.9	0.190	-0.4	0.8
2.000	50.000	10	1.480	4.2	-18.4	0.194	-0.1	0.5
5.000	0.400	2	1.772	30.1	-3.3	0.921	-19.7	2.8
5.000	1.000	5	4.083	2.0	-1.7	0.984	-1.6	1.3
5.000	2.000	10	8.019	-0.2	-0.2	0.998	0.2	0.2
5.000	1.000	2	1.650	63.4	-9.1	0.755	-28.3	6.0
5.000	2.500	5	3.395	23.5	-15.3	0.848	-11.9	9.7
5.000	5.000	10	6.061	2.8	-14.4	0.904	-1.5	8.6
5.000	2.000	2	1.565	89.3	-14.8	0.561	-28.2	7.0
5.000	5.000	5	2.973	49.1	-33.0	0.627	-15.5	14.0
5.000	10.000	10	4.897	23.2	-44.2	0.671	-7.1	17.0
5.000	5.000	2	1.464	105.1	-20.3	0.309	-19.2	4.8
5.000	12.500	5	2.477	67.0	-44.9	0.334	-10.0	8.0
5.000	25.000	10	3.579	42.9	-58.7	0.350	-5.1	7.9
5.000	10.000	2	1.383	90.5	-21.1	0.176	-9.9	2.6
5.000	25.000	5	2.084	54.7	-43.8	0.185	-4.0	3.5
5.000	50.000	10	2.678	34.0	-54.9	0.190	-1.7	2.9

the relative percent errors in the corresponding estimates computed by ignoring the coefficient of variation, i.e., by assuming that the model has a product form solution. Some important observations follow. The throughput estimates are quite accurate even at high CV's and moderate number of terminals ($N > 5$). The errors in the device response times are much larger, especially at large CV's ($CV > 5$) but decrease to tolerable levels at 5 or more terminals. Maximum errors occur when the general server utilization is about 50%. A comparison with product form solution shows that RTP approximation substantially increases accuracy when a number of terminals is 5 or more. The two queue cyclic model can be solved exactly as an $M/G/1/N$ loss system [Kobayashi 78]. Table C.6 presents the results of the study. In the table, the new variable S_1 is the service time of the exponential server. Once again, we see that the RTP approximation is a fairly effective technique, especially for moderate to large numbers of customers ($N > 5$) and low to moderate CV's ($CV < 5$).

Appendix C.B: Effect of Number of Equivalent Servers

Section C.6.1 addressed the issue of choosing the appropriate number of equivalent servers to represent a subnetwork M_i in the transformed model M. If the customer classes in M_i contend freely with each other (as in the multiclass FCFS example in Section C.5.1), using a separate server for each will eliminate the dynamic interaction present in the original system. Both the accuracy and the numerical properties of the RTP approximation will then suffer.

Table C.6: Accuracy of RTPA for two-queue cyclic models.

CV	S_1	N	R_N	ERA	ERP	X_N	EXA	EXP
0.0	0.200	2	1.801	-0.0	1.8	0.999	-1.6	-3.1
0.0	0.200	5	4.799	-1.0	-1.0	1.000	-0.0	-0.0
0.0	0.200	10	9.799	-0.5	-0.5	1.000	0.0	0.0
0.0	0.500	2	1.568	-2.3	6.3	0.937	-3.2	-8.5
0.0	0.500	5	4.377	-5.9	-4.9	0.999	-0.8	-1.5
0.0	0.500	10	9.372	-3.9	-3.9	1.000	-0.0	-0.0
0.0	1.000	2	1.368	-7.7	9.7	0.731	-2.3	-8.8
0.0	1.000	5	2.840	-10.0	5.6	0.897	-2.9	-7.1
0.0	1.000	10	5.335	-10.9	3.1	0.949	-1.7	-4.2
0.0	2.500	2	1.176	-6.2	9.3	0.374	-1.9	-3.9
0.0	2.500	5	1.329	-1.3	21.5	0.400	-0.3	-0.6
0.0	2.500	10	1.333	0.0	24.9	0.400	0.0	-0.0
0.0	5.000	2	1.094	-2.8	6.7	0.196	-1.0	-1.4
0.0	5.000	5	1.125	-0.1	11.0	0.200	-0.0	-0.0
0.0	5.000	10	1.125	0.0	11.1	0.200	0.0	0.0
0.707	0.200	2	1.816	0.1	0.9	0.984	-0.9	-1.6
0.707	0.200	5	4.779	-0.6	-0.6	1.000	-0.0	-0.0
0.707	0.200	10	9.779	-0.3	-0.3	1.000	0.0	0.0
0.707	0.500	2	1.625	-1.3	2.6	0.889	-1.1	-3.6
0.707	0.500	5	4.244	-2.5	-2.0	0.994	-0.7	-1.0
0.707	0.500	10	9.192	-2.0	-2.0	1.000	-0.0	-0.0
0.707	1.000	2	1.444	-3.5	3.8	0.692	-0.7	-3.7
0.707	1.000	5	2.923	-4.0	2.6	0.862	-1.4	-3.3
0.707	1.000	10	5.420	-4.4	1.5	0.928	-0.9	-2.0
0.707	2.500	2	1.236	-3.1	4.0	0.365	-0.8	-1.8
0.707	2.500	5	1.480	-1.0	9.1	0.399	-0.2	-0.4
0.707	2.500	10	1.500	-0.0	11.0	0.400	-0.0	-0.0
0.707	5.000	2	1.132	-1.5	3.0	0.195	-0.4	-0.7
0.707	5.000	5	1.187	-0.1	5.2	0.200	-0.0	-0.0
0.707	5.000	10	1.188	-0.0	5.3	0.200	0.0	0.0

Table C.6: (Continued)

CV	S_1	N	R_N	ERA	ERP	X_N	EXA	EXP
2.000	0.200	2	1.847	3.7	-0.8	0.955	-2.5	1.4
2.000	0.200	5	4.720	0.7	0.7	0.999	0.1	0.1
2.000	0.200	10	9.711	0.4	0.4	1.000	0.0	0.0
2.000	0.500	2	1.714	12.4	-2.8	0.824	-5.9	4.1
2.000	0.500	5	4.060	5.2	2.5	0.955	1.1	3.0
2.000	0.500	10	8.576	5.1	5.1	0.994	0.5	0.6
2.000	1.000	2	1.588	20.9	-5.6	0.630	-5.7	5.9
2.000	1.000	5	3.154	17.4	-4.9	0.760	2.1	9.7
2.000	1.000	10	5.614	17.6	-2.0	0.839	3.8	8.4
2.000	2.500	2	1.412	22.1	-8.9	0.343	-0.9	4.5
2.000	2.500	5	2.089	16.0	-22.7	0.384	2.3	3.5
2.000	2.500	10	2.515	5.4	-33.8	0.397	0.6	0.7
2.000	5.000	2	1.286	13.5	-9.3	0.189	0.9	2.3
2.000	5.000	5	1.565	3.5	-20.2	0.199	0.5	0.6
2.000	5.000	10	1.622	0.2	-22.9	0.200	0.0	0.0
5.000	0.200	2	1.855	22.0	-1.2	0.948	-15.3	2.1
5.000	0.200	5	4.698	1.3	1.1	0.997	0.0	0.2
5.000	0.200	10	9.678	0.7	0.7	1.000	0.0	0.0
5.000	0.500	2	1.743	54.6	-4.4	0.805	-25.1	6.5
5.000	0.500	5	4.010	18.2	3.8	0.921	-3.1	6.9
5.000	0.500	10	8.008	13.1	12.5	0.969	2.7	3.1
5.000	1.000	2	1.650	86.0	-9.1	0.606	-25.3	10.0
5.000	1.000	5	3.345	58.6	-10.3	0.685	-4.2	21.7
5.000	1.000	10	5.849	51.0	-6.0	0.723	8.9	25.7
5.000	2.500	2	1.540	114.8	-16.5	0.329	-14.7	9.1
5.000	2.500	5	2.791	97.0	-42.1	0.351	2.6	13.4
5.000	2.500	10	4.391	75.3	-62.1	0.366	6.6	9.2
5.000	5.000	2	1.464	103.1	-20.3	0.183	-4.3	5.8
5.000	5.000	5	2.416	65.8	-48.3	0.191	3.8	5.0
5.000	5.000	10	3.321	27.7	-62.4	0.196	2.1	2.2

One indication of the deterioration of accuracy is that the RTP approximation no longer yields the exact solution when it is applied to a multiclass product form network consisting only of load independent FCFS servers. The data in Table C.7a illustrates this. Another indication is provided by the data presented in Table C.7b. For the network under consideration, note that class 2 service time at device 1 is less than that of class 1; at device 2, they are comparable; and at device 3, which is very lightly used, class 2 has higher demand than class 1. Therefore, we expect that for equal class populations, class 2's response time should be smaller than class 1's response time. The solutions from both simulation and RTPA1 tally with this observation. But for smaller populations, RTPA2 does not. Partitioning the subnetwork by customer class also creates certain numerical difficulties. Convergence with separate equivalent servers is painfully slow (100-300 iterations). Moreover, due to incorrect intermediate values of the throughputs, servers can easily become saturated during the iteration.

There are two solutions to the saturation problem. The first one assumes that since the server is saturated, the response time is infinite, and thus, equation (C.3) reduces to

$$S_{ir}{}' = 1 / X_{ir}.$$

With this assumption, however, the solution diverges.

The second solution to the saturation problem reduces the throughput estimates in proportion to the individual class utilizations such that the total server utilization is UMAX. This method led to a slow convergence with UMAX = 0.99. However, the iteration diverged with UMAX = 0.9999.

Table C.7: Problems associated with separate equivalent
servers for a multi-class FCFS network.

(a)   Product form network

DEVICE	CLASS 1			CLASS 2		
i	V_{i1}	S_{i1}	$V_{i1}S_{i1}$	V_{i2}	S_{i2}	$V_{i2}S_{i2}$
1	10	1	10	8	1	8
2	12	1	15	12	1	14
3	15	2	30	10	2	20

POPULATION		RESPONSE TIME					
CLASS 1	CLASS 2	CLASS 1			CLASS 2		
		EXACT	RTPA1	RTPA2	EXACT	RTPA1	RTPA2
5	5	291.8	291.8	277.0	207.3	207.3	216.1

RTPA1 = 1 iteration
RTPA2 = 148 iterations
RTPA1 = RTP approximation with one equivalent server for all classes
RTPA2 = RTP approximation with one equivalent server for each class

(b)   Non-product form network [Bard 79]

DEVICE	CLASS 1			CLASS 2		
i	V_{i1}	S_{i1}	$V_{i1}S_{i1}$	V_{i2}	S_{i2}	$V_{i2}S_{i2}$
1	18	7	126	8	11	88
2	5	20	100	13	8	104
3	10	2	20	15	3	45

POPULATION		RESPONSE TIME					
CLASS 1	CLASS 2	CLASS 1			CLASS 2		
		EXACT	RTPA1	RTPA2	EXACT	RTPA1	RTPA2
5	5	1140	1115	1107	1156	1120	1228
10	10	--	2255	2048	--	2016	2444
20	20	--	4827	3749	--	3683	5436
50	50	12267	12952	11588	9070	8566	9571

-- No simulation data available in [Bard 79].

Appendix D

Implications of Bistability

in Preemptive Priority Systems

In Section 5.7.2 we studied a bistable preemptive priority system containing fixed rate server. Designers wishing to avoid bistabilities in preemptive priority systems should be wary of following two types of systems:

1. Systems with highly skewed load distribution: They are likely to exhibit such bistable behavior because, as exemplified by the network of Figure 0.1, they may have bimodal state distributions; and

2. System in which the order of priority is different at different devices: To see the instability, consider a system in which class H has priority over class L at server i and class L has priority over class H at server j. When a class H queue builds up at i, due to priority scheduling at i, class L customers get blocked at i. In this situation class H customers face little contention at j, and they cycle back to i faster. Thus, the condition persists for a while. However, due to random fluctuations, the pendulum will swing in the other direction and then the queues will build at j.

These results about the stability have an important implication about simulation of such systems. Accurate prediction via simulation is now more complicated because the "steady state" does not exist in such systems. For example, consider the U_H trace displayed in Figure 5.10. For first 100 seconds, the utilization is about 35%. After this initial period, the utilization suddenly jumps to a 95% plateau and stays there for about 25000 seconds. To an unsuspecting analyst, it will appear that after an initial transient, the system has reached steady state. With great confidence, he may assert that class H CPU utilization is about 95%. Global balance analysis will, however, yield a solution $U_H = 0.66$. The convergence analysis shows that $U_H = 0.35$ and $U_H = 0.95$ are both stable.

INDEX

The MIT Press, with Peter Denning as consulting editor, publishes computer science books in the following series:

ACM Doctoral Dissertation Award and Distinguished Dissertation Series
Artificial Intelligence, Patrick Winston and Michael Brady, editors
Charles Babbage Institute Reprint Series for the History of Computing, Martin Campbell-Kelly, editor
Computer Systems, Herb Schwetman, editor
Foundations of Computing, Michael Garey, editor
History of Computing, I. Bernard Cohen, editor, and William Aspray, associate editor
Information Systems, Michael Lesk, editor
Scientific Computation, Dennis Gannon, editor
The MIT Electrical Engineering and Computer Science Series

For information on submission of manuscripts for publication, call or write to:

Frank P. Satlow
Executive Editor, Computer Science and Engineering
The MIT Press
28 Carleton Street
Cambridge, MA 02142
617-253-1623